Bible Questions Explained

Bible Questions Explained

by
DR. LOUIS T. TALBOT
Chancellor of Biola College
and Talbot Theological Seminary

WM. B. EERDMANS PUBLISHING COMPANY

Grand Rapids   Michigan

ISBN 0-8028-1195-7

Reprinted, July 1978

PHOTOLITHOPRINTED BY EERDMANS PRINTING COMPANY
GRAND RAPIDS, MICHIGAN, UNITED STATES OF AMERICA

FOREWORD

During the twenty-five years it has been our privilege to study the Bible over the radio, we have set aside an occasional broadcast for the answering of questions that have arisen in the minds of those who "listened in" to these messages. This book contains some of the questions asked and answered during this period. We have endeavored to bring all questions under the lens of Holy Writ, so that Scripture might interpret Scripture.

We give thanks to God for the many we have been privileged to see delivered from skepticism and doubt to a saving knowledge of the Lord Jesus Christ, and to faith in the Bible as God's inspired and infallible Word.

We are also deeply thankful to God for all those who have made this radio ministry possible, and for its preservation in permanent form through the printed page.

Concerning these "Bible Questions Explained" let us remember our Lord's own words: "If any man willeth to do his will, he shall know of the teaching, whether it is of God" (John 7:17). That the Holy Spirit may take the things of Christ and show them unto us, as we study these pages, is our prayer.

To the faculty and student body of the Bible Institute of Los Angeles, whose faithfulness to the glorious Gospel of the Lord Jesus Christ and loyalty to the infallible Word of God have been a source of inspiration to the author and to thousands everywhere, this book is affectionately dedicated.

CONTENTS

I

THE BIBLE

Question: What is the difference between a manuscript of the Bible and a version?

Answer: A manuscript is a copy of the Bible in the original languages in which it was written. The Old Testament was written in Hebrew; the New Testament in Greek. We have many ancient manuscripts, all written by hand, of course, before printing was invented in Europe. The three most ancient, and, therefore, the most valuable, are: The Vaticanus, in the Vatican Library, Vatican City; The Sinaiticus, now in the British Museum, London, but until a few years ago in the library at Petrograd, now Leningrad, Russia; and The Alexandrian, also in the British Museum.

A version is a translation into some other language; there are more than 900 translations into the different languages and dialects of the world. Moreover, there are hundreds of valuable versions written by hand long before printing was invented, and found today in the great libraries of the world.

Question: Please explain II Peter 1:20, 21 and II Tim. 3:16.

Answer: These remarkable verses tell us that the Word of God was written by "holy men of God" as they were "moved by the Holy Ghost." They tell us that "all scripture is given by inspiration of God." Of course, there is more in these verses; but this is the fundamental fact; and the practical teaching is very evident.

But what is meant by "inspiration of God"? That is doubtless the question that is in your mind. The answer is that every human author of the books of the Bible was but the instrument through whom the Holy Spirit wrote; even to the very words used. He guided the pen of these writers; so that we have the veritable Word of God. Yes, I believe in the verbal inspiration of the whole Bible!

To be sure God uses the characteristic style of the men inspired, which fact accounts for the differences in the style of writing. For instance, some epistles are distinctly Pauline; others are not. But this does not change the fact that all the human authors were so fully controlled by the Holy Spirit of God that they were guarded from error concerning what they wrote.

Not only did the Holy Spirit write the Bible, but He is our only Teacher of this marvelous Book. The Lord Jesus said so repeatedly in John 14-16, His last message to His disciples. The prophet had said so, long before that: "Not by might, nor by power, but by my Spirit, saith the Lord of hosts" (Zech. 4:6). The whole Word of God teaches it. And how glad we are that "the law of the Lord is perfect, making wise the simple," so that even the little child can understand its message.

Question: Do you believe in the verbal inspiration of the Bible?

Answer: Yes. All orthodox, fundamental Bible lovers believe in the verbal inspiration of the original manuscripts, in the Hebrew and Greek languages. Moreover, we believe that God has guided the translators of our English Bible, as well as those of other tongues, seeing to it that we have the exact sense of the Word of God, simply put into language that we can understand. The greatest scholars of all time have spent literally years of their lives, comparing the different sources—manuscripts, versions, quotations from the church fathers, discoveries of archæology—they have spared neither time nor money nor effort to give to the world the exact meaning, even to the slightest shade of difference in the use of a word or phrase. The story of how our American Standard Version was translated, together with the English Version, reads like a chapter from fiction; it is so interesting. And the longest telegram ever sent over the wire was the whole New Testament in this version, transmitted from New York City to Chicago by 99 telegraph operators. Why? Just in order that Chicago might sell it on her streets promptly, as did New York and London! What is that but a testimony to the divine origin of this Book of books?

By verbal inspiratiton we mean that the Holy Spirit so controlled the pen and thought of the human author that the very words were God-breathed. That is inspiration.

"All scripture is given by inspiration of God, and is profitable for doctrine, for reproof, for correction, for instruction in righteousness" (II Tim. 3:16).

"The prophecy came not in old time by the will of man: but holy men of God spake as they were moved by the Holy Ghost" (II Pet. 1:21).

Question: What proof have we that the Bible is the Word of God?

Answer: Whole volumes have been written on this subject. Space here will permit only a brief statement of some of the reasons why we know that the Bible is the inspired Word of God, authentic, authoritative, infallible, and divine. First let us outline some of the *external* evidences of these truths:

1. *The ancient manuscripts* in the great libraries of the world go back to a very early date. Some of the manuscripts of the New Testament were written as early as the fourth century A.D. And we still have copies of the Greek translation of the Old Testament which Christ used when He was on earth. His word concerning it is sufficient! It was translated not later than 250 B.C., and is called the Septuagint Version.

2. *The versions,* or translations, of the Bible into the many languages of the earth are manifold. Some of these are older

than the authentic manuscripts. It is a well known fact that the men who made some of these translations could easily have known the apostles, all of which means that they had apostolic authority for their versions.

3. *About fifty of the early church fathers quoted the New Testament* so freely in their writings that all of the New Testament could be put together, with the exception of a few passages. These writings of the church fathers are still available to scholars today.

When these manuscripts, versions, and quotations from the church fathers are compared, verse by verse, line by line, they are found to verify the fact that our English Bible is authentic.

4. *Archaeology* has proved many facts of Bible history. Monuments and tablets have been discovered which prove beyond all doubt that they told the story of creation, the fall, the flood, and other events of Bible history. Abraham's early home, the city of Ur of Chaldea, has been discovered. These are but a few of the silent testimonies from the monuments to the eternal truth of the Word of God.

5. *History* has borne out the prophecies foretold in the Bible. What could be more striking and more convincing than the way prophecy has been and is being fulfilled concerning the Jew?

6. *The attacks of Satan upon the Word of God prove its divine origin.* These attacks have been unceasing, unmitigated, violent. Any other book would have been utterly obliterated long ago. But God has miraculously preserved the Bible against the open attacks of fire, water, and sword; and against the more subtle attacks of skeptic, critic, and "scientist falsely so called."

Why was Paul executed by the wicked Nero? Because he preached and wrote and lived the message of the Word of God. Why was John Wycliffe tried before prelate and priests? Why were his bones dug up, burned, and the ashes thrown to the River Swift? Because he gave the English people their first complete Bible in their own tongue. Why was William Tyndale kept in prison for eighteen months without book or pen, only to be strangled and burned at the stake afterwards? Simply because he gave to the world the first printed Bible. Why were Martin Luther and other reformers persecuted? Why was John Huss burned at the stake? Because they preached and taught and translated the Bible into the languages of the common people.

True enough, these things are not being done today in certain countries; but Satan's attacks are yet more subtle. He fills the minds of men with doubt concerning this wonderful Book. But the Word of our God shall abide forever! And what could furnish more abundant proof of its divine origin and authority than its miraculous preservation throughout the ages.

7. *The universal appeal of the Bible proves its divine origin.* Translated into more than 900 languages and dialects, it meets the need of the human heart, of whatever color or race, of whatever degree of education, of whatever social level. This Has never ben true of any other book. It is the world's best seller, and has been for many a year.

8. *The power of the living Word of God to regenerate the heart and change the life is unmistakable evidence of its divine inspiration.* These are but a few of the external evidences of the inspiration of the Bible.

Then there are also unmistakable internal evidences that "holy men of God spake as they were moved by the Holy Ghost":

1. *Our Lord Jesus testified to the divine origin of the Old Testament.* His word is final!

2. *The apostles also* quoted from it freely, believed it, preached it. Moreover, they testified to the inspiration of the New Testament. (See II Tim. 3:16; II Peter 1:19-21.)

3. *The fulfilled prophecies* — and they are legion — prove beyond all doubt that the Old Testament foretold the message of the New; that the New quotes and fulfills the Old.

4. *Add to all this the marvelous unity of the Book,* written over a period of thousands of years, by different human instruments of varying degrees of education, in different languages, in different styles of writing. Such circumstances would ordinarily make for anything but unity; yet we have this one Book, with one message, telling the story of the one and only Saviour of men. Prophecy and history, law and psalm, proverb, parable, and sermon, whether poetry or prose—all tell the story of salvation from sin by faith in the shed blood of the Lord Jesus Christ. Need we further proof of the divine inspiration of such a Book?

The more analytically we study it, the longer we read it, the more diligently we search its pages, comparing Scripture with Scripture, the more convinced we are of its wonders, its quickening power, and its divine inspiration; that is, if we let the Holy Spirit who wrote it be our Teacher and Guide, taking the things of Christ and showing them unto us.

For those who care to go into this subject more fully, I would suggest a little book, entitled, "HowWe Got Our Bible," by Charles Leach. It may be purchased at the Biola Book Room, 558 South Hope St., Los Angeles, Calif.

Question: Who compiled, or put together, the Old Testament Canon?

Answer: The Bible does not tell us, but tradition says that Ezra and a company of men known as "The Great Synagogue," devout Jews, compiled the Old Testament.

Moses, we know, wrote the first five books of the Bible, as the Holy Spirit inspired him. These books are often called "The Law." At the close of his life, Moses wrote, saying that God told him to place the book of the law "by the side of the ark of the covenant" (*not "in* the side of the ark of the covenant," as we read in the Authorized Version). See Deut. 31:24-26, R.V.) The ten commandments were kept *in* the ark; but the scrolls of parchment, or vellum, upon which the books of the Bible were written, were kept in the Holy of Holies "by the side of the ark of the covenant." Later on, during the apostasy of Israel, the long-hidden Scriptures were discovered in God's House, opened, and read to the people. As, one by one, the inspired books were written, they were put with the books of Moses. Then it was that Ezra and his company of devout Jews compiled the whole Old Testament.

Assuredly God overruled the work, and guided as to arrangement in the divine order. And certainly Christ acknowledged it to be the inspired Word of God.

Question: Why are some of the words in our English Bible put in italics?

Answer: All words in italics in our English Bible have been added by the translators to make the meaning clear. Sometimes it is difficult to express in the English language the meaning of the Hebrew and the Greek. Some Hebrew words, for example, are so freighted with meaning that the translators found it necessary to supply words, in order to bring out the richness of the original text. Therefore, all words in italics in our English Bible are not found in the original Hebrew and Greek. Often they do clarify the subject matter; but we need to be careful at times, lest they obscure the meaning.

Question: My pastor said that the chapter and verse divisions of the Bible were added by men, long after the Bible was written. Is this so?

Answer: Yes. The first Bible to have chapter divisions was that translated by John Wycliffe in 1382 A.D. The first to have verse divisions was the Geneva Bible, a translation made by the Puritan Party.

These divisions have been used of God, for our convenience in locating passages. Often they are logical and true to the real divisions of the subject matter. But sometimes it seems that a better division might have been made; as, for example, the twelfth chapter of Hebrews is but a continuation of the eleventh chapter. However, we are grateful to those godly men who rendered us this definite service.

Question: Why was the Revised Version necessary? I prefer the King James, or Authorized Version.

Answer: For public reading and worship, so do I prefer the King James Version. And nothing in all the English language can compare with it for beauty and majesty and dignity of style. It is still the Bible of the people. It is familiar to most Christians, and therefore desirable for public reading, to avoid confusion. These are the reasons why I use it in the church services. Moreover, it is remarkably accurate in its translation. It was the product of forty men's work; therefore, this precluded any one man's coloring the translation with his own prejudices or inclinations. Truly God guided the translators who, in 1611, under the supervision of King James of England, worked so diligently at their task!

Yet since that date, many valuable manuscripts, versions, and archæological discoveries have become available to scholars; and therefore, by careful scrutiny of these, devout, scholarly men have been able to improve on the accuracy of an English translation here and there—so far as rendering the literal meaning of the original Hebrew and Greek is concerned. Accordingly, the American Standard Version and the English Revised Version, which are practically the same in most respects, are the most accurate translations in our English language.

Again, scholars of the past generation, who made this translation, working diligently for some fourteen years, were better qualified to translate the Hebrew and Greek than were the scholars of King James's day.

Yet, to repeat for emphasis, for all practical purposes, we still cling to the King James Version, using the Revised as a kind of commentary for analytical study. And let me add that *no fundamental doctrine has been changed in the least by the later version.*

Question: What do you think of the modern versions of the Bible? I do not refer to the American Standard Version or to the English Revised Version, but to the Bible in modern speech.

Answer: While some orthodox ministers and Bible students like certain modern versions, yet I do not. I much prefer going to an analytical commentary for any clarification of the text. Perhaps my reasons are not acceptable to all; but the modern translations have, to me, lost a certain beauty and sacredness that I am loathe to give up. Moreover, some of the versions are definitely dangerous, in that they omit many of the priceless portions which have to do with our Lord's work on Calvary's Cross. I refer to "The Shorter Bible," particularly. And, knowing the theology of other translators, who deny the virgin birth of Christ, His atoning work on Calvary, the inspiration of the Scriptures, and many such doctrines—knowing how some of these men take their stand against orthodox Christianity, I should be very skeptical of their interpretation of these sacred truths. Personally, the King James and Revised Versions are "good enough for me."

Question: What is the difference between the Catholic and the Protestant Bibles?

Answer: The main difference is that the Catholic Bible includes certain Apocryphal Books, which the Protestants do not consider inspired by God, and therefore do not include in their Bible. (For a discussion of this, see "Apocryphal Books," elsewhere in this series.)

The Catholic Bible was translated into English from the Latin Vulgate, a version which greatly influenced Biblical translation for about 1,000 years. The Latin Vulgate was also one of the main sources of the King James Version, which we still use today. Therefore, the Catholic Bible is, in the main, much like our own Protestant translations, varying only in different words used by the translators to convey the same meaning. It was published in Douay France, in 1609; that is why it is called the Douay Version.

When it comes to a matter of *interpretation* of the Scriptures, there *is* a real difference between Catholics and Protestants on certain fundamental issues. Some of these differences we have discussed elsewhere in this series.

An illustration here will suffice: The word "repent" in our Protestant Bible is sometimes translated "do penance" in the Catholic Bible. However, the great doctrine of justification by faith is set forth in the Douay Version. If Catholics would only read their own Bible, they would see the fallacy of the teaching of this system concerning salvation through penance, ordinances, and the mass. They would also see the unscriptural interpretation of a host of other things that belong to Roman Catholicism.

I always recommend to Roman Catholics that they read Paul's Epistle to Romans in their own Bible. Many Catholics have come to a knowledge of the truth of justification by faith through a reading of this epistle in the Douay Version.

Question: How do you explain certain discrepancies in the Bible?

Answer: There are no discrepancies, even though man has sought to make it appear so. Or should I say Satan has sought to make it appear so? Once we remember that "the natural man (the unregenerated man) receiveth not the things of the Spirit of God" (I Cor. 2:14), we have the solution to many *so-called* discrepancies, that are not discrepancies at all. It is not in man to understand spiritual things; he must be taught by the Spirit of God. And the unregenerate man has not the Spirit of God.

There may be faulty translations of certain words, such as "world" in Matt. 28:20, which should be rendered "age": "Lo, I am with you alway, even unto the consummation of the age." But such translations are of little consequence, in so far as they touch the matter of sin, salvation, and eternal issues.

Moreover, once the Spirit-taught man analyzes these passages cited by skeptical men, he always finds that apparent variations are explained in a most plausible way. Only man's ignorance of what the Bible says; his repetition of hearsay; and his sin-darkened mind can account for what man may call a discrepancy. God does not make mistakes! And He has seen to it that His Word is inerrant!

May I quote the statement of another? It is fundamental: These so-called discrepancies of men "affect no vital doctrine" of our Christian faith!

A few illustrations of what we mean follow.

Question: How can you harmonize the doctrine of the inerrancy of the Bible with such a glaring mistake as that in Matt. 27:9, 10, which reads: "Then was fulfilled that which was spoken by Jeremiah the prophet, saying, And they took the thirty pieces of silver, the price of him that was valued, whom they of the children of Israel did value; and gave them for a potter's field, as the Lord appointed me." If you turn to the Old Testament, you will find that this quotation is found in Zech. 11:12, 13, and not in Jeremiah. Does this not prove that Matthew erred?

Answer: Not at all. It rather proves the inerrancy of the Bible. If you read the language of Matthew carefully, you will note that Matthew does not say that Jeremiah *wrote* the statement, but that he *"spake"* it. Zechariah *wrote* it, to be sure; but the Holy Spirit knew what the prophets *spake,* as well as what they *wrote.*

There is another illustration of this in Jude, which records a hitherto unrecorded utterance of Enoch. But the Holy Spirit knew what Enoch had prophesied; and He used it at His appointed time, as a warning to apostates of judgment to come upon the ungodly.

Question: How could Jude say in verse 14 that Enoch prophesied according to the quotation here, when there is no record in the Old Testament that Enoch ever made such a prophecy? "And Enoch also, the seventh from Adam, prophesied of these (meaning apostates), saying, Behold, the Lord cometh with ten thousands of his saints, to execute judgment upon all, and to convince all that are ungodly among them of their ungodly deeds which they have ungodly committed, and of all their hard speeches which ungodly sinners have spoken against him" (Jude 14, 15).

Answer: It is true that there is no such prophecy recorded in the Old Testament, as having been made by Enoch; but *Jude wrote by inspiration of the Holy Spirit;* and the Holy Spirit knew what utterances Enoch had made, even though there is no record of them. "All scripture is given by inspiration of God" (II Tim. 3:16). For the prophecy came not in old time by the will of man; but holy men of God spake as they were moved by the Holy Ghost" (II Pet. 1:21).

It is suggestive, to say the least, that Enoch, who "was translated that he should not see death" (Heb. 11:5), thus became a beautiful type of the saints who will be living on earth when the church is translated. It is interesting to know that he preached the second coming of Christ *with His saints,* to judge sin and "to execute judgment" upon the ungodly. "Known unto God are all his works from the beginning of the world" (Acts 15:18). And "the seventh from Adam," even Enoch, was God's mouth-piece many centuries ago, to warn men to "flee from the wrath to come."

Question: Please explain the difference in the time of the crucifixion, as given by Mark and John. Is there not a discrepancy here?

Answer: Not at all. The common and correct explanation is that Mark 15:25 speaks according to the Jewish computation of time, saying, "And it was the third hour"; whereas John 19:14 speaks according to the Roman computation of time of "the sixth hour." Of course, we know that Rome ruled the civilized world in the day of Christ, including the land of Palestine. And many Roman customs prevailed, along with many Jewish customs strictly adhered to by the Hebrew people.

In a word, Mark is speaking of Jewish time; John, of Roman time.

Question: I believe the whole Bible; but so many discredit the stories of the flood and Jonah that I should like some scriptural proof of the fact of these events.

Answer: The Lord Jesus verified the historicity of both events during His earthly ministry. In Matt. 12:38-42 He gave the Jews "the sign of the prophet Jonah" as typical of His death and resurrection. "For as Jonas *was* three days and three nights in the belly of the sea-monster (Revised Version, marginal rendering of the original Greek), so shall the Son of man be three days and three nights in the heart of the earth" (Matt. 12:40). (See also Luke 11:29-32).

And in Matt. 24:37-39, picturing the corruption that will

be on the earth at the end of this age, he said, "As the days of Noah *were,* so shall also the coming of the Son of man be."

Moreover, the apostles bore witness to the fact of the flood. (See such references as Heb. 11:7; II Pet. 2:5).

Again, archæology and the legends of ancient peoples prove that they knew of the flood, although many of the stories handed down from history and legend are perverted accounts of the Biblical record.

Certainly the God who created all things was *able* to perform these miracles. They are to be classed with all other miracles as *supernatural;* and, indeed, our whole Christian faith is based upon the supernatural.

Question: Please explain these words found in II Peter 1:20, "No prophecy of the scripture is of any private interpretation."

Answer: These words mean that we may not take a passage out of its context, or interpret it apart from the whole of the Word of God. It is not to be treated as an isolated verse, meaning anything under the sun we may want to make it mean. This is exactly what many would-be critics of the Bible have ever done; but they only show their ignorance, as well as their defiance of the living God, by such perversion of the inspired record.

To illustrate what I mean, let me take just one group of words, only seven, on which the Russellites base a most important doctrine, although they not only pervert the true meaning of these seven words, but also flatly contradict dozens and dozens of other passages by so doing. These seven words are found in Rev. 3:14: "The beginning of the creation of God." Without any doubt, they refer to our Lord; and mean that He is the *Author* of the creation of God. This is the interpretation given by the well-known commentators, Jamieson, Fausset, Brown, men who accept the whole Bible as the Word of God.

But what does Russellism erroneously say? It teaches blasphemy, saying that God created Jesus; and that, therefore, He is "the beginning of the creation of God." Then in order to try to prove this falsehood of Satan, they are compelled to admit that by Jesus all things were created.

Do you not see, my friend, how subtle Satan's wiles are? The same cult teaches that Jesus was not born of the virgin Mary, but that He was a created angel, even the Archangel Michael. It teaches that Jesus was the first being God created; that He did not rise from the dead bodily; that He is not eternal God. It is just one of Satan's numerous ways of attacking the deity of our blessed Lord.

We who love Him and know His Word to be infallible, authentic, and divine, accept its definite, repeated, irrefutable teaching—that our Lord Jesus always was and always will be God equal with the Father and with the Holy Spirit. And to this "give all the prophets witness," as well as Christ Himself and His apostles. Read such passages as John 1:1-14; Col. 1:14-19; 2:9; Phil. 2:5-11; Heb. 1:1-3; yes, all of the Epistle to the Hebrews—all the Bible! They speak for themselves; and yet literally thousands of poor, blinded souls will follow one Satan-inspired man, who bases a whole doctrine upon seven words which he perverted from their true meaning. In doing this "Pastor" Russell is giving these words a "private interpretation," even twisting them to mean what they do not say, but what he wants them to imply.

As we examine any separate verse of Scripture, in the light of all revealed truth, it will ever be so. All the man-made "discrepancies" will vanish away. All the Satan-inspired "contradictions" will be revealed in their true color, as Satan's lies. That is strong language, but our Lord Jesus said that Satan is "a liar, and the father of" lies (John 8:44).

II

THE TRIUNE GOD

Question: Can you explain the Trinity? I realize that there are three persons in the Triune God. Am I to understand that the Trinity is a composite personality?

Answer: The Bible clearly *teaches* the doctrine of the Trinity, but nowhere does it *explain* the Trinity. There are some things *above* reason, and the doctrine of the Trinity is one of them.

I think the expression "God the father, God the Son, and God the Holy Spirit" is somewhat misleading, though many Christians use it in all reverence for the Triune God. But this would imply that there are three Gods; whereas there are not three Gods, but three persons in one God. A better expression would be: God, the Father, the Son, and the Holy Spirit.

Of course, all this is beyond our comprehension. If man's mind could comprehend the doctrine of the Trinity, Christ would doubtless have explained it to His disciples. He had the opportunity of doing so when Philip asked, "Lord, show us the Father, and it sufficeth us" (John 14:8). But Jesus did not explain how He could be one with the Father, and yet say that He was going to the Father. He threw Philip back on faith.

And we accept this eternal truth on faith, because God has stated it definitely and repeatedly in His Word. After all, ours is a supernatural (above the natural) belief. And that is where faith enters into the Christian religion. We may believe what we cannot explain; and we may apprehend what we can not comprehend. The Bible doctrine of the Trinity is very clear.

I have a Jewish friend who accepted the doctrine of the Trinity after a study of the Hebrew word for "God" in Gen. 1:1. There we read, "In the beginning God created the heaven and the earth." In the original Hebrew the word for "God" is "Elohim," a uni-plural noun; the verb "created" is in the singular. Thus, even from the very first verse of the Bible, the Trinity is set forth as one God.

Question: Please explain Deut. 10:17, "For the Lord your God is God of gods, and Lord of lords." Is there more than one God?

Answer: There is only one God in the absolute sense, though there are many false gods—gods in the minds of men, but not in reality. This is what Moses had in mind when he wrote these words under the guidance of the Holy Spirit. He was emphasizing the sovereignty of God over all the universe. Satan is called "the god of this world" (II Cor. 4:4), and seeks worship. His desire to be "as God" led to his fall; and his desire for worship causes him to deceive multitudes, obtaining their worship.

The prophet Isaiah answered your question, as does all the word of God: "Look unto me, and be ye saved, all the ends of the earth: for I am God and there is none else" (Isa. 45:22).

Question: Did God take a body when He walked in the Garden of Eden, or was He in Spirit form?

Answer: The appearances of God in Old Testament times were pre-incarnate manifestations of our Lord Jesus Christ. God's appearance in the Garden of Eden was one of these appearances. Sometimes there theophanies, or Christophanies, as they are called by theologians, describe the appearance of God in the form of an angel. Sometimes He is called "the angel of the Lord." Angels have the power "to become visible in the semblance of human form." Thus we read that when God talked to Abraham, "three men stood by him" (Gen 18:2). This is suggestive of the Trinity; yet this appearance of God to Abraham was without doubt in angelic form.

This is something else we do not try to *explain,* any more than we try to explain the Trinity. But we do know that not until our Lord "was made flesh," in Bethlehem's manger, did He have His *human* body. In Heb. 10:5 the Holy Spirit quoted the prophetic word of the Son of the Father, when He said, "Sacrifice and offering thou wouldest not, but *a body hast thou prepared me.*"

The "angel of the Lord," called also "the angel of the covenant," is always distinct from the *created* angels. These titles refer to the pre-incarnate appearances of Christ. Some of these instances are: The angel of the Lord as He appeared in the Garden of Eden; the "captain of the host of the Lord" as He appeared to Joshua (Josh. 5:14); the One "like the Son of God" who walked with the three Hebrew children in the fiery furnace (Dan. 3:25); and "the angel of the Lord," before whom "Joshua the high priest" stood, Satan also "standing at his right hand to resist him" (Zech. 3:1). These and many other Old Testament passages refer to the appearances of Christ before His incarnation in Bethlehem's manger.

Question: How are we to harmonize Ex. 24:10 with John 1:18?

Answer: Ex. 24:9, 10 reads, in part: "Then went up Moses, and Aaron, Nadab, Abihu, and seventy of the elders of Israel: and they saw the God of Israel"; while John 1:18 tells us: "No man hath seen God at any time; the only begotten Son, which is in the bosom of the Father, he hath declared (or revealed) him."

A careful reading of the thirty-third chapter of Exodus will throw a great deal of light on your question. Here Moses was asking God to reveal Himself—to show Himself; and God said, in verse 20, "Thou canst not see *my face*: for there shall no man see me and live." That is the point you have in John 1:18. No man hath seen the face of God, except as it was revealed in the face of our Lord Jesus Christ when He became Man. The human face could not stand it. To have the glory of God manifested would be death to our human nature; and our Lord laid aside His *glory—not His deity*—when He was born in Bethlehem, later to take it again when He went back to the Father. (See John 17:5).

Yet we find recorded in Ex. 33:21, 22: "And the Lord said, Behold, there is a place by me, and thou shalt stand upon a rock: and it shall come to pass, when my glory passeth by that I will put thee *in a cleft of the rock,* and will cover thee with my hand while I pass by: and I will take away mine hand, and thou shalt see my back parts: but my face shall not be seen."

There is no place to see the glory of the Lord like the cleft of the rock. If you want to see the glory of the Lord, hide yourself at Calvary. There you can sing the song of redemption:

> "Rock of Ages, cleft for me,
> Let me hide myself in Thee."

The expression "back parts" may be translated "His receding glory," or "the departing of the Lord." God passed by and took His hand away, so that Moses saw the receding effect of the glory of God that had passed by him. That is all he saw. No man with eyes such as we have can look upon the face of God and live.

But let us think further of the words, "the cleft of the rock." They take us back in thought to the smitten rock in the wilderness journey of Israel. The people were thirsty, and murmured against Moses and against God. Then Jehovah told Moses to smite the rock on Mount Horeb. This he did, and the water gushed forth to quench the thirst of the multitude.

Paul, writing many centuries later, said that Israel "drank of that spiritual Rock that followed them: and that Rock was Christ" (I Cor. 10:4). He was smitten of God and afflicted" for a sin-sick world—that all who drink of the life-giving stream which flows from Calvary might see "the light of the knowledge of the glory of God in the face of Jesus Christ" (II Cor. 4:6). This is the lesson of the coming Redeemer that God was teaching Israel in the wilderness.

The Lord Jesus is, in very truth, eternal God. When He was on earth, certain disciples saw glimpses of His glory, as on the mount of transfiguration and after His resurrection; but during most of His earthly ministry He was the self-humbled One. When we get to heaven, we shall see the glory of the Triune God, there forever to be like Him, for "we shall see him as he is," the One "altogether lovely." And *in Christ Jesus, our Lord,* "dwelleth all the fulness of the Godhead bodily" (Col. 2:9).

Question: Why do we read in the Old Testament that God "repented" of certain things? For example, see Gen. 6:6.

Answer: When used concerning God, "repent" in all of its forms simply means that, to man, God *appears* to change His mind. "Known unto God are all his works from the beginning of the world" (Acts 15:18). In reality it is man who changes, or repents, which accounts for the *seeming* "repentance" of God.

Question: What is the teaching of Scripture concerning the universal Fatherhood of God?

Answer: The doctrine of the universal Fatherhood of God is advanced by modernist preachers and not by the Bible. Modernists have taken the teachings of the Lord Jesus concerning God as His Father, and have gone out to teach that God is the Father of all men. Some people seem to think that this teaching is in the Bible, but it is not. It is not taught in God's Book that He is the Father of all men. The Bible teaches that God is the *Creator* of all men, not the Father of all men. We are God's creatures, as the angels are His creatures, as the demons (who were undoubtedly angels before they fell) are God's created beings. Man is created by God, but is not a son of God until he is born of God. Childhood requires birth. Jesus said that He was the Father's Son; the Father had one Son. But through the Gospel alone can we be born again, and be made the children of God.

The teaching of Christ concerning God as Father is one of the precious things in this Book of books. Two verses in John speak plainly on this subject: "As many as received him (Christ) to them gave he power to become the sons of God, even to them that believe on his name" (John 1:12). "Ye (Pharisees) are of your father the devil" (John 8:44).

Question: Please explain John 5:37, "Ye have neither heard his voice at any time." Did the Jews not hear God's voice when Jesus was baptized, and "a voice from heaven" said, "This is my beloved Son, in whom I am well pleased"?

Answer: When the Lord Jesus told the Jews that they had not heard the Father's "voice," He used the term in the sense of other similar uses in Scripture: "Hear, and your souls shall live"; and "He that hath ears to hear, let him hear." The Jews did not accept the testimony of God from heaven; that was equivalent to not hearing, in the sense in which Christ used the term.

Question: Please explain Gen. 3:15. I have heard that it gives us the first promise of the Redeemer, but it is difficult for me to understand.

Answer: If you will read the pronoun "it" as it is accurately translated in the Revised Version, you will not have any difficulty in understanding the meaning of this verse. However, let me attempt to paraphrase it:

God was speaking to the serpent, pronouncing upon him the curse; and this is part of that curse: "I will put enmity between thee and the woman." Now the serpent was Satan's tool; and Satan is the enemy of man. He is called "our adversary, the devil" (I Pet. 5:8); and he is ever seeking to turn man from the worship of God to the worship of himself. Truly he is our enemy. And even the serpent, which was Satan's tool, though doubtless once a beautiful creature, is man's enemy. He hisses when man approaches; and surely man hates the serpent. But the real hatred here referred to is that between "that old serpent, which is the Devil" (Rev. 20:2) and man.

Now look at the next words: " . . . and between thy seed and her seed." Here the "seed of the woman" is none other than our Lord Jesus; and this is the first prophecy of His Virgin Birth. In many passages He is called "the seed," meaning the promised Son of Man. (Compare Gen. 21:12, where God said to Abraham, "In Isaac shall thy seed be called," with Gen. 12:1-3, where God promised Abraham the Redeemer. See also Gal. 3:19; 4:4 and many other passages.) Jesus Christ, our Lord, was in very truth "the seed of woman," *not of man;* for He had no human father. Now Satan hates our Lord, seeks in every way to thwart His great purpose for man, sought His worship and failed to obtain it—in every particular there is enmity between our sinless Saviour and the arch-enemy of our souls.

And now let us read further in Gen. 3:15: " . . . He (Christ) shall bruise thy head (God was speaking to the serpent, remember), and thou shalt bruise his heel." The head is the seat of government and all control of the body. Our Lord potentially bruised Satan's "head" when He died and rose again; and He will seal Satan's doom forever when He casts him into the lake of fire, "to be tormented day and night for ever and ever" (Rev. 20:10). But Satan has already bruised our Lord's "heel," which speaks of His physical body, when he put Him on the cross. Thank God! Death could not hold Him; and His redemptive work is finished!

Question: Are there two conflicting genealogies of Christ? I do not believe there are, for I accept the whole Word of God. But I heard a minister say that Matthew and Luke contradict each other. Please explain.

Answer: Matthew gives Joseph's genealogy; Luke gives Mary's. But why did the Holy Spirit record Joseph's genealogy, since he was not the father of Jesus? Because through him, the head of the Nazareth home, Christ had the *legal* right to the throne of His father, David. Had there been a king of the Jews in the time of Joseph, he would have been that king. And as the eldest Son of Mary, the eldest Son in that Nazareth home, Christ had every right to be King.

But back to the two genealogies: It is marvelously interesting to study them closely. In the first place, Matthew traces Joseph's ancestry back only as far as Abraham; for he was writing especially for the Jews; and this proved the point in question—that Jesus was the Heir to Abraham's land, and the Covenant-Heir to David's throne. Luke, however, traces Mary's ancestry back to Adam, "which was the son of God"; for Luke is showing that Christ is the perfect Son of Man, the Saviour of the whole world.

But please note in these genealogies how carefully the Spirit of God protects the doctrine of the Virgin Birth of Christ. Matthew uses the word "begat" *until* he comes to verse 16 of the first chapter. He does *not* say that Joseph begat Jesus; for he sacredly guards the fact that our Lord was born of the Virgin Mary. Luke, on the other hand, uses different phraseology throughout. Omitting the words in italics, which always in our English Bible are put in by the translators to make the meaning clear, we have Luke 3:23 reading as follows; "And Jesus himself began to be about thirty years of age, being (as was supposed) the son of Joseph, which was of Heli." Thus, according to Matthew, "Jacob begat Joseph"; and, according to Luke, "Joseph . . . was of Heli," that is, the son-in-law of Heli. You see, it was the custom of the Jews to keep all their genealogies in the names of men, not women. And do you note how, again, the Holy Spirit sacredly guards the truth of the Virgin Birth of Christ, according to Luke?

It is interesting to note that Joseph came through the kingly line of Judah and David and Solomon; whereas Mary came through the kingly line of Judah and David, yet through another son of David, Nathan (Luke 3:31).

Anyone who calls these two genealogies contradictory only manifests his ignorance of the way to read the original Greek— or, for that matter, our English translation; or he shows that he doubts the infallible Word of God. In either case, he belongs to the class described by Paul in Rom. 1:22, who "professing themselves to be wise . . . became fools." And so it is with all the so-called contradictions of the Bible. There are no contradictions! The Master-Mind that wrote it knew how to do it perfectly. Only the unregenerate, finite mind of some skeptic would presume to doubt it!

Question: Why do Mark and John give no human ancestry of Christ, and no record of His nativity?

Answer: Primarily Mark is presenting the Lord Jesus as the faithful Servant of Jehovah; his key verse is Mark 10:45: "For even the Son of man came not to be ministered unto, but to minister, and to give his life a ransom for many." And who asks for the genealogy or for the story of the birth of a servant? If a man came to mow your lawn, you would not ask him for his ancestry. If he came, however, to ask for the hand of your daughter in marriage, you would want to know these things.

Matthew presents Christ as the Heir to David's throne, and the Covenant-Heir to Abraham's land—Palestine. Hence Matthew traces Christ's genealogy back as far as David and Abraham.

Mark gives no genealogy because he is presenting Christ as a Servant, and no one asks for the genealogy of a servant.

Luke presents Christ as the perfect Son of Man, whose genealogy is traced back beyond Adam to God; for the body of the Lord Jesus was not only real and human; it was a body that God had *prepared*. (See Heb. 10:5).

John is writing to prove that Jesus of Nazareth always was and ever shall be the eternal Son of God. His purpose is stated in John 20:30, 31. And who would presume to say that, as eternal God, our Lord had a beginning? As the eternal Word of God (see John 1:1-14), He is the Creator of all things; He has neither beginning nor ending. Hence the opening verses of this Gospel link Him with eternity and the eternal God.

Thus it is that the Holy Spirit, who inspired all the "holy men of old" to write these sacred things, manifested His purpose by the parts omitted as well as the facts included in the record.

Let it be remembered that all four of the evangelists proved all of these things: That Jesus was the King of Israel, the faithful Servant of Jehovah, the perfect Son of Man, and the eternal Son of God. But each evangelist emphasized one of the above-named pictures of our Lord. That explains why there are *four* stories of His earthly ministry, each meeting the need of some special group of people, each meeting the need of us all, yet in different ways.

"O the depth of the riches both of the wisdom and knowledge of God! how unsearchable are his judgments, and his ways past finding out!" (Rom. 11:33).

Question: Please explain the use of the word "espoused" in the time of Christ. I believe in the Virgin Birth of the Lord Jesus, according to the flesh, but I have been asked to explain this term.

Answer: The Revised Version translates the word "betrothed." The following footnote quoted from the "Teachers' Testament," published by Thomas Nelson & Sons, New York City, gives some helpful information: "The betrothal of a Jewish maiden was more binding and significant than a similar ceremony is with us. It implied that the bridegroom had paid to the father of the prospective bride a sum of money, by which payment the control of the father over his daughter had passed to the bridegroom. Betrothal ordinarily took place a year before marriage." (Footnote on Luke 1:27).

Question: Did Jesus ever claim to be God?

Answer: Yes, very many times—by direct statement, by accepting worship as God, by doing the miracles that only God can perform, by His sinless life, by foretelling future events that only God knows, by rising from the dead by the power of His own Holy Spirit, by applying Old Testament prophecy to Himself.

Would you read for yourself some of the many passages where He definitely claimed to be God? Then read all of the Gospel according to John, noting particularly such verses as these:

"I that speak unto thee am he" (meaning the Messiah, or the Christ). (See John 4:25, 26.)

"Therefore the Jews sought the more to kill him, because he not only had broken the sabbath, but said also that God was his Father, *making himself equal with God*" (John 5:18).

"Moses wrote of me" (John 5:46). (Read all of this wonderful discourse in the fifth chapter of John for the Lord's irrefutable proof that He is God.)

"I am the bread of life . . . which came down from heaven" (John 6:35, 41, 48, 51).

"I proceeded forth and came from God" (John 8:42).

"Before Abraham was, I am" (John 8:58).

"Dost thou believe on the Son of God? He answered and said, Who is he, Lord, that I might believe on him? And Jesus said unto him, Thou hast both seen him, and it is he that talketh with thee. . . . And he worshipped him" (John 9:35-38).

Space forbids our quoting more here; but these are only a few of the many passages that might be given, not only from John, but also from the other Gospels; indeed, from all the Word of God, on this important subject. Either Christ was eternal God; or we have no Saviour, no life eternal, no hope in this world or in the world to come. Colossians and Hebrews speak much of the deity of Christ. Read them with an open mind, under the guidance of the Holy Spirit, and you will be amazed at the overwhelming testimony to our Saviour's deity.

Question: What is the Kenosis Theory?

Answer: The Kenosis Theory is held by Unitarians and modernists, and asserts that the Lord Jesus, in His Incarnation, emptied Himself of His divine attributes to such an extent that He shared the same infirmities and limitations of knowledge with the ordinary man. These say that He shared alike their ignorance and their mistakes, and that He was no better off than the fallible teachers of His day. Some theologians would go so far as to say that Christ did absolutely abandon the relationship of equality with God and His functions in the universe.

Those who hold the Kenosis Theory base their hypothesis upon the statement found in Phil. 2:5-8; we quote the passage here from the Revised Version:

"Have this mind in you, which was also in Christ Jesus: who, existing in the form of God, counted not the being on an equality with God a thing to be grasped, but emptied himself, taking the form of a servant, being made in the likeness of men; and being found in fashion as a man, he humbled himself, becoming obedient even unto death, yea, the death of the cross."

The term, "Kenosis Theory," comes from the Greek expression, rendered in our Authorized Version, "made himself of no reputation" (verse 7). As we note from the Revised Version, these words really mean "emptied himself." But Unitarians and others who hold the Kenosis Theory have read into Phil. 2:5-8 something that is not there. The text says that Christ "emptied himself" of something; but of what? Not of His deity, for that could not be. He could take manhood into union with deity, but He could not cease to be divine. He divested Himself of His rights as God the Son. He chose to come to earth to take the place of subjection.

The meaning of Phil. 2:5-8 will be made clear when two expressions are noted:

1. He was in the *form* of God.

2. He took the *form* of a servant.

According to these texts, what was changed? Only the *form*. Before the Incarnation, He was in the *form* of God, but at the Incarnation He was in the *form* of a servant. The form, and not the personality, was changed. He was ever the eternal Son. In John 8:24 our Lord said to the Jews, "If ye believe not that *I am*, (not 'I am he'; for the word 'he' is in italics in our English translation, and is therefore not in the original Greek)—if ye believe not that *I am*, ye shall die in your sins." The name "*I AM*" was the one God gave to Moses from the burning bush, and presents God as the self-existent One. Our Lord Jesus, in taking that name, declares in unmistakable language that He and the "I AM" of the Old Testament are the same.

Question: How would you explain the statement in Luke 2:52, that "Jesus increased in wisdom and stature, and in favour with God and man"?

Answer: Luke is emphasizing the real *humanity* of Christ. There was a cult in the beginning of the Christian era which denied the reality of His human body. The exponents of this cult claimed that Jesus did not have a human body at all, and that his body was a phantom, a creation of mortal mind. This is the teaching of certain present day cults, such as Christian Science. The humanity of Christ is emphasized by Luke because the Spirit of God foresaw that at the end of the age there would be a denial of His humanity, as there would be also of His deity.

Accordingly, Luke tells us that Jesus developed as other boys did He was subject to Joseph and Mary. He ate, slept, grew in wisdom and stature. We must remember that He became Man in order to die for sinners. *God cannot die;* but He devised a plan, by which He could be, at the same time, both God and Man; and as the Son of Man, He died that sinners might live. Read Heb. 2:14-18, 4:15. This is our Gospel message—that the Lord suffered, was tempted in all points like as we are, sin apart—He was not tempted to sin, because He was holy! But because He knew hunger and thirst and weariness and loneliness; because He suffered being tempted, He is able to succour them that are tempted. He is our sympathizing Saviour.

Moreover, when He became flesh, He laid aside His glory— not His deity. He became subject to His Father's will—as a Man. It is a great mystery, the "mystery of godliness," that "God was in Christ, reconciling the world unto himself." And what we can not *explain* about the Incarnation, we leave to faith! Read Phil. 2:5-11; Col. 1:14-19; I Tim. 3:16; II Cor. 5:19; John 1:1-14.

Question: How would you harmonize Mark 13:32 with the doctrine of the deity of Christ? Speaking of the time of His return to the earth, the Lord Jesus said, "But of that day and that hour knoweth no man, no, not the angels which are in heaven, neither the son, but the Father."

Answer: Modernists have used this verse in a futile attempt to prove that Jesus is not eternal God. Our Lord here seems to disclaim omniscience, but the reference is perfectly clear when one bears in mind the purpose of Mark's Gospel—to portray Jesus as the faithful Servant of Jehovah. Christ says in John 15:15, "The servant knoweth *not* what his lord doeth." How significant that Mark, who presents Jesus as the perfect Servant, should record this statement about the hour of His return as King of kings and Lord of lords. (Matthew also makes a similar statement in Matt. 24:36; likewise, Luke, in Acts 1:7).

In the aspect of His ministry *as a Servant,* our Lord made a *voluntary* surrender of certain knowledge, in order that He might walk the walk of faith, and thus be an object-lesson to all believers. While He ever remained the eternal Son of God, co-equal and co-eternal with the Father; yet as a Servant, He chose a limitation of His knowledge, bounded by the Father's will.

In like manner, we may trust God with perfect confidence, however dark and mysterious the way may be.

Question: How would you harmonize the doctrine of Christ's deity with John 5:19? I believe that Jesus Christ is the Son of God, equal with the Father. However, I find it difficult to understand this verse: "The Son can do nothing of himself, but what he seeth the Father do: for what things soever he doeth, these also doeth the Son likewise."

Answer: The words which you quote express one of the strongest affirmations of the deity of Christ in the Bible. Christ is here affirming that He, the Son, is in full union, in complete identification, with the Father; that He does nothing without the Father; but all He sees the Father do He does also. These words of the Lord Jesus do not mean limitation, but attest the complete, perfect unity which is between the Father and the Son. In His relation to the Father, the Son can do nothing independently of the Father, then He would be another God, which is an impossibility. When the Lord said, "The Son can do nothing of himself," He was stating that He would not act differently from the Father, from His own independent will.

Question: Since Christ was sinless, why was He baptized?

Answer: At least two thoughts have been suggested: (1) That this was the occasion of His public anointing by the Holy Spirit in His earthly ministry—thus proving to all the world that He was "the beloved Son of the Father" in heaven; and (2) that in this act He identified Himself with sinners, in order to fulfill "all righteousness."

The Jordan River represents death, and His going down into it was a picture of His approaching sacrifice on the cross. Our Lord came into the world to die on behalf of sinners. Here at the beginning of His ministry He identified Himself with sinners who were being baptized by John; and by so doing, He foreshadowed the purpose of His coming into the world. At Calvary He went into death on behalf of transgressors. He "who knew no sin" was made "sin for us." It was at the cross that all righteousness was fulfilled. Christ's baptism was a picture of all this.

It is noteworthy that in this event we have the Father's voice from heaven, the presence of the Son in His human body, and the presence of the Holy Spirit, descending "as a dove" upon the sinless Son of God. Here we have a beautiful lesson in the doctrine of the Trinity.

Question: How do you explain the temptation of Christ?

Answer: Certainly the temptation did not come from *within* for He was the sinless One. Our Lord was always "holy, harmless, undefiled, separate from sinners, and made higher than the heavens" (Heb. 7:26).

As the Man, Christ Jesus, He was "in all points tempted like as we are, apart from sin" (Heb. 4:15). Thus He was prepared for His earthly ministry, as well as for His present ministry as the Great High Priest at the right hand of the Father.

In other words, Christ knew what tears were. He knew loneliness, heartache, weariness, hunger, and anguish. Every pang of pain that the believer experiences is familiar to Him. And thus He is a sympathetic Saviour and High Priest in the glory. He is "touched with the feeling of our infirmities" (Heb. 4:15). However, we must bear in mind that the Lord Jesus was never tempted to sin. This is especially emphasized in Heb. 4:15, quoted above, where we read that He was "in all points tempted like as we are, *apart from sin.*" Had Christ been tempted to sin, it would have proved that He had a fallen nature, but this was not so. What is said of God in James 1:13 is true of Christ, for He is God: "Let no man say when he is tempted, I am tempted of God: for God cannot be tempted with evil, neither tempteth he any man." It is blasphemy to say that Christ could sin.

One may ask, "Then why the temptation?" And the answer is that His temptation was not to see whether He would sin, but to prove that He could not sin. Only such a One could be a Saviour.

Some time ago a bridge was built over a great chasm in Scotland. People were skeptical as to whether or not such a bridge would support a train laden with passengers and freight; therefore, they would not trust themselves to it. The railroad company demonstrated its strength by placing trains laden with pig iron on the rails over the bridge. For forty-eight hours they did nothing but shunt to and fro before an amazed and skeptical crowd. The purpose of this object-lesson was accomplished. The railroad train did not put those trains laden with pig iron on the bridge to see whether or not the bridge would hold, but rather to demonstrate the fact that it *would* hold. All doubt and skepticism passed from the minds of the people; and from that day to this, they have trusted themselves to the bridge.

It was for this same purpose that Christ was tempted. *Being God, He could not sin!*

Question: Why did the Lord Jesus address His mother as "woman"? Was this not a title of disrespect? (See John 2:4).

Answer: Not at all. When Jesus was on the cross, He addressed her in the same way: "When Jesus therefore saw his mother, and the disciple standing by, whom he loved, he saith unto his mother, Woman, behold thy son!" (John 19:26).

It is thought by some that in those days the word was almost equal to our word "lady." It was a title of respect; for when one woman went to Jesus, exercising great faith, and He wished to commend her, He said, "O woman, great is thy faith" (Matt. 15:28).

There is, however, no evidence that the Lord Jesus ever used the title "mother" when speaking to Mary after He entered upon His public ministry. A new relationship had been established the moment He stepped out of His home life at Nazareth, and began His ministry. (Compare Matt. 12:46-50.) From that time on, it was His *supernatural* parentage that He emphasized—that He was the only begotten Son of the Father in heaven.

Question: How would you explain Luke 13:32: "Behold, I cast out devils (or 'demons' R.V.), and I do cures to day and to morrow, and the third day I shall be perfected"?

Answer: The Lord spoke figuratively here of His approaching death and glory, meaning that He was not to be hurried on or turned aside from His course. God had planned His earthly career, and He would fulfill that career, and did at the hour appointed. Until His "hour was fully come," no man could touch the Son of God; for He Himself was God, as well as the humble Servant of Jehovah. Listen to His own words: "I lay down my life that I might take it again. No man taketh it from me, but I lay it down of myself. I have power to lay it down, and I have power to take it again. This commandment have I received of my Father" (John 10:17, 18).

Compare also these passages: "Mine hour is not yet come," spoken by Christ at the beginning of His ministry; and "Father, the hour is come," spoken on the way to Gethsemane, in His high priestly prayer. (See John 2:4; 17:1).

It was not by mere chance that the Son of God was crucified on the passover; He was our paschal Lamb! He came to die at a certain time; and He knew that He would be restored to His eternal glory, which He had with the Father before the world was. (See John 17:5).

Question: What is the difference between the expressions used by the Lord Jesus: "Mine hour is not yet come" and "My time is not yet come"?

Answer: There is a difference in these two expressions. When Christ said, "My time is not yet come," He was referring to events in His earthly life. For example, in John 7:6, when His disciples asked whether He was going down to Jerusalem to the feast of the tabernacles, He said, "My time is not yet come." Every step of the Lord was ordered by the Father.

We often say that we live a day at a time, but the Lord Jesus lived a second at a time. And wherever He put His foot, the same was in full accordance with the will and guidance of His Father in heaven.

The expression, "Mine hour has not yet come," always refers to the cross.

Question: What is the difference between the expres-Gethsemane when He prayed that "the cup" of suffering might pass from Him, if that were the Father's will?

Answer: Our Lord referred to the awful burden of the sins of the world when He prayed these words. Never had He for a moment, from all eternity, been separated from His Father; and He knew that, when He bore the curse of sin for us (II Cor. 5:21), His holy Father would have to turn His face away from the Son. That is why there was darkness on the earth when He was crucified. That is why the Son of God cried out on the cross, "My God, my God, why hast thou forsaken me?" Yet all the while, from all eternity, the Son had *planned* to die, knowing that this moment of separation would come; for David prophesied this very agonizing cry hundreds of years before Jesus was born in Bethlehem. (See Psalm 22:1). In that same Psalm David, writing under the guidance of the Holy Spirit, also foretold the whole crucifixion—the extreme thirst; the shameful death; the scoffing; the pierced hands and feet; the broken heart; the casting of lots for His vesture—all this is graphically foretold in this Scripture, which was written long before crucifixion was known as a means of execution.

And what does all this tell us of our Saviour's love for us? That, knowing full well the spiritual suffering before Him, to say nothing of the physical; yet He left heaven's glory and "bore our sins in his own body on the tree." He became a curse for us, bearing away forever the curse of sin for all who would put their faith in His finished redemption.

True it is that crucifixion is a terrible death; but our Lord was not afraid of pain. And other *men* have been crucified. But no other man ever suffered as He suffered, "the just for the unjust, that he might bring us to God." It was *because* He was "holy, harmless, undefiled, separate from sinners, and made higher than the heavens" (Heb. 7:26) that the spiritual suffering was so great—far beyond human comprehension!

There are some who think that Satan attempted to kill the Lord in the Garden of Gethsemane by causing a hemorrhage, in order to defeat His plan to die on the cross, as foretold in the Old Testament, and by His own words spoken on earth. They hold that when He cried out, saying, "Let this cup pass from me," He prayed to be delivered from death there, in order that He might go on to the cross. Those who hold this view base their interpretation on Heb. 5:7, 8, where we read: "In the days of his flesh, when he had offered up prayers and supplications with strong crying and tears unto him that was able to save him from death, and was heard in that he feared (in the Old Testament sense of the term, meaning 'reverential trust'); though he were a Son, yet learned he obedience by the things which he suffered."

This view is untenable because it was impossible for either man or Satan to kill the Lord before His hour had come. This is made clear all through the Gospel according to John. The real agony of Gethsemane and the cross, as we outlined it above, is found in the fact that our Lord's holy soul shrank from being "made sin for us . . . who knew no sin" in Himself. Into this suffering we can never fully enter.

Question: Why is it so hard for us to understand the love of Christ?

Answer: We shall never fully understand or fathom that love. There are statements in the Word of God concerning the love of God that stagger us; such as, "I have loved thee with an everlasting love" (Jer. 31:3). And again, in Eph. 2:1 we read that, even when we were "dead in trespasses and sins," He loved us, and died to redeem us. All through the eternal ages there will be an unfolding of the marvels of His Person and of His love and grace.

Question: Is the Holy Spirit an influence? I always believed Him to be a Person, but our pastor speaks of Him as impersonal.

Answer: The Holy Spirit is not just an influence, though rationalistic theologians and various cults so describe Him. The Word of God makes it plain that He is a Person, co-equal and co-eternal with the Father and with the Son. Moreover, the Revised Version of our English Bible always translates the pronoun referring to Him as "He" or "Him"—never "it." So does the Authorized Version, except in one or two passages, where the translation is not as accurate as the Revised Version. Our Lord repeatedly called the Holy Spirit a Person, especially in His farewell message to the disciples in John 14-16. Read these chapters to find the verses for yourself. And the entire New Testament is full of many references to the Holy Spirit of God, showing that He is one with the Father and the Son.

(For the Person and Work of the Holy Spirit in this church age, see questions on the baptism of the Holy Spirit.)

Question: Where will the Holy Spirit be after the translation of the church?

Answer: The church is "the temple of the Holy Spirit"; and when the rapture takes place, the Holy Spirit will go with the church. However, He is omnipresent; for He is God, equal with the Father and with the Son. Because He is God, and because God never leaves Himself without a witness in the world, the Holy Spirit will operate in the earth during the tribulation period, even as He did in Old Testament times. He came upon certain individuals then, anointing them for service. His mission for the church age, indwelling the members of the body of Christ, which is the church, will end at the rapture. But he will seal the 144,000 Jews during the tribulation period, and empower their testimony. The church, however, will have been completed; and He will not operate then as He does now in the world. It will be a different ministry.

Let it be remembered that there can be no conversion, in any age, without the quickening power of the Holy Spirit.

III

SATAN—SIN—DEMONS—HELL

Question: Why did God create Lucifer when He knew that he would become the devil?

Answer: We all admit that this is the great "Why?" Some sinners question the wisdom and love of God in creating the devil. They accuse God of permitting Satan to bring sin into the human heart, then holding man responsible for his inherited sin.

But look at the glorious truth recorded in Eph. 2:7. Here we learn that "in the ages to come" God is going to put on exhibition, to the glory of Christ, the redeemed sons of Adam, sinners saved by grace. One of the old Hebrew words translated "grace" means "to bestow a gift upon a bankrupt." Therefore, there had to be spiritual bankruptcy on earth before the abounding grace of God could be bestowed upon sinful humanity.

But some argue that, if God arbitrarily brought the bankruptcy, with the universal law of sin and death, He should arbitrarily bestow grace and save every member of the human family. The Universalist teaches that God will do this very thing, and redeem all the sons and daughters of Adam by the redemptive work of Jesus Christ.

This may be a consoling theory, and religious men may persuade themselves that they have some Scripture to support the theory; but the whole body of the Scripture is summed up in John 3:36, and is definitely contrary to this false doctrine: "He that believeth on the Son hath everlasting life: and he that believeth not the Son shall not see life; but the wrath of God abideth on him."

When the Lord Jesus was on earth, He referred to the devil as "Satan" and "the prince of this world." In Luke 10:18 He said, "I beheld Satan as lightning fall from heaven." Some hold that the Lord was here referring to what is going to happen to Satan when he is cast out into the earth, as prophesied in Rev. 12:7-9. But when we compare Luke 10:18 with Ezek. 28:14-19 and Isa. 14:12-17, we learn that Satan was cast out of heaven before Adam was ever created. These passages in Ezekiel and Isaiah teach us that this creature was not Satan when he was in heaven. Here he is called "the anointed cherub" and "Lucifer, son of the morning." He was perfect in the day in which he was created *until iniquity was found in him*. But several times he said, "I will . . . I will be like the Most High." So far as we know, that was the beginning of sin. Sin is saying to God, "I will," instead of "Thy will." Because the anointed cherub said, "I will," the anointed Son of God, sweating as it were drops of blood in Gethsemane, had to say, "Thy will."

But the question is asked, "If God is both omnipotent and omnipresent; if He saw in the future the wreck and chaos that Satan was going to produce, why did not God either create the anointed cherub so he could not sin, or destroy him before he wrecked the human race?" This, of course, also brings the question, "Why did God not create Adam and Eve so that they could not sin by yielding to Satan's temptations?"

We acknowledge that the "Why?" will remain a mystery until we come into the full realization of God's glory in the ages to come; but in the meantime we must be satisfied with the statement that God works all things "after the counsel of his own will." And "the Lord is not slack concerning his promise, as some men count slackness; but is longsuffering to usward, not willing that any should perish, but that all should come to repentance" (II Pet. 3:9).

Question: Why did God let sin enter the world?

Answer: If I could answer that question, I should be God; it is one of the things we have to leave with Him, knowing that "the Judge of all the earth" will always do what is just and right. (See Gen. 18:25.)

However, even with our finite minds, we can understand how God "seeketh such to worship him" as do it voluntarily, rather than because they cannot do otherwise. (See John 4:23, 24.) We ourselves want the love of those who, of their own accord, love us; we spurn favors from those who are self-seeking and selfish in their motives for acts of kindness or a show of affection. Therefore, it seems very clear to me that God permitted us, as free moral agents, to choose His love, rather than make us automatons who could do only as He commanded. For true love to express itself, there must be a choice.

God allowed the temptation, in order that man might become righteous; and righteousness is innocence tested. When God placed Adam and Eve in the Garden of Eden, He placed them in a state of perfect innocence; but innocence is not righteousness. Righteousness is what God wants, as set forth on every page of the Bible. And innocence can not become righteousness until it is tested.

Adam and Eve were the only human beings who were ever innocent. We sometimes say that babies are innocent, but this is not true. Babies are *undeveloped*. Adam and Eve were innocent; that is, they had a will, but before the temptation, they had no opportunity to exercise it, either one way or the other. God allowed the temptation, in order that they might exercise their will God-ward, and thus become righteous. Had they done this, they would have been permitted to eat of the tree of life, and thus live forever beyond the possibility of sin. However, they failed in the test by exercising their will in the direction of unrighteousness, thus becoming sinners. But God is the God of grace, as well as righteousness. And the sinful, fallen state of man gave Him the opportunity of showing His grace through His matchless plan of redemption.

Those who would accuse God for allowing sin on the earth need to remember that He was "the Lamb slain from the foundation of the world" (Rev. 13:8). For in Christ "dwelleth all the fulness of the Godhead bodily" (Col. 2:9). By Him "all things were made" (John 1:3, 10; Heb. 1:2; 2:10; Col. 1:15, 16). He was ever eternal God, our Creator; and He it was who *planned* to die for sinners! Is that not proof that He is and always was and ever shall be the God of love? He bore "our sins in his own body on the tree" (I Pet. 2:24); suffering the most shameful of deaths; being separated from His Father, with whom He had ever had unbroken fellowship—all this our Lord did because He loved us. And who would dare, in the face of such sacrificial love, harbor even for a moment the thought that He could be capable of anything less than justice and kindness and right? He is without sin!

One other word: When Satan puts such doubts into our minds, let us rebuke him, in the words of Paul, as he was inspired by the Holy Spirit: "O man, who art thou that repliest against God?" (Read Rom. 9:14-24.)

Question: Do you believe in a personal devil? Please explain what the Bible teaches about Satan.

Answer: Most assuredly I believe in a personal devil; and he is not a dragon with a red body, horns, and a forked tail, as billboards and legends picture him. He himself is the instigator of such caricature; for it is his purpose to lead men to believe that he is a myth and a joke. But he is *no joke,* let me tell you! For the Bible teaching on this important subject, let me briefly outline a few facts, which you will do well to study for yourself from the Word of God for the plain teaching of Scripture on the arch-enemy of our souls.

1. Before Satan fell through pride, he was a cherub, beautiful, bright, and wise. He was called "Lucifer, son of the morning" and "the anointed cherub that covereth." (See Isa. 14:12-

17; Ezek. 28:12-19.) (Names are given to only two other angels in the Bible: Gabriel and the archangel Michael; while the "angel of the Lord" is often mentioned in Old Testament Scripture as the appearance of God in angelic form before Christ came into the world.) Very evidently, Satan was a powerful angel. While there is no definite statement in the Bible to prove that, in his unfallen state, he was given dominion over the earth in its original beauty; yet there are inferences and intimatitons which seem to point to this fact.

As we have explained in answer to another question in this series of studies, the Lord Jesus called him "the prince of this world" (John 14:30; 16:11); while Paul wrote of him as "the god of this world" (II Cor. 4:4). The Lord Jesus did not deny his right to offer Him "the kingdoms of the world" in His temptation (Matt. 4:8). Many Bible students think that the fall of Satan may have been accompanied by the chaos into which the world was thrown, out of which, at an indefinite time later, God renovated the earth and created all life. In these things we dare not be dogmatic; for beyond what God has seen fit to reveal in His Word, we may not go.

2. The Lord Jesus said, in Luke 10:18, "I beheld Satan as lightning fall from heaven." This, by the way, is a remarkable proof of the deity of Christ. Satan's fall certainly preceded the fall of man—possibly a long, long time; and Adam and Eve sinned about 4,000 years before Jesus was born in Bethlehem. Yet the eternal God and our Creator, even Jesus, "beheld Satan as lightning fall from heaven."

3. Satan tempted Eve in the Garden of Eden, speaking through the serpent (Gen. 3:1-13).

4. Though Satan will one day be in hell, which was "prepared for the devil and his angels" (Matt. 25:41), yet he is not in hell today, nor has he ever been. No one ever returns from the lake of fire! And Satan is still "going to and fro in the earth . . . walking up and down in it" (Job 1:7; 2:2). Even

as he had access to the presence of God when he accused Job—
you see, he is still an angel, though a fallen angel; and as a
spirit-being, he still has access to God, though he was cast out
of heaven as his place of abode—but even as he accused Job, so
also he is still "the accuser of our brethren" (Rev. 12:10). He
is our "adversary" and "as a roaring lion, walketh about, seeking whom he may devour" (I Pet. 5:8). It is Satan's delight
to have occasion to accuse us to God, yet we should be ashamed
to give him such occasion. When we do, however, "we have
an Advocate with the Father, Jesus Christ the righteous" (I
John 2:1). And our risen Lord is more powerful than Satan
and all his hosts! (See also Luke 22:31; Heb. 2:14.)

5. As "the prince of the power of the air, the spirit that
now worketh in the children of disobedience" (Eph. 2:2), he
is very powerful. "For we wrestle not against flesh and blood
(other human beings), but against principalities, against powers,
against the rulers of the darkness of this world, against spiritual
wickedness in high places" (Eph. 6:12). Thus we see that the
earth and the air are the scene of his untiring activity. And
his many demons go forth at his bidding. Thank God! It will
not always be so!

6. Satan's certain doom was pronounced in the Garden of
Eden, when God said that "the seed of woman" (the Lord
Jesus) would "bruise" Satan's head. For the terrible picture
of his eternal torment, read Rev. 20:10.

**Question: Why does the New Testament speak so often
of "devils" when there is only one devil?**

Answer: Evidently you refer to the King James or Authorized Version of our English Bible. The Revised Version more
accurately translates the word "demons" when it does not refer
to Satan, the only devil. In other words, there is only one
devil; there are many demons, his emissaries. The context

always makes clear which is meant, even if you do not possess a copy of the Revised Version.

Question: Please explain James 2:19, "The demons also believe, and tremble."

Answer: If you read the context, you will see that James, in writing to the man whose empty *profession* of faith does not bear fruit, says, in substance, "Thou believest that God is one; thou doest well (or, in paraphrase, 'so far so good') : the demons also believe (that God is one) and tremble." And why do they tremble? Because they know that their doom is sealed, and that they will one day be cast into the lake of fire with the devil and all his wicked angels. Theirs is a head-knowledge, but not a heart-knowledge.

The same might be said of any human being who knows that there is one God, yet refuses the atoning work of Christ on the cross. He trembles at the thought of judgment—unless Satan has so blinded him that he has deceived him into a false sense of security.

When the Lord Jesus was on earth, the demons recognized Him as "the Holy One of God." On one occasion they "cried out saying, What have we to do with thee, Jesus, thou Son of God? *art thou come to torment us before the time?"* (Matt. 8:29). Here they express a knowledge of certain doom.

When the Lord Jesus "suffered them not to speak" of Him as the Son of God, it seems as though He would not receive this testimony from demons.

Question: Do you believe in a literal place of burning hell and torture for all the wicked? If so, how do you reconcile that doctrine with the love of God?

Answer: The only way I have of knowing what God will do is by observing what He has done in the past, and by turning to His Word to see what He says He will do in the future. From Jude 5-7 I learn something of His dealings with "the angels which kept not their first estate"; of the terrible judgment that befell Sodom and Gomorrah, and how the inhabitants of those wicked cities suffer the punishment of *fire* that is *eternal*.

No one ever spoke words more solemn in regard to the destiny of the wicked than did the Lord Jesus. His statements pluck up by the roots all such teaching as annihilation of the wicked and universalism. Take, for instance, the words of the Lord in Matt. 25:46, "And these shall go away into eternal punishment: but the righteous into eternal life" (R.V.). Every effort has been made to make the word "eternal" mean something else besides what it obviously does mean. But it is the same Greek word that is translated "eternal" in connection with the destiny of the righteous. Unversalists have attempted to show that the Greek *aionion* means simply "age-long," implying that there will be a limit to the punishment of the wicked. However, the same word is used seventy-two times in the New Testament: Three times, about the eternity of the existence of God; three times about the Holy Spirit; four times about heaven; and sixty-two times, about the destiny of the wicked. Surely this startling fact speaks for itself! And surely God has not failed to warn man of the consequences of rejecting the only Saviour from sin!

Yet again, the words of the Lord Jesus in John 3:36 settle the question once for all: "He that believeth on the Son *hath* eternal life; but he that believeth not the Son shall not see life, but the wrath of God *abideth* on him." The words "shall not see life" put an end to the argument of universalists; while the words "the wrath of God abideth on him" put an end to annihilation; for "abideth" is in the present progressive tense. The wrath of God could not "abide" on someone who does not exist because of annihilation.

How do we reconcile this doctrine with the love of God? My friend, we do not shrink from proclaiming "the wages of sin" because we have another side of the message to tell forth: "For God so loved the world, that he gave his only begotten Son, that whosoever believeth in him should not perish, but have everlasting life" (John 3:16).

Personally, I have never seen that there is anything to be gained by questioning whether or not the torment of hell is literal fire or some other kind of punishment. If God had wanted us to take it figuratively, would He not have told us? And whether literal or figurative in its meaning, the term definitely expresses fearful suffering. To be shut out from the presence of God forever; to be denied all the light and joy and comfort that even the wicked shade in this world as the by-products of Christianity; to know undying remorse and shame and sin— are not these things suggestive of bitterness of soul, whatever comes? Why, then, trifle with the subject?

I have often heard people dare to ask, "How can a God of love send men to hell? Let me tell you, in the first place, that God does not send any soul to hell. Every man decides for himself whether or not he will accept or reject the Lord Jesus, the only Saviour from sin. Moreover, the wicked could not stand the glories of heaven, even if they could get there. As the naked eye cannot look upon the sun without going blind, so also the regenerate could not bear the presence of our holy God. We read in Rev. 6:15-17 a terrible picture of what will happen when the wicked will hide themselves "in the dens and in the rocks of the mountains" and cry out to the mountains and rocks, saying, "Fall on us, and hide us from the face of him that sitteth on the throne, and from the wrath of the Lamb: for the great day of his wrath is come; and who shall be able to stand?" No, my friend, the wicked could not bear the light of heaven and the presence of the Lamb of God, even if they could get there.

And, too, heaven would not be heaven if sin could enter there. Our holy God can not bear the presence of sin. Yet He loved a sinful world so much that, before "the foundation of the world," He planned to die for sinners (Rev. 13:8). Is that not love? Dare we question the wisdom and justice of such a God? We shall do well to take Him at His Word; love Him because He first loved us; and seek rather to warn men to flee from the wrath to come, than waste time by trying to make Scripture mean what it does not say, thus helping to lull sinners to sleep with a false sense of security.

Question: What is the meaning of the expression, ". . . everlasting fire, prepared for the devil and his angels" (Matt. 25:41)? Would this not imply that hell is not for man?

Answer: It does imply that hell was no*t "prepared"* for man. Hell was *"prepared"* for the devil and his angels. When man fell into sin, God "prepared" *salvation* for him. But it is clearly stated that, if man rejects that prepared salvation, he will find himself in the place prepared for the devil and his angels.

Question: What does the Bible teach about the fallen angels?

Answer: Two New Testament passages speak plainly:

"God spared not the angels that sinned, but cast them down to hell, and delivered them into chains of darkness, to be reserved unto judgment" (II Pet. 2:4).

"The angels which kept not their first estate, but left their own habitation, he hath reserved in everlasting chains under darkness unto the judgment of the great day" (Jude 6).

It has been conjectured that perhaps the fallen angels sinned when Satan exalted himself as God, and wanted to be worshipped as God. He evidently had a following in these now fallen angels. We do not know, because the Bible does not tell us. Therefore, we dare not go beyond the revealed truth of God's Word. Matt. 25:41 would lead us to associate these fallen angels with Satan: "Then shall he say also unto them on the left hand, Depart from me, ye cursed, into everlasting fire, prepared for *the devil and his angels.*"

Question: I Cor. 6:3 states that Christians shall "judge angels." Who are these angels, and when will this judgment take place?

Answer: The angels are those referred to in Jude 6: "And the angels which kept not their first estate, but left their own habitation, he hath reserved in everlasting chains under darkness unto the judgment of the great day." (Cf. II Peter 2:4.)

The likelihood is that the judgment of those angels will take place at the great white throne, where wicked men are to be judged, though there is no definite statement to that effect in the Word of God.

The part Christians will have in judging angels is not revealed. And what God has not seen fit to tell us, we leave with Him, accepting His Word for it, on faith.

Question: What is the unpardonable sin?

Answer: While the final rejection of the Son of God as the only Saviour *is* unpardonable, and fixes destiny; yet a careful reading of Matt. 12:22-32; Mark 3:22-30; Luke 11:14-23 makes it clear that "the unpardonable sin" is the accusation that the Lord Jesus Christ was in league with Beelzebub, and that His miracles were performed by the power of the devil.

This unpardonable sin cannot be committed during this age, because the Lord Jesus is not on the earth. He must be on earth, performing mighty acts in the presence of people, in order that such a sin may be committed. This is the explanation of the words, "Whosoever speaketh against the Holy Ghost, it shall not be forgiven him, neither *in this age,* neither *in the age to come*" (Matt. 12:32). The "age to come" is the millennium, when Christ will be on the earth to reign. If in that coming age anyone attributes His mighty works to Satan, then that will be *the* "unpardonable sin" as referred to in the above-named Scriptures, even as it was *the* "unpardonable sin" for the Pharisees to hold that He cast out demons by the power of Beelzebub when He was on the earth nearly two thousand years ago.

When Christ spoke these words concerning this sin against the Holy Spirit, the church age was yet a "mystery"; that is, something not then revealed to man. The Lord Jesus was speaking at the close of the dispensation of law, which culminated at the cross. "The age to come," as known by the Jew, and as foretold in the prophetic Scriptures, is the time when the kingdom will be established. The present church age, then a "mystery" to the Jews. Christ passed over, because it was to be revealed later through Paul.

Question: What is "the second death"?

Answer: There are several references in the book of Revelation to "the second death." They tell us that it is "the lake of fire." (See Rev. 2:11, 20:6, 14.) The term is used in the sense of eternal punishment, separation from God, remorse, suffering, and sorrow; not in the sense of physical death, as the whole body of Scripture makes plain.

You must bear in mind that death, in the Bible, never means cessation of existence. It means separation. The prodigal son was separated from his father and from his father's house. Consequently, the father said, "This my son was *dead,* and is alive again" (Luke 15:24). The father did not mean that his son had ceased to exist, but that he was separated from him, and in the far country.

Paul has the same thought in mind in Eph. 2:1, where he says, "You hath he quickened, who were dead in trespasses and sins." Before their conversion these Ephesians were "dead" because they were alienated from God and afar off.

Physical death also means separation of the spirit from the body. "The body without the spirit is dead" (Jas. 2:26).

All these things need to be borne in mind because of the teaching of the Russellites and other annihilationists, who claim that death means absolute non-existence. The "second death" of Revelation is separation of both body and spirit from God.

IV

THE EARLY HISTORY OF MAN

Question: As only about 6,000 years have passed since Adam was created, how do you account for all the millions of years scientists claim for the age of the earth?

Answer: Between the first two verses of Genesis there could have elapsed all the time of all the geologic ages. "In the beginning God created the heaven and the earth." Possibly that was millions of years ago. Then something happened to mar God's perfect, original creation; for verse 2 reads, "And the earth was [*became*] without form and void." (Cf. Jer. 4:23-26; Isa. 24:1; 45:18.) Note the real meaning of the word "became." How long the earth remained in this chaotic condition, God has not seen fit to tell us; but certainly there is room here for all the time of all the ages. Then out of this chaos, God brought a *renovated* earth about 6,000 years ago; created all life; made man in His own image, even as the inspired record states.

Just what happened to ruin God's original creation, He has not seen fit to tell us; yet there is scriptural ground for believing that the fall of Satan and the wicked angels *may* have been associated with the judgment that came upon the earth. That Satan fell through pride, we know. (Read Isa. 14:12-17; Eezk. 28:12-18.) That he seems to have been given dominion over the earth before he fell, while he was still a beautiful angel, seems to be beyond all doubt. (See John 12:31; 14:30; II Cor. 4:4; Matt. 4:8, 9.) When Satan offered the Lord Jesus all the kingdoms of this world, if He would worship him, Christ did not deny Satan's power to give possession of "the world." These and other Scriptures seem to imply that the earth was Satan's domain before he fell through pride. He sinned by seeking worship as God. He caused man to fall by the same appeal to pride—"Ye shall be as gods." He sought in vain to obtain worship from the sinless Son of God. He is, even yet, in a sense the "god of this world," by which Paul means the God-dishonoring, Christ-rejecting, Spirit-resisting world.

Thank God! It will not always be so. One day our Lord will come and claim that which is His by right of creation, and which He has purchased from its fallen state by right of His atoning work on the cross.

Our God is a God of science and order. But ever remember Paul's admonition to Timothy: "O Timothy, keep that which is committed to thy trust, *avoiding profane and vain babblings, and oppositions of science falsely so called"* (I Tim. 6:20).

Question. Was there a race of beings upon the earth before the Garden of Eden and the creation of Adam and Eve?

Answer: There are a few passages in the Scriptures that would lead us to believe that there was a race of beings on the earth before Adam was created. For example, in Gen. 1:28, following the record of the creation of man, we read the words of God to Adam and Eve: "And God blessed them, and God said unto them, Be fruitful, and multiply, and replenish the earth . . ." The word "replenish" here is the same that was given to Noah after the flood, and the inference is that the earth had been inhabited before Adam's day.

We must bear in mind, however, that the pre-Adamic race —if there was one—was not a race of human beings. In all probability they were an angelic host led by Satan before his fall, while he was called Lucifer. There are indications in Scripture that Satan once had the same dominion over this earth as was given to Adam, which dominion Adam lost through his fall. This would account for Satan's interference with the world and with the human race.

The description of the Eden in which Lucifer was placed, as recorded in Ezek. 28:13, may refer to the earth before the chaotic period of Gen. 1:2. But we do not know that it was entirely separate and different from the Eden into which Adam was placed.

The many fossils that are discovered today, which would indicate life upon this earth millions of years ago, may be the relics of the pre-Adamic days, to which the Scriptures here and there allude. Jer. 4:23-26, for example, says in part: "I beheld the earth, and lo, it was without form and void: and the heavens, and they had no light . . . and, lo there was no man, and all the birds of the heavens were fled . . ." (Cf. Isa. 24:1; 45:18.) The words "no man upon the earth" would indicate that this may be a description of a condition before the advent of man.

Question: Is there any proof as to how long man has been on the earth? The text books my children use tell of prehistoric man and the stone-age man. But what proof has a Christian as to the time man has inhabited the earth? Perhaps you can refer me to some author who has presented this answer in simple form.

Answer: Let me suggest that you get our book of radio messages on "God's Plan of the Ages." I believe it will help you a little in your study of original man. The footnotes of the Scofield Reference Bible also give much light upon the scriptural teaching concerning the original creation, chaos, and the renovation of the earth.

In the preceding questions we have touched briefly upon related topics. But let me add here that Adam was created about 6,000 years ago. The so-called prehistoric man and the stone-age man do not prove the fairy tale of organic evolution. They rather prove the account of the first chapter of Romans, where we are informed that, when men departed from God, they went into the depth of sin and degradation. This answer satisfies the Christian, who takes God at His Word.

Hundreds of text books used in our school system today substitute supposition for fact; fancy for theory; man's human philosophy, which leaves God out, for the "Thus saith the Lord" of Holy Writ.

Question: Were the six days of creation solar days of twenty-four hours each, or were they longer periods of time?

Answer: I believe they were solar days of twenty-four hours each. However, there are those who think that II Peter 3:8 implies that they may have been longer periods of time: "One day is with the Lord as a thousand years, and a thousand years as a day."

The insurmountable difficulty in believing that the Genesis days were ages is that the Word says that each of the "days" of creation was divided into two parts: The light was called "day," and the darkness was called "night." If the night had consisted of thousands of years, all vegetation would have died. All vegetable life must have light in order to survive.

The motive back of certain critics in estimating these six days of creation as longer periods of time, is to seek to apply the theory of evolution to the creation story. Certainly the God of all creation is *able* to do all things; and He could assuredly create all things in six solar days, or less time than that if He chose to do it. And our God did *not* bring human life into the world by such a process as organic evolution. To accept such a theory, is to deny the infallible Word of God.

Question: Why do you not accept the theory of the organic evolution of man? I do not accept the atheistic

theory — that there is no God, and that man sprang from a so-called "First Cause." But if I believe that God created man by this method, then what is wrong with that? In other words, I had a science instructor who calls himself a theistic evolutionist, meaning that he believes that God created all life by this method.

Answer: Many volumes have been written on this subject; but space here will permit only the most brief discussion. I am familiar with the arguments set forth by the so-called "theistic evolutionists." But that term is misleading. It deceives the unwary. I know that such scientists "falsely so called" admit that the Biblical story of the *order* of creation is scientific, and try to build a parallel *theory,* saying that, before there could be plant or animal life, there had to be light. *Even so the Biblical record is scientific in the true sense of the term!* The God of all wisdom is the God of all true science! I realize also that these theistic evolutionists reason thus: That "one day is with the Lord as a thousand years, and a thousand years as a day."

But what these people fail to see is that *the evolution theory is a flat denial of the fall of man;* and thus they play into the hands of Satan, who would ever deceive man and try to lead him to believe that there is no sin, no need of a Saviour, no fall, no regenerating power in the shed blood of our Lord Jesus Christ. To grasp this truth is fundamental; and it settles the issue forever. If man evolved, then he was not made "in the image and likeness of God" *in the beginning,* and the Bible does not mean what it says. If man was evolved from a lower form of animal life, then he did not fall through sin, and God's great plan of redemption—all the Word of God—is to be set at naught. According to this theory, man is ever climbing upwards, and will someday be "as gods"—Satan's falsehood! Do you not see, my friend, how subtle Satan's attack has ever been, and still is, in deluding thousands of would-be intellectuals, seeking to turn them away from Calvary's cross? The Holy Spirit says, through Paul, that such as these, "professing themselves to be wise . . . became fools" (Rom. 1:22).

Moreover, while variations within a given species are abundant, yet science has yet to show a single instance of where one species brought forth another species. Cattle do not bear reptiles; and fish do not bear fowl. Neither can one species "evolve" into a higher species. God's Word can not be broken; each form of animal life brings forth "after his kind." This, too, is fundamental.

If any man prides himself on his superiority over the pagan blacks of Australia or Africa; if he thinks he has won this place of superiority by his own development, or by that of his forefathers, let him remember that only by the grace of God did his forefathers have the Gospel; only by the grace of God is he what he is—whether Christian, or simply enjoying the by-products of Christianity. Let him remember that the savage heathen is what he is today because of the long-continued sins of his race. (See Rom. 1:18-32.)

Let me add also that many great scientists today have stated that this theory of organic evolution is false. And even its most ardent supporters always have to admit that, at best, it is only a *theory*—which is another name for a *supposition*.

Over against this Satan-inspired *theory* we have the eternal *fact* of God's Word. "Thus saith the Lord" is not to be refuted. And man would do well to believe the Word of the unchanging, eternal, all-wise God.

Question: Do we have any scriptural proof for the location of the Garden of Eden?

Answer: Yes, while the exact boundaries of the Garden of Eden are not named, yet the general location is definitely stated.

At least four proper names recorded in the second chapter of Genesis may be located on the maps of history: "Ethiopia . . . Hiddekel (the ancient name for the Tigris River) . . . Assyria ' ' . Euphrates River" (Gen. 2:13, 14).

Secular history calls the Tigris-Euphrates valley, or Mesopotamia, "the cradle of civilization," and rightly so, according to the Genesis story of creation.

Question: Were Adam and Eve clothed with a garment of light before the fall? In your book, "God's Plan of the Ages," you state that before the fall, man was clothed with such a garment. I showed this statement to my pastor, and he said that it is not so. To prove his point, he quoted Gen. 2:25: "They were both naked, the man and his wife, and were not ashamed." How would you answer this objection?

Answer: If Gen. 2:25 is to be understood as referring to an absolute nakedness, we must have an odd idea of Adam's and Eve's knowledge, or rather, of their ignorance, at being naked and not knowing it; for according to this supposition, they were not ashamed because they knew not that they were naked; but only after they had sinned, "the eyes of them both were opened, and they knew that they were naked."

It is an inconceivable thing that Adam and Eve should be as naked before the fall as they were afterwards, and yet be so blind as never to see this, or so ignorant as not to know it. It is unthinkable that their sight in this regard should come with their apostasy from God. Such is unreasonable.

The meaning, therefore, of the words must be this: That although Adam and Eve had no such material garment before the fall as they had afterwards, when God clothed them with the skins of animals (Gen. 3:21); yet they had no reason for being ashamed, because they were clothed with a luminous garment that more than made up that want. The whole story of the fall is suggestive in this regard. They evidently lost *something* in the way of clothing, because they immediately began to make for themselves a covering.

Just one word further in regard to the statement that Adam and Eve were clothed with a garment of light before the fall: Psalm 104:1, 2 reads: "O Lord my God, thou art very great; thou art clothed with honour and majesty. *Who coverest thyself with light as with a garment.*" And Gen. 1:26, 27 says plainly: "And God said, Let us make man *in our image after our likeness* . . . So God created man in his own image." Does it seem far-fetched to take the Word of God literally on this matter; Only after man sinned was he afraid of God, ashamed to stand in His presence. But made in the image and likeness of God—and He clothed Himself "with light as with a garment"—how beautiful and majestic must man have been when he first came from the hands of the Creator!

Question: Why did God reject Cain's offering, and accept Abel's?

Answer: Because Cain brought a bloodless sacrifice, in spite of the fact that God had taught him that "without shedding of blood is no remission" of sin (Heb. 9:22). Abel, on the other hand, brought "the firstlings of his flock" (Gen. 4:4), a blood sacrifice, that showed his faith in the coming of Christ, "the Lamb of God, which taketh away the sin of the world" (John 1:29). Heb. 11:4 leaves no room for doubt; for there we read that "*by faith* Abel offered unto God a more excellent sacrifice than Cain." And in Heb. 12:24 the blood of Jesus is called "the blood of sprinkling, that speaketh *better things* than that of Abel." Here the type is definitely explained.

Every Old Testament saint is in heaven today because he believed God's promises—and they were many, given in plain statement, in shadow, and in type—that the only Redeemer was to come to die for a sinful world. And every lost soul of every age will be in hell because he spurned God's only way of salvation, which is the way of the cross. "There is none other name under heaven given among men, whereby we must be saved" (Acts 4:12).

Question: Please answer this question for an elderly man who has been in the false religion known as Unity and Theosophy: How could Cain know what kind of an offering to bring if God did not tell him? (See Gen. 4:4, 5.)

Answer: God did tell him. Abel, his brother, knew the kind of offering to bring, and he brought it. Cain also knew, but he refused to bring it. "By *faith* Abel offered unto God a more excellent sacrifice than Cain" (Heb. 11:4); and faith is taking God at His Word.

Cain is the type of the natural man, who refuses to believe in vicarious suffering. But you may ask, "How did he know what offering to bring?" Why, from his parents, Adam and Eve. They would surely relate to their sons the story of the fall, and how God had made clear that sin carried with it a penalty to be atoned for only by the shedding of blood. They would tell their children that the only approach to God was by faith in the promised Redeemer (Gen. 3:15).

But God also told Cain to bring the animal sacrifice. Read Gen. 4:5-7: "But unto Cain and to his offering he had not respect. And Cain was very wroth and his countenance fell. And the Lord said unto Cain, Why art thou wroth? and why is thy countenance fallen? If thou doest well, shalt thou not be accepted? And if thou doest not well, sin lieth at the door." In the Hebrew the same word is used for "sin" and "sin-offering." Thus Cain's sin is here identified with the sin-offering—the animal sacrifice—that crouched at his "tent door."

In spite of God's explicit exhortation, to say nothing of what Adam and Eve without doubt had taught Cain, even then Cain deliberately went out and killed his brother because of envy and jealousy. This shows that his heart was untouched by God's exhortation. The hardest, meanest man in the world is the self-righteous man, of whom Cain is a type.

Question: Where did Cain get his wife?

Answer: This question is just one of the skeptic's "stock in trade." But by asking it, he shows his ignorance of the Bible. If he would but read the fourth and fifth chapters of Genesis, he would see that, after Cain killed Abel, God gave Adam and Eve another son to take Abel's place. His name was Seth. Adam was 130 years old when Seth was born (Gen. 5:3); "and the days of Adam after he had begotten Seth were *eight hundred years: and he begat sons and daughters*" (Gen. 5:4). "And all the days of Adam were nine hundred and thirty years" (Gen. 5:5).

Many have surmised that no sons and daughters were born to Adam and Eve between the death of Abel and the birth of Seth, but they have not found any such statement, or grounds for such a supposition, in the Bible. Undoubtedly children were born to Adam and Eve during the years between the death of Abel and the birth of Seth, for Adam was 130 years of age when he begat Seth. How many sons and daughters could have been born before God gave them "another son to take the place of Abel, whom Cain slew"?

But even if there had been no sons and daughters born to Adam and Eve between the death of Abel and the birth of Seth, eight hundred years is a long time! And for 800 years after Seth was born, other sons and daughters were given to our first parents. Surely that allows time for one of Cain's sisters to grow up and marry Cain. And surely the God who created man in the beginning was able to set aside His usual laws of nature, and thus to permit the human race to increase in the earth! Cain married his sister, which was according to God's plan.

In this connection, let us recall Gen. 20:12, where we read that Abraham's wife, Sarah, was his half-sister: "And yet indeed she is my sister; she is the daughter of my father, but not the daughter of my mother; and she became my wife." God evidently permitted the men of these early days to marry relatives, though later, in the Law of Moses, He forbade one to marry a sister or certain close kin.

There are those who ask this question, trying to believe that Adam was not the first man. But in I Cor. 15:45 we read that *"the first man Adam* was made a living soul."

Let us keep in mind that, in the book of Genesis, God is not giving us an account of the history of all humanity, but rather the divine record concerning the ancestors of the "seed of woman," even the Lord Jesus Christ, who was born of the Virgin Mary.

Some, untaught in the Scriptures, claim that Cain *found* his wife in the land of Nod, but the Bible makes no such statement. When Cain went out from the presence of the Lord, certainly he took his wife with him. What the Bible does say is that, having gone to the land of Nod, "Cain *knew* his wife" (Gen. 4:16, 17). Every student of the Bible knows that this word is used here in the same sense as that of Matt. 1:24, 25: "Joseph . . . knew her not (meaning Mary) until she had brought forth her firstborn son: and he called his name Jesus.

Much unbelief today is due to misunderstanding in regard to what the Bible teaches. What the Bible says is one thing; what people often say it teaches is another thing entirely. Skeptics raise questions that only show their ignorance of the Word of God; and would-be skeptics foolishly repeat what they hear, not searching the Scriptures to see if these things are so.

Question: Was Cain ever saved?

Answer: There is nothing in all the Bible to indicate that Cain was ever saved; whereas there is everything to imply that he died a lost soul. In the first place he tried to offer to God a bloodless sacrifice, the works of his own hands—and this in open rebellion against God.

In the second place, we read that "Cain went out from the presence of the Lord" (Gen. 4:16); and having turned his back upon God, he and his descendants built a godless civilitation, which became so corrupt that it had to be wiped out in the flood.

Question: We often read in the Bible of how people were "troubled" at the appearance of angels. Was this because the angels were holy; and in their presence man was conscious of his sinfulness?

Answer: Undoubtedly. And the very fact that the appearances were supernatural also greatly troubled those to whom the holy angels appeared. However, when we get to heaven, the sight of all the myriads of angels and of the archangels will not trouble us; for heaven will be "home." Home is the place where there is no embarrassment and no strangeness. One of the most beautiful descriptions of heaven is found in the word "home." We shall not be troubled there. We shall rejoice to look upon the sinless Son of God, unafraid in his presence, because we are washed in His precious blood.

Question: Please explain Gen. 6:2, "The sons of God saw the daughters of men that they were fair; and they took them wives of all which they chose."

Answer: I take it that these "sons of God" were from the godly line of Seth; whereas the "daughters of men" were from the godless line of Cain. Satan is ever endeavoring to break down barriers that God has set up. God has in all ages called His people to walk the pathway of separation. But from the very beginning Satan's aim has been to destroy this characteristic mark of God's people, thus bringing about an unholy union between the saved and the unsaved. How often this occurs in marriage relationships of the present hour, and what tragedy has followed in its wake! God ever warns His people to be "separate" from the Godless world. (See II Cor. 6:14-18; James 1:27, as well as repeated warnings to His people, Israel, not to intermarry with the heathen nations about them, not to worship their idols—to remain a separate people.)

There are those who teach that these "sons of God" were the fallen angels. But all Scripture contradicts such an interpretation. The angels are never spoken of as having sex; on the contrary, our Lord definitely denied that they do in His statement found in Matt. 22:30.

Question: Please explain Gen. 9:25: Cursed be Canaan; a servant of servants shall he be unto his brethren." Does this refer to the Negro race?

Answer: Canaan was the fourth son of Ham. (See Gen. 10:6.) The "Bible Cyclopedia," by Fausset, says, in part: "From Ham came four main races: Cush (Ethiopia); Mizraim (Egypt); Phus (Nubia); and Canaan." Canaan "comprised six chief tribes: The Hittites, Hivites, Amorites, Jebusites, Perizzites, and Girgashites, to which (in the narrow sense) the Canaanites being added make up the mystic number seven . . . The Hamitic descent of Canaan was formerly questioned, but is now proved by the monuments."

As we well know, Ham had sinned. (Read Gen .9:20-27.) Then Noah uttered the three-fold prophecy of these verses: That special blessing would come from God upon Shem (Christ and the Bible came through this son of Noah); that Japheth would be the father of the "enlarged" races, and would share the blessing of Shem; and that Canaan should serve his brethren.

To quote Fausset further: "In Ham's sin lies the stain of the whole Hamitic race, sexual plofligacy, of which Sodom and Gomorrah furnish an awful example. Canaan probably shared in and prompted his father's guilt towards Noah; for Noah's 'younger son' probably means his 'grandson' (Gen. 9:24), and the curse being pronounced upon Canaan, not Ham, implies Canaan's leading guilt, probably being the first to expose to Ham Noah's shame."

In any case, the curse upon Canaan was a curse upon Ham —a sorrow and a grief to any parent. And without any doubt Ham sinned in this act, whether in partnership with Canaan or on his own initiative.

"The Pulpit Commentary" adds this thought: "Possibly Canaan was already walking in his father's evil steps . . . Possibly Noah foresaw Canaan's depravity; certainly God did, And this was a *prophecy,* as well as a curse . . . The doom of servitude was sovereignty imposed . . . In after years . . . the peculiar sins for which the Canaanites were destroyed were allied to those which are referred to in the text." We need only read Moses' repeated warnings to Israel against the vile sins of the Canaanites, to know something of the depths of degradation to which these people had sunk. Thus Israel was "the divinely appointed instrument to purge the land of transgressors hopelessly depraved: 'Defile not yourselves in any of these things, for in all these the nations are defiled that I cast out before you, and the land itself vomiteth out her inhabitants' (Lev. 18:24). The Canaanites had the respite of centuries, the awful example of the plain (Sodom and Gomorrah), and the godly example of Abraham, Melchizedek, and others; but all failed to lead them to repentance." (Fausset).

"So Canaan was to be 'servant of servants'; i.e., the most abject slave. Such his race became to Israel (I Kings 9:20, 21). Canaan more than any other of Ham's race came in contact

with and obstructed Shem and Japheth in respect to the bless-
ings foretold to them (excepting the Egyptians, descendants
of another son of Ham). The Hamite races, originally the most
brilliant and enlightened (Egypt, Babylon, Canaan) had the
greatest tendency to degenerate, because the most disinclined to
true religion, the great preserver of men" (Fausset).

The "Critical and Explanatory Commentary" goes even
further and says: "This doom has been fulfilled in the destruction of the Canaanites, in the degradation of Egypt, and in the
slavery of the Africans, the descendants of Ham."

Let us remember, however, that *all* the descendants of Ham
are *not* Negroes, as in the case of the early Babylonians, the
Egyptians and the Abyssinians.

Two quotations from secular history are at least of interest,
in this connection, both taken from Fausset's work, already referred to above. One is from Procopius, Belisarius' secretary,
who "confirms the Scripture account of the *expulsion of the
Canaanites,* for he mentions a monument in Tigitina (Tangiers)
with the inscription, 'We are *exiles* from before the face of
Joshua, the robber.'" (Tangiers is in northern Africa!)

The other quotation is from Rabbi Samuel ben Nachman:
"Joshua sent three letters to the Canaanites, before the Israelites
invaded it, proposing three things: Let those who choose to
fly, fly; let those who choose peace, enter into treaty; let those
who choose war, take up arms. In consequence, the Girgashites
(descendants of Canaan), fearing the power of God, fled *away
into Africa;* the Gibeonites entered into league, and continued
inhabitants of Israel; the 30 kings made war and fell."

Students of anthropology and ethnology are strangely silent
on the origin of the Negro race, except as many of them try
to make all mankind fit into the unscriptural theory of evolution. And as we shall see in answer to our next question,
scientists differ as to the reason for their being black. But it
does not seem a difficult thing for the child of God to take

God at His Word, and believe Him for what He says. Is it at all improbable that some of the descendants of Canaan migrated to Africa, and there became the forefathers of the enslaved Negro? Surely not! Even as the secular historian and the Jewish rabbi said, some of these could easily have fled to Africa, "the land of Ham" (cf. Psa. 78:51; 105:23). Not only is this the scriptural explanation of this question; to us it seems also the most plausible.

Let it be remembered that the God of Shem has always offered salvation to the sons of Ham, as well as to "all the families of the earth," through Jesus Christ our Lord.

And let it ever be remembered by the child of God that the inspired record of "how" and "why" the nations were divided in the earth after the flood, as found in the tenth and eleventh chapters of Genesis, is one of the most valuable documents in all literature. It has been verified by archæology, ethnology, and history. What more does any man need, let alone the man of faith, who needs only the "Thus saith the Lord"?

(Everyone familiar with the Genesis record knows that the sin of man at the tower of Babel tells us "why" the nations were divided, why the earth was no longer "of one language, and of one speech" (Gen. 11:1). And Gen. 10:32 surely is very plain as to "how" the nations were scattered over the face of the earth: "These are the families of the sons of Noah, after their generations, in their nations: *and by these were the nations divided in the earth after the flood.*")

Question: Since Shem, Ham, and Japheth were brothers, why are their descendants of different color: Some white; some yellow; some black?

Answer: Before we discuss this question, let us note the meaning of some of the names associated with this topic:

"Ham" means "heat," "hot," "black."

"Ethiopia" means "sunburnt," or "blackness." Compare Jer. 13:23: "Can the Ethiopian change his skin, or the leopard his spots?"

"Negro" comes from the Latin "niger," meaning "black."

Color is only one characteristic that differentiates the races of man; the hair, the skull, the size of the body, facial characteristics—these are some of the things considered in distinguishing the races.

But to return to your question, while climate is usually given as an important reason for differences in color of the races; yet some people of tropical countries are *not* black, as are the Negroes. Therefore, we can not attribute all of the racial characteristics of the Negro to his environment. My personal opinion is that, while environment does make many differences, yet it still remains true that Gen. 9:25 gives us the only real reason for the difference between the blackness of the race that is a "servant of servants" (Negroes) and the comparative darkness of the skin of other peoples who inhabit countries equally as hot as tropical Africa. Indeed, why are the Egyptians not as black as the Negroes? Both are descendants of Ham. Why are the Abyssinians, also children of Ham, not Negroes? They live in the same latitude as do the blackest of people. I think the answer lies in the fact that the Negroes came from Canaan, who was under the curse; whereas the Egyptians and the Abyssinians were descended from other sons of Ham.

Even so, could the omnipotent God not use the laws of nature, which He made, to bring this to pass, if He so desired, in so far as color and other racial characteristics are concerned? Or, was He not able to put a difference between the sons of Canaan and the other sons of Ham in a moment's time, if He so desired, by His decree that it should be so? We do not have to *explain* all the ways of our sovereign God, you know.

It is irrefutable that He has stamped the Negroes with characteristitcs which forever distinguish them from other races—

characteristics, of which color is only one. And it is not by chance that the Negro has been "a servant of servants." This fact is but prophecy fulfilled. (See the next question for our responsibility to the Negro.)

Without any doubt whatever, the degradation and ignorance and superstition of any race, of whatever color, are the result of long-continued sin. We do not need the scientist to tell us that! In fact, many scientists "falsely so called" place the lowest of men at the bottom of the evolutionary "family tree," all of which is contrary to the Word of God. Read the first chapter of Romans to see how man *"became* degenerate, having fallen from the exalted position of Adam, made in the image and likeness of God, even unto the degradation of heathenism.

However, let us not trouble our minds too much about the matter of racial differences. If God had wanted us to know more than He has told us, would He not have written it in His Word?

At the same time, the discoveries of science are both interesting and profitable; for true science always verifies the Bible. Therefore, having sought to find out what anthropology and ethnology have said upon this subject—though finding little of definite help—yet we are quoting here a few excerpts which may or may not be of any value to the reader. These are taken from "The Races of Man," by J. Deniker, Sc.D. Among other positions of honor held by Dr. Deniker are these: Chief Librarian of the Museum of Natural History, Paris; Honorary Fellow of the Anthropological Institute of Great Britain. These quotations are given with no thought of the author's religious creed; we refer to him only as one recognized in his field of science:

"The differences between the 'races' are shown in the somatological characteristics which are the resultant of the continual struggle in the individual of two factors: Variability, that is to say, the production of the dissimilar; and heredity, that is to say, the perpetuation of the similar. . .

"The distribution of the pigment which gives colouring to the skin, to the hair, to iris, varies much according to race. . . According to race, the microscopic granules of pigment of a uniform brown are very unequally distributed around the nuclei of the cells, to which they give the most varied tones from pale yellow to dark brown, almost black. As the pigment exists in all races, and in all parts of the body, it is to its more or less plentiful accumulation in the cells that the colouring of the skin and its derivatives is due. Further, there must be added, for certain races at least, the combination with the tint of the blood of the vessels, as seen through the skin. . .

"I can scarcely treat here as fully as I could wish such interesting questions as the influence of external circumstances, of acclimatation and crossings or hybridisation, inasmuch as they are still very little and imperfectly studied. The direct influence of environment has rarely been observed with all the scientific exactness to be wished. Ordinarily we have to rest satisfied with phrases which do not mean a great deal. . .

"I cannot refute here all the erroneous assertions in regard to the assumed influence of environment. . . It is enough to give some examples. Negroes are not black because they inhabit tropical countries, seeing that the Indians of South America, who live in the same latitudes, are yellow; Norwegians and Great Russians, who are fair and tall, live side by side with the Laplanders and the Samoyeds, who are dark and of very low stature."

The above quotations are but a few of many such that might be cited, setting forth the fact that—as the student of the Word of God sees it—man can offer no theory for the origin of the Negro race half as satisfying or plausible as that suggested by the words of Gen. 9:25: "Cursed be Canaan; a servant of servants shall he be unto his brethren." As for other variations in the races, it seems logical that diet, climate, variability, heredity, and hybridism could well be responsible for these.

Question: What is the Christian's responsibility to the Negro? I have known some professing Christians who have mistreated him. Should there be inter-racial marriages?

Answer: Let me say, in the first place, that all that has been stated in the two preceding answers was an honest effort to give what God has said and what history has verified concerning the Negro race. When it comes to a matter of the Christian's attitude and responsibility to these people, there is only one thing the Christian can do, as I see it—and that is to treat them as human beings for whom Christ died; to go to them with the Gospel; and to encourage them in every effort to live for Christ. Let us not forget that God's promise to Abraham includes a blessing for every son of Adam: "In thee shall *all* families of the earth be blessed." That promise was fulfilled, in part, when God gave Christ and the Bible to the world through the nation of Israel; it will yet be fulfilled completely when our Lord returns to reign through the house of Israel in the millennial earth. The Gospel of our crucified and risen Lord is for "red and yellow, black and white." Our God is "no respecter of persons" (Acts 10:34). And some of the most saintly Christians I have known have been Negroes.

Having lived both in the North and in the South of these United States of America, I think I can understand what you mean by your question concerning the Negro. While the old prejudices resulting from the Civil War are fast passing away, yet I do feel that often *individuals* in the different parts of the country fail to understand one another on this vital question.

Personally, I think the Negroes are far happier with their own race. Furthermore, I am convinced that God intended that it should be so, and that the two races should not intermarry.

On the other hand, we owe them a chance to do the best they can for themselves. We should treat them as fellow-Christians, or as those who need our Saviour, and love their souls for Christ's sake. That is why we send missionaries to Africa. Shall we do less for the Negro who was brought as an unwilling slave from his native land?

And finally, as law-abiding citizens, shall we not grant all of our fellow-men such rights and privileges as the laws of our respective states demand? To do less, is to flout the law; to do it grudgingly, is to manifest an unchristian spirit.

Question: Please explain Heb. 7:1-3. Was Melchizedek an appearance of God in the form of an angel?

Answer: Some Bible teachers do hold the view that Melchizedek was an appearance of God in angelic form, basing this opinion on Heb. 7:3, but most students of the Word of God hold the other view, that he was merely a man, a type of Christ in His High Priestly Person. I am convinced that this latter interpretation is correct, for the following reasons:

1. He was king of Salem, the ancient site of the city of Jerusalem, which means "the city of peace." "Salem" means "peace"; therefore, as king of peace, Melchizedek was a type of Christ, the Prince of Peace and King of Peace.

2. He was also "by interpretation king of righteousness," a type of the Lord Jesus, who one day will rule in righteousness.

3. As priest of the most high God, he was a type of Christ, our Priest.

4. Nothing is written of Melchizedek in all the Bible except the story recorded in Gen. 14:17-20; the statement that he is a type of Christ in Psalm 110:4; and the explanation of the type in Heb. 6:20; 7:1-28. Very evidently the Holy Spirit omitted all reference to Melchizedek's parents, in order that

he might be a type of the eternal Son of God, who verily has "neither beginning of days, nor end of life." In this connection, please note the Revised Version for the word "descent" of the Authorized Version of Heb. 7:3. Accurately translated, it means, "without father, without mother, without *genealogy*"; in other words, without *recorded genealogy,* in order that he might be a type of the eternal Son of God.

Let it be remembered that the whole argument presented in Hebrews is that, as Melchizedek was greater than Aaron, the first high priest in Israel, so also Christ is greater than Aaron in His eternal priesthood. The Holy Spirit was seeking to lead Christian Jews away from Judaism to Christ Himself. The Aaronic priesthood had served God's purpose, and had been done away in Christ; therefore, why return to Judaism? That, in fact, is the argument of this entire weighty epistle.

Just one further word to show how Melchizedek, was greater than Aaron: (1) Abraham, Aaron's forefather, was blessed by Melchizedek; (2) Abraham paid tithes to Melchizedek; (3) having no *recorded* genealogy, he is type of the eternal High Priest, even Jesus. Aaron and his sons died; Christ abideth a Priest continually, unchanging, ever living to make intercession for us.

Moreover, Aaron was only a priest, from the tribe of Levi; Christ was from the kingly tribe of Judah, according to the flesh; and is, therefore, both King and Priest.

Again, Aaron and his sons were made priests without an oath (Heb. 7:20, 21); Christ was proclaimed a Priest forever after the order of Melchizedek—not after the order of Aaron— when the Father confirmed His Word by His oath.

Once again, the Levitical priests had to offer sacrifices for their own sins; animal sacrifices; many sacrifices; whereas Christ had no sin for which to atone; He offered Himself; He offered one sacrifice forever!

This is a profound, yet a very important truth. Every Christian needs to realize what many seem not to comprehend, that in the glory the Man Christ Jesus is our Advocate with the Father, our Intercessor, our eternal, unchanging High Priest. As Melchizedek is a type of His *Person,* so Aaron is a type of His *work* on Calvary's cross. And to quote another, Melchizedek is a type of the "priestly work of Christ in *resurrection,* since he presented only the *memorials* of sacrifice, bread and wine.

Question: Why do some Christians say that the church began with Abraham, speaking of Old Testament believers as Christians?

Answer: It seems to us that they do not rightly divide the "word of truth." In the first place, the church began on the Day of Pentecost, as recorded in Acts; and in the second place, "the disciples were called Christians first in Antioch" (Acts 11:26).

Those who "spiritualize" the meaning of all of God's definite promises to Abraham make the prophecies mean what they do not say; and they ignore fulfilled prophecy, in God's dealings with the Jew. While they are saved, if they believe in the deity of Christ and His finished work on the cross, yet they miss one of the greatest sources of joy — to know that He Himself will one day return to put down sin. The world does not have to wait for the church to "bring in the kingdom" by the preaching of the Gospel. Christ will do that—we hope, very soon! Surely the chaotic condition of nations today, nearly two thousand years after men have had the Gospel, is not an encouraging sign that the church will convert the world!

Concerning the beginning of the church, much might be said. The Old Testament saints did not even know that the church, the bride of Christ, was in the mind of God; He revealed this "mystery" to Paul, as all New Testament teaching proves. Again, Christ Himself said, following Peter's great confession that Jesus was the Son of the living God, "Upon this rock I *will build* my church" (Matt. 16:18).

The church began at Pentecost, and will continue on the earth until the last member of the body of Christ is won to Him. God alone knows the time when that will be; but when it comes to pass, then He will translate the church to be forever with Himself.

Question: Since human sacrifices were an abomination unto the Lord, why did God tell Abraham to offer Isaac on Mount Moriah?

Answer: God was teaching Abraham and Isaac and future generations a beautiful lesson of the coming Redeemer, even our Lord Jesus Christ. Moreover, God knew what He intended to do, and that He would not let Abraham offer up His son. Bible students have often acknowledged that the whole incident is a lesson in obedience on the part of Abraham and Isaac; but too often they have missed the very heart of the God-given object-lesson in type: That one day He would send His only begotten Son, and offer Him upon a mountain of Israel for the sins of the whole world. Jesus Himself said when He was on earth: "Abraham rejoiced to see my day: and he saw it, and was glad" (John 8:56). Surely one of the times when, by faith, Abraham saw the day of Christ, was the time when he was willing to offer his "only begotten son" of promise (Heb. 11:17).

Note other striking analogies: The journey of three days, during which Abraham's heart was sad; compare the fact that Christ was three days and three nights in the tomb; Isaac's carrying the wood for the altar up Mount Moriah, even as Christ bore His cross up Mount Calvary; Abraham's faith in a resurrection hope, pointing on to Christ's resurrection (cf. Heb. 11:19); Isaac's obedience to his father, even as our Lord

Jesus was "obedient even unto death," ever doing His Father's will.

But Isaac was saved from death, the ram being his substitute. Not so our blessed Lord; He was our Substitute on Calvary, bearing the shame and curse and suffering in our stead.

To be sure, there *is* a beautiful lesson in faith and obedience on the part of Abraham and Isaac; but we miss the main message of the story, if we lose sight of the "shadow of the cross," which it plainly casts upon the inspired page.

Question: Was God pleased with "Jephthah's awful vow," the story of which is recorded in Judges 11:30-40?

Answer: The Bible makes no comment, one way or the other, about Jephthah's vow; but Jephthah is listed in Heb. 11:32 as one of the heroes of faith. And certain it is that he worshipped the God of Israel.

As reliable a commentator as Fausset thinks that Jephthah did not offer his daughter, his only child, as a human sacrifice; for that was an abomination unto the Lord. The heathen nations of Palestine did offer human sacrifices to their false gods; but Jehovah repeatedly warned Israel not to do this very thing. Since Jephthah was a God-fearing judge of Israel, and since he knew that human sacrifices were an abomination to God, Fausset thinks he offered his daughter as a "spiritual burnt-offering" unto the Lord, in the sense that she was set apart for His service, forever to be a virgin. (See verses 37-40.)

However that may be, these were his words to God when he "vowed a vow unto the Lord, and said, If thou shalt without fail deliver the children of Ammon into mine hands, then it shall be, that whatsoever (literally, whosoever) cometh forth of the doors of my house to meet me, when I return in peace . . . shall surely be the Lord's, and I will offer it up for a burnt offering" (Judges 11:30, 31).

Even if he did offer his daughter as a human sacrifice, *because* he had foolishly made such a vow; yet he very evidently did it without the approval of God. Many of God's children make grievous mistakes. David sinned wilfully and woefully; but his sin did not rob him of his salvation; and God forgave him, even as He often has to forgive us. So that our only conclusion must be that God honored Jephthah's *faith*. And as the Scriptures are silent as to a more definite outcome of the story, so we, too, must be silent in our own conclusions concerning the matter.

Question: Why did God tell the children of Israel to "borrow" from the Egyptians "jewels of silver, and jewels of gold" when He knew they would not return to Egypt to pay them back? (See Exod. 11:2).

Answer: This expression is used many times in the book of Exodus; but it does not mean "borrow" in the literal rendering of the term. On the contrary, it means "ask" and is so translated literally from the original Hebrew. The King James Version renders the word "borrow," but the Revised Version translates it correctly "ask."

And why did God tell His people to ask these things from the Egyptians? Because they had earned them! For four hundred years they had been slaves, building cities for Pharaoh, yet not having received their hard-earned wages. Therefore, God told them to ask for what was theirs by rights.

If you will read carefully the whole book of Exodus, you will see one important reason why God told them to take these costly jewels with them. They were to build the tabernacle, a beautiful, costly structure, temporary though it was. The golden candlestick alone cost $29,085, made from "a talent of pure gold" (Exod. 25:39). Then there were the pieces of furniture covered with brass; some covered with gold. There were the sockets of silver for the boards. There was the mercy seat of pure gold. There were the precious stones in the breastplate and on the shoulders of the high priest. Do you see that for this tabernacle alone Israel had to have great wealth? And God provided it by giving them their just wages, earned over a long period of time.

Question: How were men saved before Christ died for the sins of the world?

Answer: By faith in the coming Redeemer, even Jesus. The Old Testament is full of definite prophecies of His coming into the world to die for sinners. Throughout the entire Old Testament there is "the scarlet thread of sacrifice," by which God taught men that they could be saved only by faith in One who was to come. They were saved by putting their faith in the Christ of prophecy; we are saved by trusting in the Christ of history, who fulfilled the prophecies of His coming to die for the sins of the world. It is the blood of Christ alone that cleanses from sin in any age.

Here are just a few of the many prophecies of His coming to die for sinners, as set forth in the Old Testament:

1. Adam and Eve made fig-leaf aprons to make themselves fit for God's presence—the work of their hands; but God made "coats of skins and clothed them" (Gen. 3:21). The innocent animal had to die—a faint type of the innocent Lamb of God who died, that we might be clothed in the righteousness of Christ.

2. Cain brought the fruit of the ground; Abel brought the blood sacrifice—by faith!

3. Gen. 3:15 is the first promise of the coming Redeemer. (It is explained in answer to another question in this book. See "First Promise of Redeemer.")

4. The passover lamb was a picture of "Christ our passover" who "is sacrificed for us" (I Cor. 5:7).

5. Isaiah 53 and Psalm 22 are two of the most graphic prophecies of the suffering Messiah.

There are dozens of other prophecies, pointing on to the Christ who was to come to die for sinners.

V

THE SOVEREIGNTY OF GOD

Question: Please explain Isaiah 45:7, "I make peace, and create evil." Is God the author of evil, as this text suggests?

Answer: Isaiah is not speaking of *moral* evil. The Hebrew word for "evil" (to quote Dr. Scofield) is "translated 'sorrow,' 'wretchedness,' 'adversity,' 'afflictions,' 'calamities,' but never translated 'sin.' God created evil only in the sense that He made sorrow and wretchedness to be the sure fruits of sin'.'

James 1:13 distinctly says, "Let no man say when he is tempted, I am tempted of God: for God cannot be tempted with evil, neither tempteth he any man."

Jeremiah used the word as Isaiah did, often warning a wayward people of the consequences of their sin. Take, for example, Jer. 42:10: "If ye will still abide in this land, then will I build you, and not pull you down, and I will plant you, and not pluck you up: for I repent me of the evil I have done unto you." Jeremiah was addressing the backslidden people of Judah. They had gone away into idolatry, and the prophet was warning them of the chastening hand of the Lord. In this connection he foretold the invasion of Nebuchadnezzar, and the Babylonian captivity, as God's method of chastening His people.

It is not, therefore, moral evil that Isaiah and Jeremiah had in mind. God is holy, and can not be tempted with evil. "Neither tempteth he any man!"

Question: What does the Bible teach about predestination and election? I have been brought up to believe that God chose some for salvation before the foundation of the world; and that, whether they want to or not, they have to

be saved; or if God did not choose them, no matter how
much they try to trust Christ, they can not be saved, because God did not choose them. Is this the real doctrine of
election?

Answer: There is no such teaching between the covers of
the Bible! God's predestination is according to His foreknowledge. I Tim. 2:3, 4 tells us that "God . . . will have all men
to be saved, and to come unto the knowledge of the truth."
Mr. William Kelly translates this passage in this way: "God
. . . *wishes* all men to be saved." Since our Saviour does wish
all men to be saved, then how could He, from before the foundation of the world, condemn some to eternal perdition, so
that they have no power to accept Christ and be saved?

My friend, God has predestined; but Rom. 8:29 says that
we are predestined *according to His foreknowledge.* The same
truth is plainly stated in I Pet. 1:2: "Elect according to the
foreknowledge of God the Father,"—so the apostle addresses
the Christian Jews of the dispersion.

God knows whether a man will love Christ; He knows
whether a man will spurn Christ; and God has chosen from the
foundation of the world—but whom has He chosen? All who
will believe unto eternal life. The Lord Jesus Christ died for
the whole world; and if every man in the world *would* come
to Christ and trust Him, *all* would be saved. My friend, if you
come to Him, He will in no wise cast you out. (See John 6:37.)

**Question: Why did God say in Rom. 9:13: "Jacob have
I loved, but Esau have I hated"?**

Answer: It is very important that we get clearly in mind
this fact: Paul was quoting Mal. 1:2, 3; and Malachi wrote
more than a thousand years *after* Esau despised his birthright,
and turned his back upon the privileges of the firstborn son.
Again, we are to think of these words "loved" and "hated" as

expressing a comparatitve approval and disapproval of the attitude of the two sons of Isaac toward the things of God. Our God hates sin, but always loves the sinner. Otherwise, He would not have planned to die for sinners.

Moreover, this whole subject comes under the much-discussed question of the sovereignty of God, which we have attempted to set forth in answer to other questions.

Again, when God chose Jacob, even before the sons were born, it was because He knew Jalob would seek spiritual things, in however faltering and grasping a manner. And He chose Jacob as the one through whom "the seed," even Christ, should come. He did nothing to hinder Esau from being a saved man! Remember that. If Esau repented of his sin, and put his faith in the coming Redeemer, then his soul was saved. The Scriptures do not tell us whether he did or not; but he seems to have been a man of the world, seeking his satisfaction in the things of the flesh.

Question: Please explain why God said to Moses, concerning Pharaoh, "I will harden his heart, that he shall not let the people go."

Answer: In the first place, before God hardened Pharaoh's heart, Pharaoh hardened his own heart against God. Then, in order to show to the world what comes from rebellion against Him, God made an example of that wicked king, as a warning to others against similar rebellion. Read the whole story carefully, and you will see that repeatedly Pharaoh made such blasphemous statements as this: *"Who is the Lord, that I should obey his voice and let Israel go? I know not the Lord, neither will I let Israel go"* (Ex. 5:2).

Again, it is a matter of the sovereignty of our all-wise and all-loving God. Read once more Rom. 9:14-24. And trust Him who "doeth all things well" to take care of such things as our

finite minds can not comprehend. Remember also—always—
that He is the God of infinite love; and as such, He can not be
unjust or unrighteous. He is the God of all holiness and truth.

**Question: Since God is the God of love, why did He tell
His people, Israel, to fight against the heathen nations
about them?**

Answer: These nations had had their opportunity to receive
the truth of God; but they had turned their backs upon the
light. They were idolaters, corrupt in their lives, and a menace
to the people of God. Time and again Israel fell into their
snares, worshipped their idols, intermarried with them—all
contrary to God's explicit commands. Since the nations refused
to go God's way, there was nothing left for Him to do but to
cut them off, in the interest of His chosen people.

When a certain part of the human body becomes diseased,
it is often necessary to amputate a limb, in order to save the
whole; and this was true in the body politic. The command
God gave for the extermination of the depraved nations suggests the depths of degradation into which they had sunk; and
in permitting them to exist, nothing would have been accomplished except the release of corrupting influences affecting
surrounding people.

This act reveals God in His concern for the human race
as a whole. And it reveals Him in His concern particularly for
the nation of Israel.

But, some may ask, why did God choose Israel? He chose
the Hebrew nation in order to give the *whole* world the
Redeemer and His eternal Word. To Abraham God said,
"In thee all families of the earth shall be blessed" (Gen. 12:3).
Therefore, it was in the interest of the whole world, as well as
Israel, that God protected them from those who would defile
them.

Our God *is* a God of love. He does not send a single soul to
eternal torment. But He has given man a free will; and when

man deliverately chooses to forsake God, there is nothing left for him but judgment.

This truth applies to all questions that people raise concerning God's dealings with those of Old Testament times who brought upon themselves the righteous judgment of God. But what if it did not, "O man, who art thou that repliest against God?" (Rom. 9:20).

Question: What is the explanation of Exodus 22:18, "Thou shalt not suffer a witch to live"?

Answer: We shall have no difficulty in understanding this command, repeated and enlarged upon in Lev. 19:31; 20:6, 27; Deut. 18:9-14, if we get clearly in mind the character of witches in the days of Moses and Joshua. They were the greatest enemies of God's truth, even as the witch-doctors of Africa are today. Their hands were steeped in blood; they were the exponents of immorality. Therefore, God commanded that they should be cut off, in the interest of His people.

The heathen nations, among whom Israel dwelt, had turned their backs upon God. And sometimes God had to "cut off" the wicked who refuse to obey Him, in order to protect His people.

Missionaries today tell us of these Satan-possessed witch-doctors of pagan lands. They are unspeakably cruel, vile, and horrible in their evil practices. Nor do we have to go to heathen lands, so-called, to find demonism or spiritualism in its most subtle form. The Christian should avoid all contacts with spiritualists, fortune-tellers, and necromancers, except as he may be used of God to lead such as these out of spiritual darkness into the light of God's truth. Either they are fakes—and who wants to be the dupe of a deceiver? Or they are demon-possessed—and what child of God would dare play into the hands of Satan, with his eyes open to his deed?

Question: Will the heathen be lost? Will there not be, at least, a probation for them after death, since they have died in ignorance and superstition?

Answer: There is nothing in the Word of God to justitfy even the slightest inference that there will be probation after death for *anyone;* on the contrary, there is positive teaching to the effect that what one does with the Lord Jesus Christ in this life determines forever his eternal state. All must stand before Him; for He is the Judge of all the earth, and the Father has committed all judgment unto Him. (See John 5:22, 25, 27-29.)

The best answer to your question about the heathen is found in Rom. 1:18-32. There we read that the "invisible things of him from the creation of the world are clearly seen, being understood by the things that are made, even his eternal power and Godhead; *so that they are without excuse;* because that, when they knew God, they glorified Him not as God, neither were thankful; but became vain in their imaginations, and their foolish heart was darkened. Read on in this terrible indictment of sinful man, "without Christ." It is one of the darkest pictures in the Bible, one of the most graphic descriptions of the baseness and the vileness of the human heart that has gone to the depths of sin.

What God is saying here is that, because the nations, which we call heathen, refused to have God in their knowledge; because they deliberately and persistently turned their backs upon His truth, He "gave them up." And the righteous judgment of God awaits all who refuse to "have God in their knowledge." Let it be remembered, however, that when anyone *seeks* the light, God gives light, and in grace comes to him again, offering salvation in Christ.

No, my friend, "there is none other name under heaven given among men, whereby we must be saved," except by the

name of Jesus. And there is no second chance after death.
(See Acts 4:12.) That is why our responsibility is so great,
why we are impelled by the grace of God to take the message of
salvation to the heathen world. But let no man dare to question
the justice or the wisdom of God in this matter. He is ever the
God of love, who died for sinners. And what our finite minds
cannot grasp, concerning His ways with men, we do well to
leave with Him, who "doeth all things well." His wisdom and
justice and mercy are infinite!

**Question: How do you harmonize II Pet. 3:9, "The
Lord is . . . not willing that any should perish," with portions of the ninth chapter of Romans, which seem to indicate that God made some to be wicked, to show forth His
power and glory?**

Answer: This question is discussed in connection with
other passages of Scripture, referred to in this series; but we
shall add here a word in the light of this particular question.
Romans 9 is very deep and difficult, but a careful study of it
will reveal that God does not will that any man should be lost,
or determine any man's doom to eternal punishment. For example, note verse 22, which is perhaps one of the most difficult
in the chapted: "What if God, willing to shew his wrath, and
to make his power known, endured with much longsuffering the
vessels of wrath fitted to destruction?" Who fitted these people
for destruction? Not God, surely; nor does the text say so. On
the contrary, God's attitude toward them has been one of
"longsuffering." These unbelievers *fitted themselves,* by rejecting God's grace, by rejecting the only Saviour, the Lord Jesus
Christ.

**Question: Does not the statement in John 12:39, 40
teach fatalism? And would not one deduct from the teaching of these verses that God is the author of man's destruc-**

tion? It seems that the people had no choice in the matter, that their unbelief was absolutely necessary, in order that this prophecy might be fulfilled, and that God ordained that it should be so.

Answer: These verses teach neither fatalism nor extreme predestination. But first let us read them: "Therefore they could not believe, because that Esaias said again, He hath blinded their eyes, and hardened their heart; that they should not see with their eyes, nor understand with their heart, and be converted, and I should heal them."

God foreknew that Israel would not believe, and therefore Isaiah spake these words. But long before the Lord spake these words through Isaiah, the Jewish people had deliberately hardened their hearts and turned away from God.

The Lord Jesus wept over the city of Jerusalem. He wept over the nation of Israel. And He said, "How often would I have gathered thy children together, even as a hen gathereth her chickens under her wings, *and ye would not!* Behold, your house is left unto you desolate. For I say unto you, Ye shall not see me henceforth, till ye shall say, Blessed is he that cometh in the name of the Lord" (Matt. 23:37-39). Because Israel persisted in unbelief, judicial blindness fell upon them.

You must remember, my friend, that God is sovereign in punishing, and may mete out judgment as He pleases. Some He cuts off suddenly, the moment they sin. Others He gives over to judicial blindness, and ceases to strive with their consciences. Something like this will come upon professing Christendom after the true church is translated. Then II Thes. 2:1-12 will be fulfilled. The Antichrist will be revealed to the world, and will deceive those who have rejected the truth of God as it is in Christ Jesus, "because they received not the love of the truth that they might be saved. And for this cause

God shall send them strong delusion, that they should believe a lie, that they all might be judged (R.V.) who believed not the truth, but had pleasure in unrighteousness." This will be judicial blindness.

This is a solemn and an awful subject, and should awaken those who know the truth and have light, yet are rejecting the same.

Question: Did God predestinate the fate of Judas?

Answer: If by this is meant, "Did God arbitrarily foreordain that Judas could not believe and be saved?" then our answer is emphatically, "No!" One who knows the God of the Bible could never believe in such predestination. It was, indeed, foretold that Judas would betray the Lord; for God knows what men will do. But Judas was a free moral agent; and what he did, he did of his own volition.

Please note what is said of Judas in Acts 1:16-25: "Men and brethren, this scripture must needs have been fulfilled, which the Holy Ghost by the mouth of David spake before concerning Judas, which was guide to them that took Jesus. . . And they prayed, and said, Thou, Lord, which knowest the hearts of all men, shew whether of these two thou hast chosen, that he may take part of this ministry and apostleship, from which Judas *by transgression fell.*" Please note those last three words, They do *not say* that Judas *by predestination fell,* or *by fore-ordination fell,* but *by transgression fell.* That is, Judas by his own transgression fell. These words leave no doubt whatsoever as to the answer to this question.

VI

LAW AND GRACE

Question: If salvation is all of grace, and works do not have a part in God's plan of redemption, why did Christ answer the lawyer's question in Luke 10:25 as He did? The lawyer asked, "Master, what shall I do to inherit eternal life?" Christ answered by telling him the story of the good Samaritan. Then He said, "Go, and do thou likewise." Surely this proves that works play a part in the scheme of salvation.

Answer: If you read the chapter carefully, you will have no difficulty in understanding why the Lord so answered the lawyer. The man was seeking to justify himself by keeping the law. He asked, "What must I do to inherit eternal life?" He desired to know how to get to heaven on the ground of *"doing."* The Lord answered by quoting the law, and gave the story of the good Samaritan, that he might know how to interpret the meaning of the word "neighbor." The Lord's answer was to *convict* him, and to show him his inability to be saved on the ground of works.

The same lesson was taught by the Lord to the rich young ruler. That young man also sought salvation by "doing," but was both unable and unwilling to keep the whole law by loving his neighbor as himself. Only our sinless Saviour was *able* to keep the whole law; that is why He could be our perfect Substitute on the cross. If a man is going to try to get to heaven by the works of the law, then let him keep the whole law, or he has *broken* it and "come short of the glory of God" (Rom. 3:23). "For whosoever shall keep the whole law, and yet offend in one point, he is guilty of all" (James 2:10).

[97]

"Wherefore then serveth the law? It was added because of transgressions, till the seed (Christ, Gal. 4:4, 5) should come. . . Wherefore the law was our schoolmaster to bring us unto Christ, *that we might be justified by faith.* But after that faith is come, we are no longer under a schoolmaster" (Gal. 3:19, 24, 25.) Read all of Galatians; Eph. 2:8-10; Titus 3:5; Rom. 3:19-28.)

Question: How do you harmonize your statement that we can not DO anything to be saved with Rom. 2:13: "Not the hearers of the law are just before God, but the DOERS of the law shall be justified"?

Answer: When Paul wrote these words, under the guidance of the Holy Spirit, he was writing to people who believed *just as you do.* That is why he said this. They were trusting in the law; they gloried in the fact that it was given to them; and yet the very law in which they gloried condemned every one of them, because they did not—they could not—keep it. Paul was only reminding them that, if they intended to be saved by keeping the law, then they had to *keep* it, not merely hear it. Later he says, in the third chapter: "Now we know that what things soever the law saith, it saith to them who are under the law: that every mouth may be stopped, and all the world may become guilty before God. Therefore by the deeds of the law there shall no flesh be justified in his sight: for by the law is the knowledge of sin" (Rom. 3:19, 20).

My friend, do you honestly believe that you are a "doer of the law"? Of course, you will emphasize the fourth commandment about keeping the seventh day. But let me ask you, do you keep it? I can show you that, in listening over the radio this morning, you are breaking the Sabbath; for you are using electricity; and the fourth commandment says that we shall do no work of any kind; nor shall we permit our sons or daughters or servants to do any work. The men who control the electric power are verily your "servants" in this respect; and you let them work for you; yet you think you are keeping the Sabbath.

Verily Paul says, "Not the hearers of the law are just before God, but the doers of the law." If one is to be saved by *doing,* then the law must be *done, not heard.*

Question: You said yesterday over the radio that we do not have to DO anything to be saved. Later on in your message you quoted Matt. 26:27, 28, which tells us that Jesus instituted the Lord's Supper, saying to His disciples, "Drink ye all of it." Just how do you harmonize your statement with this command to DO this? And how do you harmonize it with Christ's command that we be baptized?

Answer: My friend, this and your next question show how confused the legalists are in regard to the plan of salvation; that is, how a sinner is really brought to a saving knowledge of the Lord Jesus Christ. When He said to His disciples, "Do this in remembrance of me," He was not talking of those who needed salvation, but to those who already possessed it. He had already told them to rejoice because their names were written in heaven, in the Lamb's book of life. How were they saved? How did they get their names written in heaven? By partaking of the Lord's Supper? No! A thousand times, no! They got their names there when they believed the exhortation of John the Baptist, "Behold the Lamb of God, which taketh away the sin of the world" (John 1:29).

My friend, one does the "doing," not in order to be saved, but because he *is* saved. If you are resting in *your doing,* as you evidently are, you are going to be a very disappointed man one of these days when you meet Him who said over and over again that salvation is all of grace, without works of any kind.

Question: What does Paul mean in Phil. 1:19, "I know that this shall turn to my salvation"?

Answer: The apostle here refers to his bodily salvation, in his approaching trial before Nero. He was a prisoner at Caesar's court (Phil. 1:13); willing to live or die for Christ; knowing that, if God willed, the prayers of his Christian friends at Philippi would be answered, and he would be set free.

There is nothing in the passage to intimate that Paul referred to the salvation of his soul. This letter was written some ten years after Paul and Silas had told the Philippian jailer, in no uncertain terms: *"Believe* on the Lord Jesus Christ, and thou shalt be saved" (Acts 16:31).

Question: What is the meaning of Phil. 2:12, "Work out your own salvation with fear and trembling"?

Answer: Mark you, this verse does *not* say, "Work *for* your own salvation, but work *out* your own salvation." It is your *own* salvation that you are to work out.

The text is best explained when considered in connection with the verse which follows: "For it is God which worketh in you both to will and to do of his good pleasure." The entire passage means that the Christian is to manifest, or show forth to the world, his salvation by a godly and careful walk. This he can not do in his own strength; he can do it only by the power of God. "Not by might, nor by power, but by my Spirit, saith the Lord of hosts" (Zech. 4:6).

Question: If salvation is all of grace, and works play no part in our redemption, then why do we read in Rev. 22:14, "Blessed are they that do his commandments, that they might have right to the tree of life, and may enter in through the gates into the city"?

Answer: Read this verse in the Revised Version, and you will have your answer: *"Blessed are they that wash their robes, that they might have the right to come to the tree of life, and may enter in by the gates into the city."* Works do not give the right to the tree of life. It is the grace of God that cleanses "our robes" in "the blood of the Lamb of Calvary." And every believer on the Lord Jesus Christ has right to the tree of life only on the ground of His finished redemption.

Question: Please explain John 5:45, 46: "Do not think that I will accuse you to the Father: there is one that accuseth you, even Moses, in whom ye trust. For had ye believed Moses, ye would have believed me: for he wrote of me." How could the Jews "trust" Moses, and yet not "believe" Moses?

Answer: Thousands of people are doing that very thing today. What does Moses represent? The Law. There are thousands today who are trusting the law, but they do not believe what Mosts wrote about "the sufferings of Christ, and the glory that should follow" (I Peter 1:11). When Moses gave the law, because he knew that Israel could not keep the law, he gave them a sacrifice. The sacrifice was a part of the law, and part of the teaching of Moses. Israel presumed to try to keep the law, but rejected Christ, of whom the sacrifice spoke. They, like many Gentiles today, sought to obtain righteousness by the deeds of the flesh, rather than by the free gift of God's grace. And because the Pharisees in the day of Christ refused to give up the law and receive Christ absolutely, they were not saved. Then their nation was set aside—not cast away, but set aside during this church age, when God is "calling out a people for his name."

This is the trouble with the Seventh Day Adventists, and with thousands of others, even church members, who are seeking salvation on the ground of works. They trust Moses (the law), and yet that law is a witness against them, because they have not kept it, and they *can not* keep it. No one but the Son of God has ever kept it; and none other ever will. If you do not believe that the law is a witness against such as these, then read Deut. 31:24-26: "And it came to pass, when Moses had made an end of writing the words of this law in a book, until they were finished, that Moses commanded the Levites, which bare the ark of the covenant of the Lord, saying, Take this book of the law, and put it in the side of the ark of the covenant of the Lord your God, *that it may be there for a witness against thee.*"

The law never witnesses *for* anybody, and the law will not witness for your salvation, my friend. If you are not trusting Christ, and Christ alone, the law will witness against you. But you may ask, "Wherefore then serveth the law?" (Gal. 3:19). You will find the answer to that question in the words which follow this quotation from Galatians. The law was given to Israel to show them their need of the Messiah; it was given till Jesus should come. It was never given to Gentiles; and when the Lord Jesus came, offering salvation by faith alone, the law had done its work and passed away.

This the Pharisees refused to believe. Therefore, Jesus said to them, "You *trust* Moses, but you do not *believe Moses.*" And this is true of everyone who thinks he has anything to do with the law. Many trust the law, yet they do not believe what the law says about the necessity of the shed blood, as an atonement for the soul. (See Lev. 17:11.) As soon as Moses had come down from Mount Sinai, as soon as he had told the people what the law was, then he told them also to build a tabernacle, that they might bring their *offerings* for their sins. In all this Moses spoke of the curse of the law, and of Israel's need of redemption through One who was to be "the Lamb of God, which taketh away the sin of the world."

Question: I heard a Sunday School teacher say that, because we are not under law, but under grace, we should not teach children the ten commandments, or tell them to try to keep them. Please explain.

Answer: It is a serious mistake to make such a statement as that teacher did; for *"all* scripture is given by inspiration of God, and is profitable for doctrine, for reproof, for correction, for instruction in righteousness" (II Tim. 3:16). I think, however that I know what the Sunday School teacher meant. Let me explain by approaching the question from her point of view.

Very often children, and older people too, are taught that they must keep the ten commandments, in order to be saved. That is legalism; and no man was ever saved by keeping the law. It is God's holy standard, "our schoolmaster to bring us unto Christ"; for "by the law is the knowledge of sin." It reveals to us the holiness of God and the utter inability of man to keep it in his own strength—or to keep it at all, for that matter.

To teach thus is but to discourage any soul who would be saved, yet thinks he must observe the law for redemption. The law is exacting. The law is stern. And the penalty for breaking it is death.

Now we know that Christ was "born under the law," that He kept it absolutely, perfectly, because in Him was no sin. We know also that He kept it for us! and that by faith in His nished work on the cross, we are saved. God sees us as identified with Christ. We are justified; God's holy law is vindicated and magnified. And we are no longer under law, but under grace. This is evidently what the Sunday School teacher meant. She was right in her motive, but over-zealous and unwise in her extreme view. We *should* emphasize the *grace* of God, making children and older people to see first of all the love of God in Christ unto salvation. But, on the other hand, we should also teach them the ten commandments to show them God's holy standard, to show what our Lord did for us in keeping the law, and in delivering us from the curse of the law. Moreover, the ten commandments have a restraining influence on anyone who will study them. And, finally, "the great commandment," which sums up the law, is "the law of love"; "Thou shalt love the Lord thy God with all thy heart . . . and thy neighbor as thyself."

Question: Why are some modernistic ministers always reading the Sermon on the Mount, whereas other ultra-dispensationalists say that this sermon, including the Lord's Prayer, is not for the church age? Does this beautiful discourse not have a message for us also?

Answer: Your question is two-fold. First, let me say that this sermon does have a distinct message for every Christian "All scripture is given by inspiration of God, and is profitable for doctrine, for reproof, for correction, for instruction in righteousness" (II Tim. 3:16). To rob the child of God of these comforting, instructive lessons from the lips of our Lord, would be to "take away from" the Book of His Word, and to rob His children of priceless truth.

As to your question concerning the frequent use of the Sermon on the Mount by modernistic ministers, let me say that they quote from these "laws of the kingdom" of our Lord, seeking in their whole theology to work out a plan of salvation by works alone, in self-righteoueness, deliberately discarding the many other passages that tell us of the cross of Christ. They will not go to Calvary, there to bow as sinners before the feet of the only Saviour. I refer to those who deny His vicarious atonement for sin. Yet these same "wolves in sheep's clothing" will quote these matchless words from our Saviour's lips, trying to build up a code of ethics, which alone they seek to follow, in order to get to heaven. Thus they lead the erring into a false hope. They call themselves Christian, yet deny the deity of the Lord, whose name they claim to bear.

Now, on the other hand, the ultra-dispensationalists, to whom you refer, go to the extreme concerning the Sermon on the Mount, recorded in Matt. 5-7. It is true that, primarily, these chapters do set forth *the laws of Messiah's kingdom;* that Israel rejected her King, and that these laws will yet be obeyed when He comes again in glory to rule over a purified earth. But there are many fundamental, spiritual lessons for every child of God, in every age, to be found on these pages. Therefore, let us be careful not to rob ourselves and others of this portion of the Word of God.

Personally, I can pray the Lord's Prayer from a heart of worship and praise to God—yes, with those who love Him, yet do not see "eye to eye" with me on dispensational truth. So long as they believe in His finished work on the cross for their salvation, they are children of "the household of faith"; and I can worship the same Lord with them.

Let me add, however, that there is one petition in the Lord's Prayer that is strictly on legal ground: "Forgive us our debts, as we forgive our debtors." By the grace of God, He has forgiven us, even though we did not deserve forgiveness. And we dare not measure our own frail, human forgiveness by His unlimited mercy. Therefore, when we utter this petition in public assembly, or no any other occasion, we should ever be mindful of this important fact: That we ask forgiveness for sin only on the ground of the grace of God, not because of any merit of our own. And can we not have this in mind, even as we join with other fellow-Christians in this prayer?

Question: I live a moral life and try to conform to the teachings of the Sermon on the Mount. Even though I do not make a profession of faith in Christ, why do I not stand as good a chance of getting to heaven as the man

who says he is a Christian and yet does things I would not do?

Answer: Your question is two-fold. First, let me deal with your own case; then with the other man's. You are trying "to get to heaven" by your own efforts, and that can never be done. According to God's Word, "there is none other name under heaven given among men, whereby we must be saved" (Acts 4:12). "Believe on the Lord Jesus Christ, and thou shalt be saved" (Acts 16:31). "Without shedding of blood is no remission" of sin (Heb. 9:22). There are dozens and dozens of Scriptures that I might quote to you; but these will suffice to show that God has plainly told us how to be saved—by faith in the shed blood of the Lord Jesus Christ, and by faith alone. My friend, read the New Testament prayerfully, carefully, for the teaching of Christ and the apostles on this all-important subject. Ask the Holy Spirit to teach you; and as you read the Word of God under His direction, you will be convinced— and converted. "Behold the Lamb of God, which taketh away the sin of the world" (John 1:29). Good works *are* important, very important. But we are saved first; then good works should follow our profession of faith in the Lord Jesus.

As for the man who professes to be a Christian, yet does questionable things, let me say first of all that only God and that man know the true state of his heart. He *may* be a hypocrite. He may be a true believer on the Lord Jesus, yet a weak Christian. There is no excuse for his being a weak Christian; for the Holy Spirit will give power over sin to all who claim the promises of God. If he *is* truly born again, then he ought to be ashamed of his testimony, and ask forgiveness for failing to witness to the saving power of Calvary's cross.

But whatever the state of that man's heart, you who are out of Christ are "without excuse" for rejecting His free salvation. Go to Him, confess your sins, and accept His finished redemptiton for eternal life. Read John 3:36 and John 5:24.

Question: Was the Sabbath ever changed from the seventh day to the first day of the week?

Answer: First let us quote from Exodus 31:16, 17: "Wherefore the children of Israel shall keep the sabbath, to observe the sabbath throughout their generations, for a perpetual covenant. It is a *sign* between me and the children of Israel for ever: for in six days the Lord made heaven and earth, and on the seventh day he rested, and was refreshed." Here we learn that the Sabbath was a *sign* between Jehovah and the nation of Israel.

There is not a single Scripture to show that God ever gave the Sabbath for members of the body of Christ in this day of grace. The believer today is delivered from the law, is dead to the law, and is not under the law.

In Gen. 2:1 we read that God rested, or "sabbathed," on the seventh day. But God's rest was of short duration. Satan came on the scene; and four thousand years later the Lord Jesus said, "My Father worketh hitherto, and I work" (John 5:17). From the sin of Adam until the time Israel left Egypt, twenty-five hundred years later, there is not a word concerning the Sabbath. Noah found grace in the sight of God. Abram believed God, and was declared righteous. But both Noah and Abram rested in a *Person,* not in a day!

On Mount Sinai the Sabbath was given to Israel in connection with the covenant of the law. Israel had a Sabbath, but no rest. God "sabbathed" after He had done a perfect work. At Sinai God gave to Israel the law, which demands perfection. When Christ was on earth, He said to Israel that none of them had kept the law. They were zealous Sabbath-keepers, but they killed the Son of God. Before He went to Calvary, He said to Sabbath-keepers, "Come unto me . . . and *I* will give you *rest*" (Matt. 11:28).

In this day of grace, believing sinners find rest in a Person, not in a day. That Person is the Lord Jesus Christ. Concerning Him we read in Heb.. 10:12 that He rested in a perfect work of redemption.

The Lord Jesus was dead, and His body was in the sepulchre on Israel's Sabbath. By His death God blotted out "the handwriting of ordinances," according to Col. 2:14. And, as we read in Col. 2:16, believers in this age are not to be judged "in respect of . . . the sabbath."

The first day of the week speaks of resurrection, and believers today are resurrection people. But the first day of the week is not the Christian Sabbath; it is the Lord's Day, and speaks of the *new creation,* of which every believer is a part. (See next question.)

Question: Why do Christians keep the first day of the week, instead of the Jewish Sabbath, which is our Saturday?

Answer: Because on the first day of the week our Lord rose from the dead. Sabbath observance was a part of the Mosaic Law, which in Christ has been done away; for He kept the law for us, and we are under grace. That is why He deliberately healed and taught on the Sabbath Day, stirring up the wrath and indignation of the legalistic Pharisees. He showed thereby that "the Son of man is Lord even of the sabbath day" (Matt. 12:8). He showed thereby that He came to usher in a new order, a new covenant.

Yet let no Christian think that this gives him license to make a day of idleness and amusement out of the Lord's Day. One-seventh of our time still belongs to God. And the Christian who can go with the godless world to places of amusement on this day, shows his lack of love for the Lord who bought him, and fails to give a good testimony before the Christ-rejecting world as a born-again soul.

For a detailed discussion of this question, see pages 85-89 of our printed radio Bible messages on "God's Plan of the

Ages." In fact, the two chapters entitled "The Two Coven-
ants" and "The Age of Law" might be considered in this connection. The following brief excerpt from these pages is reprinted here:

The Jewish Sabbath	*The Christian Lord's Day*
1. The 7th day of the week.	1. The 1st day of the week.
2. Commemorated God's creation rest on the seventh day.	2. Commemorates Christ's resurrection from the dead on the first day.
3. Commemorated a finished creation.	3. Commemorates a finished redemption.
4. Compulsory obedience demanded.	4. Voluntary worship and service expected.
5. "Whosoever doeth work therein shall be put to death" (Ex. 35:2; compare Num. 15:32-36).	5. Christ went about doing good on the Sabbath Day to show that He is Lord of the Sabbath, as well as "the end of the law to him that believeth" (Matt. 12:1-8).
6. Represents the old creation.	6. Represents the new creation (II Cor. 5:17).
7. Given to Israel under the law.	7. Given to the Christian under grace.

**Question: In a special delivery letter this question is
asked: Did Christ not make the Sabbath Day? You teach
from Hebrews that He made all things. If so, why do you
disannul what He has made?**

Answer: In the first place, I did not disannul the Sabbath,
or any other Old Testament shadows which the Lord Himself
has fulfilled and "done away." He did make the Sabbath, just
as He made the other shadows. He it was who commanded that
the paschal lamb should be offered, a type of Christ, "the Lamb
of God, which taketh away the sin of the world" (John 1:29).

He it was who commanded that the burnt offering, the sin offering, and all the offerings should be made by a sinful people, manifesting their faith in the coming Redeemer. The Lord Himself caused these shadows to pass away, filling them full. In Col. 2:14-17 the Sabbath is given as one of the "shadows" of good "things to come; but the body is of Christ."

Question: Should a Christian tithe his income, since we are "not under law, but under grace"?

Answer: Although it is true that we are not under the Mosaic Law, yet it seems to me that the tithe is the least the Christian should want to give to the Lord. It was instituted long before Moses was born, and seems to be the scriptural basis for all giving. Abraham gave a tithe 400 years before the law was given. (See Gen. 14:20; cf. Gen. 28:22.)

On the other hand, there is no instruction given in the New Testament about the tithe. God does say through Paul that we should give "upon the first day of the week"—regularly; "as God hath prospered" us (I Cor. 16:2); first giving our own selves to the Lord (II Cor. 8:5); cheerfully (II Cor. 9:7); with joy; and out of a sense of gratitude to God who has given His all for us. Read carefully all of chapters eight and nine of II Corinthians.

To make tithing a binding command in this age of grace, is to return to legalism; but many Christians testify to the fact that, as they have let the tithe be the *beginning* of their giving, God has prospered them to such an extent that they have had all the more to give. Yet let it be remembered that God does not always prosper His saints accordingly; some of the most liberal, devoted Christians never have much, in a material way, in this life.

Therefore, to summarize what we have said: Every child of God should be consistent, faithful, systematic, cheerful in his giving. And the tithe seems to be the scriptural principle.

God's people under the law were servants; God's people under grace are sons. And though, under grace, tithing is not obligatory; yet why should God's people in this dispensation give less than the less favored people under the law?

"Ye are not your own. For ye are bought with a price" (I Cor. 6:19, 20).

"He which soweth sparingly shall reap also sparingly; and he which soweth bountifully shall reap also bountifully. Every man according as he purposeth in his heart, so let him give; not grudgingly, or of necessity: for God loveth a cheerful giver" (II Cor. 9:6, 7).

Question: Is it right to give part of one's tithes to radio programs?

Answer: Certainly it is right to support any cause which is proclaiming the Gospel of our crucified and risen Lord. One's first responsibility, "as unto the Lord," is to the body of believers in his own church, who have pledged themselves to take care of certain missionary responsibilities, both at home and in the foreign field. Yet one does not need to give all his tithe to any one church, it seems to me. Although we need to be very careful in our giving, lest we are deceived by those who are not true to the Word of God and the Christ of the Bible, yet I can think of no more effective way of getting the message of salvation to the world than over the air.

VII

THE ETERNAL SECURITY OF THE BELIEVER

Question: How do you harmonize the doctrine of the eternal security of the believer with the following passages of Scripture: Heb. 6:4-6; II Pet. 2:20-22; Rom. 11:22; Matt. 12:43-45; 24:13; John 15:2, 6; I Cor. 9:27; Rev. 3:5?

Answer: Some years ago I answered this question at length, in a series of radio messages, published in a leaflet entitled, "The Eeternal Security of the Believer." Excerpts from this printed leaflet, dealing with the above-named verses, are quoted here, including also the discussion of one other passage of Scripture, Heb. 10:26-38:

Hebrews 6:4-6

"For it is impossible for those who were once enlightened, and have tasted of the heavenly gift, and were made partakers of the Holy Ghost, and have tasted the good word of God, and the powers of the world to come, if they shall fall away, to renew them again unto repentance; seeing they crucify to themselves the Son of God afresh, and put him to an open shame." In these words the Holy Spirit refers to Hebrews, many of whom were *intellectually* convinced that Jesus was the Messiah. But because of bitter persecution, they were going away from the light they had, returning to Judaism.

Four things are said of the privileges these Hebrews were rejecting:

1. *They were "enlightened."* So also is every man who hears the Gospel, whether he accepts Christ or not. These were *enlightened, but not born again.*

2. *They had "tasted of the heavenly gift."* Now it is one‧ thing to taste; it is another thing to eat. Christ Himself is the

[112]

Heavenly Gift. How many sinners have been under conviction, have admired the beautiful life of our Lord, have acknowledged that He died for a lost world, have even admitted that they expect one day to accept Him as a personal Saviour, and yet have refused to open their hearts to Him. They are among those who have only "tasted of the heavenly gift."

3. *They had been made "partakers of the Holy Ghost."* "Now the word "partakers" in the Greek means those who had been "going along with" the Holy Spirit, "in company with" Him. Every Jew who witnessed the descent of the Holy Spirit on the Day of Pentecost and heard Peter's sermon, as recorded in the second chapter of Acts, was "in company with the Holy Spirit. But, you will remember, the record tells us that some mocked and said, "These men are full of new wine" (Acts 2:13). To witness the power of the Holy Spirit is one thing; to be baptized by the Holy Spirit is another.

4. *They had "tasted the good word of God, and the power of the world (or age) to come";* that is, they had heard the Word of God, and had seen the dead raised, the leper cleansed, the eyes of the blind opened—enough to convince them that Jesus was their Messiah and Lord.

Concerning these the Holy Spirit says: "It is impossible . . . if they shall fall away, to renew them again unto repentance." If they deliberately refuse to accept Christ as the only One who can save them, then they are doing the very same thing their fathers did; for they "crucify to themselves the Son of God afresh, and put him to an open shame."

Moreover, if this passage of Scripture was written concerning Christians, it is very discouraging to those who hold "the falling away" doctrine; for *they* say a man can be saved, "fall away" or be lost, and then be converted again; whereas this passage from the Word of God says, *"It is impossible . . . if they shall fall away, to renew them again unto repentance."*

Do you not see the fallacy of this doctrine, my friend? This one passage alone contradicts it definitely and finally.

But please note further the illustration given by the Holy Spirit in the verses which follow; it bears out the fact that verses 4-6 were written concerning those who had been "enlightened," but not regenerated. In other words, the saved man "bringeth forth" fruit; but the man who rejects the Heavenly Gift bears "thorns and briers." We are not saved *by* our good works; but we are saved *unto* good works. And "by their fruits ye shall know them."

Yet another convincing proof of the fact that verses 4-6 describe the enlightened, but unregenerate, is seen in verse nine and the following verses. Here the Holy Spirit turns, as it were, from a description of those who had rejected Christ, and addresses the truly born-again Hebrew Christians. He calls them "beloved." And He says, *"But, beloved, we are persuaded better things of you"*—He had referred to the unregenerated as "those" (verse 4). Of *"you,"* "beloved of God, "we are persuaded better things" than merely an intellectual knowledge. "We are persuaded . . . *things that accompany salvation."* These words unmistakably prove that, in the preceding verses, the born again souls were not in view at all.

And in verses 13-20, which follow, we find one of the strongest passages bearing upon the eternal security of the believer to be found in all the Word of God. The illustration is given of Jehovah's promise to Abraham, at which time God confirmed His Word by His oath. According to the law of Moses, two or three witnesses were required to establish a fact in point of law. And here we read that by God's Word and God's oath—by these two "immutable," unchangeable things, we have a hope, "an anchor of the soul, both sure and stedfast." What could be more plain, more reassuring, my friend? God's Word is unchanging; His promise is sure!

II Peter 2:20-22

In this passage also the Holy Spirit is writing of the unregenerate. Even a casual reading of the entire second chapter of this epistle reveals the fact that those described here are "false prophets," "false teachers" (verse 1). They are repeatedly referred to as "they" and "them"—never as "you" or "beloved.' Peter was describing those who perhaps through the influence of godly parents, perhaps through the environment of a godly home, those who in some way had "escaped the pollutions of the world" in large measure (verse 20). Restraint had kept them from much that is evil for a time. Then, still unregenerate, such as these had deliberately turned to the world with all its vices. And since God holds us responsible according to the light we have, "it had been better for them not to have known the way of righteousness, than, after they have known it, to turn from the holy commandment delivered unto them" (verse 21). The man who hears the Gospel and rejects it is in a worse condition than the man who has never heard; his responsibility is greater, and his punishment will be all the more severe. Some "shall be beaten with many stripes"; others, "with few stripes" (Luke 12:47, 48).

Furthermore, Peter proves that he is describing the enlightened, but unregenerate, when he adds in verse 22: "But it happened unto them according to the true proverb, The dog is turned to his own vomit again; and the sow that was washed to her wallowing in the mire." The man referred to here was a "dog" all the time—not a "sheep"; a "sow"—not a "lamb." Spurgeon once said, "If this dog had been born again, and had gotten a sheep nature, he would never have returned to his vomit." The sheep in the mire is unhappy, even as the Christian is not satisfied when he is out of the will of God; but the hog enjoys the mire. Even after he has been "washed" by his environment of good resolutions, the unsaved man still possesses the old nature. He is a sinner still.

Hebrews 10:26-38

What we find in this passage belongs in the same class with such references as Hebrews 6:4-6 and II Peter 2:20-22. These words were all addressed to Jews, Christian Jews, who were being warned against the empty profession of those who were intellectually convinced that Jesus was their Messiah, but who were not really saved. Many of these enlightened, but unregenerate ones had *seemed* to embrace Christianity for a time; but when persecution came, they had returned to Judaism. And their example the Holy Spirit uses as a warning against rejecting Christ, the only Way of Life.

Romans 11:22

"On them which fell, severity" — what do these words mean? Again let us note the context. Romans 11:13-24 is addressed to Gentiles, not to individual believers. The matter of personal salvattion is not in question here. The whole passage deals with Jewish responsibility not assumed. Israel is called the "olive tree"; Gentiles are the "wild olive tree." Some of the "natural branches" in Israel were broken off through unbelief; and the wild branches, Gentiles, were "graffed in among them." And the fact that the natural branches were broken off is given as a warning to the Gentiles, lest they too be not spared. The Jews, as a nation, rejected their Messiah; and in this church age God is visiting the Gentiles, "to take out of them a people for his name" (Acts 15:14). Then He will once again deal with His ancient people, Israel; the natural branches shall "be graffed into their own olive tree. . . And all Israel shall be saved." (See Rom. 11:24-27.) This, in brief, is the meaning of Romans 11:13-27.

Matthew 12:43-45

These are the words of Christ: "When the unclean spirit is gone out of a man"; that is, when he *is gone out* of his own accord—not *cast out* by the Lord Himself—when by self-reformation a man seeks to clean up his life, he still belongs to "this wicked generation" (verse 45). In another place the Lord Jesus said, "Ye must be born again." These words in Matthew were spoken to the Pharisees, who had attributed to Beelzebub the works of Christ. The house of Israel had been "swept" and "garnished" of the spirit of idolatry in the Babylonian captivity; but still unregenerate, these leaders of the nation were self-righteous hypocrites. The Lord Jesus said so. And this passage in Matthew 12:43-45 described their state, not the state of the redeemed who had fallen into sin.

Matthew 24:13

"He that shall endure unto the end, the same shall be saved." In our study of Matthew we saw that this entire passage refers to "the great tribulation" that shall come upon the earth; and the Lord Jesus referred to that period when He uttered the words of verse 13. He had in mind the faithful remnant in that day. "Many false prophets shall rise, and shall deceive many . . . But he that shall endure unto the end, the same shall be saved" (verses 11-13).

However, the principle set forth here I accept. If a man does not "endure unto the end," he only reveals what he was all the while, a mere professor, not a born-again soul.

John 15:2, 6

But someone asks, "Does not John 15:2, 6 prove the fallacy of the doctrine of eternal security?" No, my friend. A careful examination of the text makes it very clear that we have in this passage: (1) What God does with a fruitless branch; and (2) what *men* do with a fruitless branch. But the branch is united to the vine all the while!

What does God do with the fruitless branch? "He taketh it away" (verse 2). Where does He take it? To heaven. In

Corinth, because of a misuse of the Lord's Supper, Paul says, "Many are weak and sickly . . . and many sleep" (I Cor. 11:30). Then he adds, under the guidance of the Holy Spirit: "For if we would judge ourselves, we should not be judged. But when we are judged, we are chastened of the Lord." But, my friend, chastening of the Lord is one thing; eternal condemnation is another. "Whom the Lord loveth he chasteneth" (Heb. 12:6). The branch which the Lord "taketh away" represents the Christian who is saved, "yet so as by fire" (I Cor. 3:15). He loses his reward, but not his salvation. Fruit-bearing *follows* conversion, and is not a *means* of conversion.

There are two ways of going to heaven. One was Paul's way; for he was able to declare with joy: "I have fought a good fight, I have finished my course, I have kept the faith: henceforth there is laid up for me a crown of righteousness, which the Lord, the righteous judge, shall give me at that day" (II Tim. 4:7, 8). The other way of going to heaven is that of the child of God who dies without having "finished the course," without having won souls for Christ, without having consecrated all to His service after conversion.

Many of our Bible Institute students go home every year, rejoicing over a diploma, a reward for work done. They have finished their course, as it were. But sometimes we have the sad duty of dismissing a student. He goes home, but not with rejoicing. My Christian friend, are you getting ready to meet your Saviour with the victory of a life spent in His service, to the praise of His glory?

But let us look again at our text. What do *men* do with the fruitless branch? *"Men* gather them, and cast them into the fire, and they are burned" (verse 6). *Men* have no way of judging the sincerity of our profession, except by the testimony we give before the world. The *Lord* looketh on the heart. It is very important that we witness to Him by our works before a sinful world. But it is reassuring to know also that the branch is united to the True Vine, which is Christ. It is reassuring to know that our eternal security depends upon His perfect work on Calvary, rather than upon our imperfect, faltering work, even after we are born again.

I Corinthians 9:27

Who is "a castaway"? To find the answer, let us read the entire passage here. Paul is discussing rewards for service, not salvation. And he uses the illustration of the Olympian games to show the meaning of running the Christian race. Only free-born citizens could contend in these games; and only born-again children of God can run the race as Christians. Salvation is not the goal; it is the starting place. The judgment seat of Christ is the goal.

Now the word "castaway" in the Greek means "disapproved." The prize went to the victor in the Olympian games; and the crown awaits the Christian who is not "disapproved," in so far as his service is concerned, at the judgment seat of Christ. Salvation is not a reward; it is a free gift. And Paul was not writing about salvation in this passage, as the context clearly shows.

Revelation 3:5

But someone asks, referring to Revelation 3:5, "How can a name be blotted out of the book of life if it is not first entered therein?" It is only by inference that "the falling away" doctrine can be built upon this quotation from the Scriptures. On the other hand, these words mean just what they say, and give us the blessed assurance that God will *not* blot our names out of the book of life if we are trusting in the finished work of Christ. Moreover, "no prophecy of the scripture is of any *private* interpretation" (II Peter 1:20); and if specific passages are considered in their relation to the whole body of truth, as set forth in the Word of God, no contradictions will be found.

When Christ promised: "My sheep . . . shall never perish," He meant exactly what He said.

"Jesus Paid It All"

Space forbids a further consideration here of selected passages bearing upon this theme; but the same principle of interpretation will never fail. As we let the Holy Spirit who wrote the Word of God take the things of Christ and show them unto us, He will be our unerring Teacher. As we read each passage in the light of its context, comparing Scripture with Scripture, we arrive at the same conclusion: "By two immutable things (God's Word confirmed by His oath), in which it was impossible for God to lie, we . . . have a strong consolation, who have fled for refuge to lay hold upon the hope set before us: which *hope we have as an anchor of the soul, both sure and stedfast*" (Heb. 6:18, 19).

Good works *are* important. God expects His blood-bought children to bear "much fruit." An empty profession before a world lost in sin is dead. But good works can not save the sinner. Salvation must come first.

My unsaved friend, do not trust in your own efforts. You need a Saviour. And that One is Jesus of Nazareth who died for you. Look to Him by faith, and you will become one of His "sheep." You will "never perish"; for His Word is the Word of the eternal God! It is forever established in heaven. You will want to witness before the world to His measureless wisdom and limitless love. Then if you fall into sin, you will not be lost; but you will be unhappy until you have confessed your sin to your Great High Priest, even Jesus, who will cleanse you from all unrighteousness. You will be Christ's for time and eternity. And you will be among that blood-bought company, of which He Himself has said: "My sheep . . . shall never perish." Will you not take Him at His Word, and be saved today? If you will, then you can sing with assurance the words of the old hymn:

> "Jesus paid it all:
>   All to Him I owe;
> Sin had left a crimson stain;
>   He washed it white as snow."

Question: Does Heb. 10:26 not destroy all hope for the backslider? It reads: "For if we sin wilfully after we have received the knowledge of the truth, there remaineth no more sacrifice for sins."

Answer: Although this verse is discussed briefly in connection with a group of similar passages on another page of these studies, yet we shall look at it again here. The apostle is addressing Hebrews; and the warning is based upon the perfection of the one sacrifice of Christ, as the context clearly shows. "The "sinning wilfully" here is the definite turning away from, or the refusal of, that one perfect sacrifice — the finished work of Christ. To do so means eternal ruin, because there is no other sacrifice that can meet the sin question.

The apostle is not discussing the failures that all too often are found in the life of a Christian. For such a discussion, see I John 1:9; 2:1, for some of the clearest passages.

In Heb. 10:26 the Holy Spirit is speaking of the wilful definite rejection of Christ's atoning sacrifice. In other words, He is saying that if, after examining what the Old Testament Scriptures teach concerning Christ and His work; if, after comparing these prophecies with the New Testament presentation of Christ, thus obtaining a knowledge of the truth; if, in the light of all this knowledge, one deliberately and permanently rejects Christ, then God has nothing more to say to him, except to mete out judgment. Why? Because in the Lord Jesus Christ the Triune God has offered the only way of salvation. Christ crucified is "the wisdom of God." That is the only way of salvation the wisdom of God has devised.

The backslider is not in view in this text at all. It is the man who has "trodden under foot the Son of God, and hath counted the blood of the covenant an unholy thing," who is under consideration here (Heb. 10:29).

Question: What if a person has been truly converted, but goes back to the world, and never seems to repent of his backslidden state? Will he be eternally saved?

Answer: Let me answer your question in three statements:

1. Many so-called backsliders have never "slid forward"; that is, they were never regenerated. We call them mere professors, not possessors of salvation. A real Christian will be chastised, will confess his sin, and live for Christ, however falteringly it may be.

2. Such Christians as we call backsliders are carnal Christians. They will be losers at the judgment seat of Christ, in so far as their rewards for service are concerned. (See I Cor. 3:1-4; 11-16.)

3. A real Christian may become a backslider, but he can never become an apostate—and an apostate is one who denies the old faith, the Bible, even the Lord Jesus, who is the only Saviour.

Question: Was Judas saved before he was lost?

Answer: There is not the slightest suggestion in any portion of Scripture to intimate that Judas was ever a saved man. In fact, the very contrary is taught. In John 6:64, 65 we read: "But there are some of you that believe not. For Jesus knew from the beginning who they were that believed not, and who should betray him. And he said, "Therefore said I unto you, that no man can come unto me, except it were given unto him of my Father." Here we learn that Judas, with the others who rejected Him, was an unbeliever. And then the Lord Jesus added these words, recorded in the same chapter: "Jesus answered them, Have not I chosen you twelve, and one of you is a devil? He spake of Judas Iscariot the son of Simon: for he it was that should betray him, being one of the twelve" (John 6:70, 71). Here we learn that Judas is called "a devil." Therefore, it is altogether contrary to sound doctrine and plain scriptural teaching to say that Judas was ever a saint, and that he became a sinner, thus losing his salvation. Such a position is taken by some Christians who deny the doctrine of the eternal security of the believer.

Question: If the believer in Christ is eternally secure, why should the Lord give him the warning of Rev. 3:11: "Hold that fast which thou hast, that no man take thy crown"?

Answer: The Lord Jesus did not say, ". . . that no man take thy *salvation"*; but He did say, ". . . that no man take thy *crown."* And these two statements mean entirely different things. Salvation is the free gift of God. The crowns are rewards for service rendered in Jesus' name and for His Glory, *after* one has been born again. They are to be given at "the judgment seat of Christ," where only the redeemed shall stand before God and His holy angels. (See Rom. 14:10, II Cor. 5:10.)

I can not see any difficulty in this passage. If you are a really born-again soul, no one can take your salvation from you. But if you neglect your duty, and allow others to step in and do what Christ intends you to do, then they will receive your crown, or reward.

A careful reading of I Cor. 3:11-15 makes very clear the meaning of rewards, as distinguished from the gift of salvation. "If any man's *work* abide," which he has done in the service of Christ—after believing in His finished work on Calvary, he shall receive a reward." But suppose a Christian is spiritually proud, self-seeking, vain-glorious—and Satan all too often causes the Christian's testimony to be so marred—to such a man the Holy Spirit says, "If any man's *work* shall be burned, he shall suffer loss; *but he himself shall be saved; yet so as through fire*" (R.V.). With Job, such a man could say, "I am escaped with the skin of my teeth" (Job 19:20); except that Job referred to physical suffering, whereas the man described in I Cor. 3:15 is saved from eternal condemnation—just barely saved. That man who barely gets to heaven will have no trophies of grace, in the form of souls won to Christ, to be to the praise of His glory. He will have received his reward from *men* here on earth, of his motives in service were selfish. If he endowed a hospital, for example, just to make a name for himself, yet in the name of Christian charity, he will have received his praise from men. Then why should he expect a "Well done" from the Lord Jesus? He will be saved, but will have no crowns laid up in glory for soul-winning, for sacrificial service for Jesus' sake.

Yes, there will be degrees of reward in heaven, as well as degrees of punishment in hell. The God of all justice will rightly reward the Apostle Paul in ways that the repentant thief on the cross does not deserve; for think of the difference in the work accomplished by these two for the glory of God!

And would you, my friend, seek God's best—in service to Him here, and in reward and praise to Him throughout all eternity? Then read what He says about the crowns He offers for those who will put Christ first:

1. *"The Crown of Life"* (James 1:12). "Blessed is the man that endureth temptation (or 'trials,' Revised Version): for when he is tried, he shall receive the crown of life, which the Lord hath promised to them that love him."

2. *"A Crown of Righteousness"* (II Tim. 4:8). When Paul was nearing the end of his earthly pilgrimage, he wrote these

familiar words: "I have fought a good fight. I have finished my course, I have kept the faith: henceforth there is laid up for me a crown of righteousness, which the Lord, the righteous judge, shall give me at that day: and not to me only, but unto all them also that love his appearing."

3. *"An Incorruptible Crown"* (I Cor. 9:25). "Every man that striveth for the mastery is temperate in all things. Now they do it to obtain a corruptible crown; but we an incorruptible"—for running the Christian race with singleness of purpose.

4. *"A Crown of Glory"* (I Pet. 5:4). "And when the chief Shepherd shall appear, ye shall receive a crown of glory that fadeth not away." The context shows that this reward is to those who are faithful in feeding "the flock of God."

5. *The Martyr's Crown* (Rev. 2:10). "Be thou faithful unto death, and I will give thee a crown of life."

6. *The "Crown of Rejoicing"* (I Thess. 2:19, 20). "For what is our hope, or joy, or crown of rejoicing? Are not even ye in the presence of our Lord Jesus Christ at his coming? For ye are our glory and joy." This is the soul-winner's crown.

But concerning the *free gift of salvation,* read also: Rom. 1:16, 17; 5:6-8; Eph. 2:8-10; Col. 1:14; Titus 3:5; I Pet. 1:18, 19; 2:24; and literally dozens of similar passages!

Question: Please explain John 8:34, 35: "Verily, verily, I say unto you, Whosoever committeth sin is the servant of sin. And the servant abideth not in the house forever: but the Son abideth ever." What did the Lord mean when He said, "The servant abideth not in the house for ever: but the Son abideth ever"?

Answer: If you will read this passage in the Revised Version, you will note that the word "son" in the last clause is written with a small letter, and does *not* refer to Christ the Son. It refers to a child of God, who is a "son of God."

The Lord Jesus means that a *servant of sin* is not to abide forever; "but the *son* abideth ever." The contrast here is in the fact that servitude is temporal, but sonship is eternal; that servitude is not forever; that even though a man is a servant of sin, that position of servitude can be changed. And that is a blessed thing. Jesus said, "Whosoever committeth sin is the servant of sin." But that position of servitude can be changed; "the servant abideth not in the house for ever." That is, a man can change *masters,* but he can not change *fathers.* If you are born a child of God, you are born once and forever. God is your Father; and you never can be anything else but a child of God. If you are a servant of sin, you can change that position. You can be taken out of that servitude to sin, and be made a child of God. If that is accomplished, then that is "forever."

VIII

THE BAPTISM OF THE HOLY SPIRIT
THE TONGUES MOVEMENT
DIVINE HEALING

Question: Who will receive the baptism of the Holy Spirit? And is there ever a visible sign accompanying this baptism?

Answer: Every Christian is baptized with the Holy Spirit the moment he is born again; for it is the quickening power of the Holy Spirit which regenerates the soul. We shall enlarge upon this a moment; but first let us state the answer to your second question. In this present age there is no visible sign accompanying the baptism of the Holy Spirit; there is a change of one's life and testimony. But there is no visible sign, such as accompanied the descent of the Holy Spirit on the Day of Pentecost and in the house of Cornelius, as recorded in the book of Acts. This, too, we shall discuss more fully, a little later.

The work of the Holy Spirit is as clearly set forth in the Word of God as is the work of the Father, and as is the work of the Son. Let us summarize a few important truths:

The Holy Spirit convicts of sin, and regenerates the heart of the sinner, as stated in John 16:8-11; 3:8.

The Holy Spirit's relation to the believer is as follows:

1. *Every believer is indwelt by the Holy Spirit,* as evidenced by Gal. 4:5, "Because ye are sons," not because of anything else, but "because ye are sons, God hath sent forth the Spirit of his Son into your hearts, crying, Abba, Father." (See also such passages as John 14:16, 17, 26; 15:26; 16:7, 12-15; Rom.

8:14-17; I Cor. 12:3.) This last verse is striking, "No man can say that Jesus is the Lord, but by the Holy Spirit." In other words, you and I could not acknowledge that Jesus of Nazareth is Lord of lords, if we did not have the baptism of the Holy Spirit. He teaches us the truth of God as it is in Christ, in whom "dwelleth all the fulness of the Godhead *bodily*" (Col. 2:9).

2. *Every believer is baptized with the Spirit,* as plainly stated in I Cor. 12:12, 13: "For by one Spirit are we all baptized into one body, whether we be Jews or Gentiles, whether we be bond or free; and have been all made to drink into one Spirit." When the apostle wrote, saying, "WE are all baptized into one body" by the Spirit, he was writing to the Corinthians, the most carnal of all the apostolic churches. Paul made it very clear that "the baptism of the Spirit" is that operation of the Spirit, by which a believer is made a member of the body of Christ. The baptism of the Spirit is *not an experience following conversion;* it is a dispensational act, whereby God unites the born-again soul to the true church, which is the Body of Christ. There is no such thing as a Christian who is not a member of the body of Christ.

3. *Every believer is sealed with the Holy Spirit,* even as Paul wrote to the Ephesians, saying, "After that ye believed, ye were sealed with that Holy Spirit of promise, which is the earnest of our inheritance until the redemption of the purchased possession, unto the praise of his glory" (Eph. 1:13, 14). In other words, Paul said here that the Holy Spirit is the pledge given to every believer by the Father, guaranteeing the redemption of the *body* when it is raised from the dead, because the *soul* has already been redeemed by faith in the shed blood of the Lord Jesus. The seal is the mark of ownership, and we belong to God.

4. *Every believer, however, is not filled with the Holy Spirit.* It is possible for us to "grieve the Holy Spirit of God," even

though we have been baptized with the Spirit—to our own shame we must admit this; we should *not* grieve the Holy Spirit by permitting unconfessed sin in our lives. (See Eph. 4:30-32.)

We are commanded in Eph. 5:18 to "be filled with the Spirit." *Never* are we commanded to be "baptized with the Spirit"; for this is an act which God alone can work in our hearts by grace. And He does it the moment we put our faith in the atoning work of Christ for salvation.

Question: You say we are baptized with the Holy Spirit the moment we are born again. Please explain why the disciples were baptized with the Spirit after they were saved?

Answer: The disciples lived both *before* and *after* the Day of Pentecost. And it was on that memorable day nearly two thousand years ago that the church began, when the Holy Spirit came upon believers with miraculous power. That day's experience was in fulfillment of our Lord's express promise. Listen to such words as these:

"The Holy Spirit was not yet given; because that Jesus was not yet glorified" (John 7:39).

"It is expedient for you that I go away," He said to His disciples; "for if I go not away, the Comforter will not come unto you; but if I depart, I will send him unto you" (John 16:7). "And, behold, I send the promise of my Father upon you: but tarry ye in the city of Jerusalem, until ye be endued with power from on high" (Luke 24:49). (Compare Acts 1:4, 5, 8.)

So, you see, the disciples were already born again by faith in Christ *before* the Holy Spirit came on the Day of Pentecost. That is why they had the *added* experience of the baptism of the Holy Spirit. But all who have been born again *after* Pentecost have been baptized with the Spirit the moment they were saved.

For proof of this, note that the three thousand souls who were added to the believers on the Day of Pentecost did not have to wait at all for the baptism of the Holy Spirit. (See Acts 2.) In Gal. 3:13, 14 we read that Christ hung on the accursed tree, "that we might receive the promise of the Spirit through faith." Dozens of Scriptures might be quoted to illustrate this fundamental truth. The baptism of the Holy Spirit is never the future experience of the believer in this day of grace. There is no salvation outside of the body of Christ; and every saved person becomes a member of that body by divine baptism.

Question: If all believers receive the Holy Spirit at conversion, why did Paul ask certain disciples at Ephesus, "Have ye received the Holy Ghost since ye believed?" (See Acts 19:2.)

Answer: The Scriptures clearly teach that a believer is indwelt by the Holy Spirit when he believes. Gal. 4:6 speaks plainly: "And *because ye are sons,* God hath sent forth the Spirit of his Son into your hearts, crying, Abba, Father." One becomes a son of God when he believes on the Lord Jesus Christ, as John 1:12 definitely states: "As many as received him, to them gave he power to become the sons of God, even to them that believe on his name." "Because ye are sons"— not because of anything else—"God *hath* sent forth the Spirit of his Son into your hearts."

Now for the objection: Let us examine Acts 19:1-7 carefully. Here we read of a company of men to whom Paul puts this question: "Have ye received the Holy Ghost since ye believed?" "And they said unto him, We have not so much as heard whether there be any Holy Ghost. And he said unto them, Unto what then were ye baptized? And they said, Unto John's baptism" (Acts 19:2, 3).

Let us pause here to note that their very answer to Paul's question shows that *they were on Old Testament ground,* as Paul himself goes on to state in verses 4-6. When Paul explained to them that they had to believe in the Christ whom John preached, then "they were baptized in the name of the Jord Jesus. And . . . the Holy Ghost came on them" (Acts 19:5-6). Up until this time, they were not believers in the New Testament sense at all. They had been looking forward to a work which they expected God to do for them, being ignorant of the fact that He had already finished that work on Calvary. They admitted that they knew nothing of what had taken place at Pentecost; and they admitted also that they knew nothing of the meaning of Calvary—till Paul explained it to them.

It is just as impossible for you and me to have the experience of these men as it is for us to have the experience of the twelve disciples who accepted the claims of the Lord Jesus while He was on earth, then later received the Holy Spirit at Pentecost. All of these belong to the same class who lived both before Calvary and after Pentecost.

There is a similar objection offered by some; that is, the experience of the Samaritans. Again, we raise the question, "Does every believer on this side of the cross receive the Spirit the moment he believes?" And our answer is, "Yes; it has ever been true except in the case of the Samaritans." Read the story as recorded in Acts 8:14-17. The Spirit did not fall on them until some apostles from Jerusalem went down and laid hands on them. Why? Because the Jews had "no dealings with the Samaritans" (John 4:9). There was a schism between the Jews and the Samaritans which dated back to Old Testament times. And if the Spirit had come upon the Samaritans without the healing of this old quarrel, this schism would have been carried into the church. Therefore, Christ withheld the

Spirit until certain ones went down from Jerusalem—Jews—
and had fellowship with them. Jerusalem had to go down, and
Samaria had to receive Jerusalem. Then and there the schism
was wiped out. It was the Holy Spirit's way of settling what
would have been the source of great trouble in the church. But
this is the only exception in all the Word of God to the truth
herein set forth. All other believers on this side of the cross
were indwelt by the Spirit the moment they accepted Christ as
Saviour and Lord.

**Question: What is meant by the words of John the Bap-
tist, recorded in Matt. 3:11: "He that cometh after me is
mightier than I. . . . He shall baptize you with the Holy
Ghost, and with fire"? Is a believer baptized with fire, as
well as with the Holy Spirit?**

Answer: Not at all. John was speaking to a mixed company of the saved and the unsaved. The saved were to be
baptized with the Holy Spirit. The unsaved were to be baptized
with the fire of judgment at the return of Christ. Verse 12
makes it very clear that this is the meaning of John's words:
"Whose fan is in his hand, and he will thoroughly purge his
floor, and gather his wheat into the garner; but he will burn up
the chaff with unquenchable fire." The doctrine concerning the
church, revealed later by Paul, comes in between the preaching
of John the Baptist and the return of Christ in glory.

You will note in Acts 1:4, 5 that, just before His ascension
into heaven, our Lord referred to John's words, and told His
disciples to "tarry in Jerusalem" to "wait for the promise of
the Father." Then He added, "For John truly baptized with
water; but ye shall be baptized with the Holy Ghost not many
days hence." In addressing *believers,* the risen Lord made no
reference to fire; for believers shall not "come into judgment,"
but have "passed out of death into life" (John 5:24).

Compare these passages with II Thess. 2:7-9: "The Lord Jesus shall be revealed from heaven with his mighty angels, in

Question: Does Matt. 28:19 refer to the baptism with the Holy Spirit, or to water baptism? "Go ye therefore, and teach all nations, baptizing them in the name of the Father, and of the Son, and of the Holy Ghost."

Answer: This verse refers to water baptism. Men do not baptize with the Holy Spirit; only God can do this; and He does it when the sinner is born again, by faith in the finished work of Christ on Calvary's Cross.

Question: Why do you say that speaking in "tongues" is not for this age?

Answer: Let me quote from one of our former radio messages, found in the printed booklet, entitled "The Baptism of the Holy Spirit—Is It Something for the Believer to Seek?"

Those who claim that speaking in tongues is an evidence of the baptism of the Spirit overlook the plain teaching of Paul, that the gift of tongues was only a temporary gift, as were the gifts of prophecy and of supernatural knowledge. The apostles were given supernatural wisdom, in order that they might write the New Testament, even as all prophecy came from God. But let us remember the words of Paul: "Whether there be prophecies, they shall fail; *whether there be tongues, they shall cease;* whether there be knowledge (supernatural knowledge), *it shall vanish away*" (I Cor. 13:8). In the beginning of the Christian era, before men had full revelation of God's will, as set forth in His complete, written Word, He worked in supernatural ways to convince sinners of the claims of Christ. While the New Testament was being written, He worked miracles through the apostles. But God's Word was complete when John wrote the twenty-second chapter of Revelation on the Isle of Patmos. And "when that which is perfect is come," Paul said, "then that which is in part shall be done away" (I Cor: 13:10).

This verse in I Cor. 13 refers to the complete revelation of God and the passing of temporary gifts, which include tongues and supernatural knowledge. At the time Paul wrote Corinthians, the New Testament was in the process of formation; and therefore the gift of tongues was still in the church. In I Cor. 14 he gives instructions concerning how this gift was to be exercised. You will please note that special instructions were given to women to remain silent in the assembly. It would seem that in the Corinthian Church the women were prominent in the "tongues movement," even as they are today. There is not an intimation in the New Testament that a woman was ever given this gift; for in I Corinthians the instructions are to "him," never to "her." But in reading such instructions in I Cor. 14, ever bear in mind what Paul says in chapter 13, that "tongues" would vanish away. When? "When that which is perfect is come." In other words, now that we have the full, complete, perfect revelation of God, there is no need for this *then temporary gift*. We have the whole Bible and the unerring Holy Spirit to teach us all these things in an orderly, sane, dignified way, becoming to the child of God who bears the wonderful name of Christ. Let us not drag that name down to confusion and shame.

For emphasis, let me repeat: The descent of the Holy Spirit on the Day of Pentecost was accomplished by miracles, in order to show to all men that God was doing a new thing in the world, that "the promise of the Father" had come. It was a dispensational act of God. And ever since apostolic times, the Holy Spirit has been regenerating sinners who will accept the Lord Jesus, working quietly, even as our Lord foretold. "The wind bloweth where it will, and thou hearest the voice thereof, but knowest not whence it cometh, and whither it goeth; so is every one that is born of the Spirit" (John 3:8).

Question: Is speaking with tongues of God or the devil?

Answer: In answering this question, we should say, rather, that speaking with tongues, like other signs, is not unscriptural, but that it is altogether undispensational.

This is taught in I Cor. 13:8-13. In speaking concerning the sign-gifts, the apostle there wrote that when he was a child he spake as a child; but that afterwards he became a man, and put way childish things. In this connection, he said, "Tongues shall be done away," as we have already seen in answer to our preceding question.

In I Cor. 13:13 we read further: "And now abideth faith, hope, love, these three; but the greatest of these is love." We find that, after Paul penned these words, he spoke more than one hundred times of faith, hope, and love. It is very significant that in the last seven epistles which he wrote, several of which are frequently referred to as the "prison epistles," there is not a single mention of signs, miracles, visions, tongues, healings, discerning of spirits, or any of the sign-gifts mentioned in I Cor. 12.

Again, the disciples of Christ who, on the Day of Pentecost, spoke with tongues did not speak in *unknown* tongues which required an interpreter. These messengers of the Lord simply gave forth the Lord's message in the tongues, or languages, of the different nations represented in Jerusalem on that day. There were "devout Jews from every nation under heaven" assembled there fifty days after the death and resurrection of Christ. They had gathered there to keep the Feast of Pentecost, according to Jewish custom. And the disciples simply preached Jesus, and explained the fulfillment of the prophecy of Joel concerning the descent of the Holy Spirit, speaking in the different languages of these Jews. There was no muttering in the so-called "unknown tongues," of which we hear so much today.

Concerning the rushing mighty wind and the supernatural phenomena of that eventful day, we can truthfully say that there has never been anything like it since then. In Acts 10:46 and Acts 19:6 we have the record of how certain believers spoke with tongues as an evidence that they had received the Holy Spirit and salvation—in that day of transition, when men did not have the complete Word of God.

But concerning speaking with tongues, as is the custom in Pentecostal assemblies today, the divine instructions are found in the fourteenth chapter of I Corinthians. The first statement which we would emphasize in this chapter is found in verse 33: *"God is not the author of confusion."* Again, in order that confusion might be avoided, specific instructions were given in verses 27 and 28. Here the apostle said that, if any speak with tongues, it must be two or three; and if there were no one in the assembly with the gift of interpretation, then there should be no speaking with tongues. Very important also is this command of verse 34: *"Let your women keep silence in the churches."* What I am about to say, I say in all kindness; for I do not fail to appreciate the devoted service of Christian women. But it is a known fact that, if women were taken out of the tongues movement, the movement would soon cease to move.

Therefore, inasmuch as there is not such an assembly in this country, where the speaking with tongues is permitted and practised, that is conducted in line with the plain teaching of God's Word, we dogmatically affirm that speaking with tongues in public meetings is not of God.

Let us not forget the warning of the Lord Jesus, that "an evil and adulterous generation seeketh after a sign" (Matt. 12:39); or the Bible prophecy that the Antichrist is coming "with all power and signs and lying wonders" (II Thess. 2:9).

Our attitude in this day of grace should be in accordance with the words of the Lord, as recorded in John 20:29: "Thomas, because thou hast seen me, thou hast believed; blessed are they that have not seen, and yet have believed."

Question: If we have faith enough, why can we not claim divine healing for our bodies now? I have been taught that at conversion the body belongs to Christ, and we have no more to say about it; that we are dead, and it is Christ who now lives in us; that sickness is a sin; and that we are not to go to doctors, or use medicine; but rather, that we are to pray and have faith. I am so confused. Please explain.

Answer: No wonder you are confused! We need not be confused, however, on this subject; for the Bible speaks plainly. Those who teach such doctrine as you have outlined claim that there is physical healing in the atonement for this present hour. Some even go so far as to declare that they have already received their resurrection bodies. A man came into my office some time ago, and claimed that he belonged to the 144,000 of Revelation. He said that he had already received his resurrection body. I took one look at him, and lost interest immediately! Some are "ever learning."

Rom. 8:23 makes it very clear that our bodies are not yet redeemed: "We ourselves groan within ourselves, *wailing for* the adoption, to wit, *the redemption of our body.*" If we may have the redemption of our bodies *now, why wait for it?*

My friend, not until the Lord returns for His church will "this corruptible . . . put on incorruption, and this mortal . . . put on immortality" (I Cor. 15:53). "Our citizenship (R.V.) is in heaven, from whence also we *look for* the Saviour. the Lord Jesus Christ: who shall change our body of humiliation, that it may be fashioned like unto this glorious body" (Phil.

3:20, 21). Many other passages of Scripture bear out this truth.

Without a doubt, divine healing is meant for this age, *but only in so far as it may please God to grant it.* Sometimes He heals; sometimes He does not. What of the millions of His dear saints who have died? Did they lack faith? What of God's abundant blessing upon the ministry of Christian missionary doctors and nurses, to say nothing of those in so-called Christian lands? What of the very evident blessing of God upon medical science in the world today? Do you not see where this false teaching leads one? It is both unscriptural and unreasonable in its argument. Assuredly we need to pray for the sick; but then we must leave the issue with God, using the means He has given us to heal the sick.

Question: When we pray for the restoration of a dear one's health, should we add, "Thy will be done"? I have been told that, to do this, shows a lack of faith, and that we are to claim healing.

Answer: In matters like bodily healing, we should be submissive to the will of God; in fact, we should always *glory* in the will of God, whatever that will should bring.

Sometimes it is contrary to the will of God that we should be healed, as in the case of Paul. In II Cor. 12:7-10 he tells us that, lest he should "be exalted above measure," become proud because of the revelation given unto him from God, he was given a "thorn in the flesh," to keep him humble. Bible students generally agree that this "thorn in the flesh" was very poor eyesight. Paul prayed thrice that it might be removed; but God said, rather, "My grace is sufficient for thee; for my strength is made perfect in weakness."

We should not *demand* things of God, regardless of His will. The proper attitude of faith is to submit one's self unto Him, knowing that His will is best.

Bodily healing is not on the same basis as salvation. If it were so, we should not have to wait for Christ to return to redeem the body, as shown in answer to another question in this series.

My book on the *Mystery of Suffering* goes into fuller discussion of this matter.

IX

THE CHRISTIAN LIFE

Question: What should be the Christian's attitude toward earthly pleasures? I want to be a consecrated Christian; but my friends think I am rather queer and fanatical in my views?

Answer: In the first place, we have the direct command: "Come out from among them, and be ye separate, saith the Lord, and *touch not the unclean thing;* and I will receive you, and will be a Father unto you, and ye shall be my sons and daughters, saith the Lord Almighty" (II Cor. 6:14-18). Again, we have other very definite Scriptures, such as, "Love not the world, neither the things that are in the world. If any man love the world, the love of the Father is not in him" (I John 2:15-17). And yet again we are urged to keep our garments "unspotted from the world" (James 1:27). These are but a few of the many passages.

By "the world" in such Scriptures, the Holy Spirit means the God-dishonoring, Christ-rejecting, Spirit-resisting world. We are to be *"in* the world, but not *of* it."* We are to mingle with our fellow-men, seeking to point them to Christ, loving their souls, but hating their sins. In other words, we are not to find our *satisfaction* in doing the things that dishonor the name we bear.

In the second place, we are repeatedly exhorted not to do *anything* that causes the "weaker brother to stumble." Perhaps you or I could do many things the world does, yet come out unharmed, to a certain extent; whereas another following in our steps would go down in utter defeat. Paul wrote to the Corinthian Christians, saying that meat offered to idols was just the same to him personally as other meat; that is, it made

[140]

no difference to him at all; but if another looking on, who thought there was some virtue in such meat, saw Paul eating it and stumbled thereby, then, Paul said, he would not touch meat so long as the world stood. The application is plain.

So far, we have considered only the negative side of the question. Let us look for a moment at the positive side. If we truly love the Lord; if we find our joy and our satisfaction in His Word and will, then these matters will not trouble us. He will give us so much to think about, so much to do for Him, that there will be no time for or enjoyment in the things that dishonor or displease Him.

As for our being considered fanatical or too "religious," our Lord told us that it would be even so. These are but a few of His many words on this subject: "If the world hate you, ye know that it hated me before it hated you. If ye were of the world, the world would love his own . . . In the world ye shall have tribulation: but be of good cheer; I have overcome the world" (John 15:18-20; 16:33). "The servant is not greater than his lord."

Having said all this, may I add a word of advice? Sometimes we *invite* unnecessary criticism, from those who can not understand our position, by taking what the world calls a sanctimonious, "holier-than-thou" attitude; or by being unduly harsh in our criticism of others; or by being eccentric in our dress. Personally, I feel that we accomplish more by the silent testimony of our lives, and by presenting *Christ* in all His power and beauty and holiness, than we do by "harping" on the so-called social evils. This is not to say that we must not take our stand for right against wrong. But if we give people Christ: if He takes possession of their very lives; then all these other issues are taken care of, definitely and finally. "The things of earth will grow strangely dim in the light of His glory and grace." We shall be doing a constructive work, rather than one that is destructive in the main, yet lacking in the appeal that only the Gospel message can give.

And may I add, in regard to the matter of dress, I am convinced that we should be conventional without being unchristian; "in style" without being extreme; one with our fellowmen, making our whole personalities as attractive as possible; for nothing is too good for our Lord. How can we attract people to Him if we take no pride in our personal appearance, are freakish or not well groomed? God has given us a common sense and good judgment, which He expects us to use—for His own glory.

Question: Do you think it is becoming in Christian women to wear slacks or pajamas, even on the beach?

Answer: Speaking generally, I can not understand why women should desire to dress as men. One very seldom finds men dressing as women. It is one of the characteristics of the end of the age.

Now when it comes to a matter of life on the beach, or of mountain climbing, it may be more convenient and more modest for a woman to wear slacks. If some women on the beaches wore slacks instead of the little they do wear, they would look far more modest than they do.

There is a command in Deut. 22:5 forbidding both men and women to wear the clothes of the opposite sex: "The woman shall not wear that which pertaineth unto a man, neither shall a man put on a woman's garment: for all that do so are an abomination unto the Lord thy God." There are reasons to believe that in those days the wearing of men's clothes was the way the harlot advertized herself as such.

Some would maintain, regarding this command, that God gave it to Israel, and that we are not under the Mosaic Law, but under grace. It is true that we are not under law; yet it is also true that many of God's fundamental laws governing mankind found definite expression in the Mosaic Law, and have even been carried over into governments of our own day. Surely many of them find expression in "the law of love" of our Christian faith. Why should this general principle regarding dress be altered or done away?

Perhaps what I am about to say is stretching a point too far; but it would seem that when God said to Eve, "Thy desire shall be to thy husband, and he shall rule over thee" (Gen. 3:16), that He set forth a real difference in His plans for the man and for the woman. "Male and female created he them." And any attempt on the part of either sex to ignore or set aside God's fundamental laws of nature, would seem unbecoming, to say the least. Personally, I believe that such an attempt is definitely contrary to God's will.

Every truly cultured person knows that the well dressed woman does not attire herself in such a way as to call attention to herself. And the matter of one's apparel is easily determined by the child of God who remembers the precious truth that her body is "the temple of the Holy Spirit" (I Cor. 3:16; 6:15-20).

Question: Should we support a church that denies the deity of Christ and His finished work on Calvary?

Answer: No. We should first make every effort, through prayer and influence, to maintain a testimony that is true to Christ and the Bible in whatever church we may join. Then failing that, we should withdraw our membership, and put it where we may share in giving the Gospel to the world, as well as feed our own souls on the Bread of Life. Certainly anyone or any church that denies the deity of our Lord and His finished work on the cross should not have the support of a Christian's gifts or time or interest. Except as we can win them to Christ, we should not have fellowship with them.

Question: What do you think of church suppers and bazaars as a means of raising money for the Lord's work?

Answer: While many well-meaning Christians work hard, getting up these programs; yet such methods of "raising money" for the Lord's work seem to us dishonoring to God.

In the first place, God does not need or want money from the godless world. And when the self-righteous unsaved give to such causes, they often think they have won merit thereby, deceiving themselves.

In the second place, the Lord's work should be supported by the gifts and offerings of His own people. Not only is it the duty of the child of God, thus to support His work in the world; it is a source of untold blessing and joy: "Bring ye all the tithes into the storehouse, that there may be meat in mine house, and prove me now herewith, saith the Lord of hosts, if I will not open you the windows of heaven, and pour you out a blessing, that there shall not be room enough to receive it" (Mal. 3:10).

It is interesting to note what God said to Israel in Exod. 35:5 concerning an offering for the building of the tabernacle: (1) "Take from among you (not from a stranger) an offering unto the Lord"; Israel was God's blood-bought people. (2) "Whosoever is of a *willing heart,* let him bring it, an offering of the Lord."

Again, even as the Lord Jesus cleansed the temple of money-changers when He was on earth, so also we are convinced that He would cleanse His "house of prayer" from all buying and selling and money-making schemes of man.

Question: Is it right for a Christian to carry life insurance? Or does it show a lack of faith to do so?

Answer: To carry life insurance is but to make a business investment, in order to provide for one's family in the event of death. And Paul wrote, saying, "If any provide not for his own, and specially for those of his own house, he hath denied the faith, and is worse than an infidel" (Tim. 5:8). The life insurance companies do a legitimate business, in compliance with the law; and it is entirely legal, business-like, and Christian to take advantage of this means of fulfilling one's obligation to his own. If any Christian feels otherwise about the matter then let him follow the dictates of his own conscience; but to us there seems nothing contrary to Christian principles in such a business matter.

Question: What do you think of "The Passion Play" and motion pictures which impersonate Christ?

Answer: My answer is found in the fact that, to me, it is nothing short of plasphemy for any sinful human being to impersonate our sinless Lord. Moreover, the highly commercialized moving picture business, in presenting Biblical stories, is not furthering the Gospel of our crucified and risen Lord. It is a money-making scheme, for entertainment, often produced by unbelievers.

God has given us a beautiful portrait of Himself in His infallible Word. Why trust those who often do not even know Him to attempt to portray Him and His truth? To me it is a sacrilege.

Question: How do you explain Luke 14:26? "If any man come to me, and hate not his father, and mother, and wife, and children, and brethren, and sisters, yea, and his own life also, he cannot be my disciple."

Answer: The parallel passage in Matt. 10:37 explains this verse. There Christ says, "He that loveth father or mother more than me is not worthy of me: and he that loveth son or daughter more than me is not worthy of me." These words show that the Lord is not talking of an actual hatred, but rather of what would seem hatred by way of comparison with the God-given love, implanted in the heart of the born-again child of God, implanted there by the Holy Spirit alone. If I desire to follow the Lord Jesus Christ, yet allow myself to be turned away from that object by my father, my mother, my wife, my children, then I am not worthy of the Lord Jesus, and can never be His disciple so long as this condition of heart remains.

This text does not teach that natural relationships, as such, are to be repudiated; but Christ must be first, and His claims set before all else, even one's own life.

Question: Did Paul teach in I Cor. 7 that the unmarried state is better than the married?

Answer: If you read the chapter carefully, you will note that Paul advocated celibacy in this chapter "only for the then present distress," not for all time. And even then he did not insist upon it. In I Tim. 4:13 he expressly warns against the teaching of those "forbidding to marry," and declares it to be the "doctrine of demons."

Question: What does the Bible teach about divorce?

Answer: God has *permitted* divorce because of sin, "but from the beginning it was not so" (Matt. 19:8). According to our Lord's explicit words, there is only one scriptural ground for divorce, and that is adultery.

For Christ's teaching on this subject, read Matt. 5:31, 32; 19:3-12; Mark 10:2-12; Luke 16:18. Paul also wrote on this subject in I Cor. 7:10-16.

Question: What Scripture is there to sanction the re-marriage of a divorced person, even though that divorce was obtained on the ground of adultery?

Answer: I have always looked upon Matt. 5:31, 32 as scriptural justification for the innocent person to re-marry, when divorce has been obtained on scriptural grounds. It seems to me that Jesus is speaking there not only of divorce, but also of re-marriage; and He makes the one exception—"saving for the cause of fornication."

Question: Matt. 5:32 tells us that the Lord Jesus said, "Whosoever shall marry her that is divorced committeth adultery." (Compare Matt. 19:9.) Before I was converted, I married one who had been divorced for other than scriptural reasons. I did not know or care what the Scripture said. Now that I have been born again by the blood of Christ, I do want to do His will. What is the right thing to do — to leave the one to whom I am now married, or try to win that one to Christ? We are happy together, but I am perplexed as to what the Lord would have me do.

Answer: There is no definite statement in the Bible to answer your particular question, unless you take the one you quoted, Matt. 5:32, literally in this respect. I realize that some sane, devout, scriptural Bible teachers hold that the thing for you to do would be to be separated from your present companion. Yet I cannot see it that way. After careful, prayerful consideration of the whole subject, I have been convinced that this is but one of all your sins that have been put under the blood of Christ. It was done before you were born again; and to break up another home, would be but to add sorrow to trouble. It seems to me that, having confessed this sin, together with other sins, covered by the shed blood of the Lord Jesus, you should go on seeking to lead your present companion to Christ. (However, this would *not* apply in the case of a *Christian* who deliberately marries a divorced person, knowing that he is going contrary to God's express command. That is, it does not give him license to go deliberately against the known will of God in this matter.)

Question: Although I was saved while still in my teens, yet I married an unbeliever, in spite of the fact that my pastor and Christian friends told me that II Cor. 6:14-18 and other passages of Scripture teach that we should not be "unequally yoked together with unbelievers." Since my marriage I have consecrated my all to Christ. What would He have me do — leave my husband, or try to lead him to the Lord by keeping our home unbroken and seeking to witness before him to the power of Christ in the life?

Answer: The very definite answer to your question is found in I Cor. 7:12-16, which says, in part, "And the woman which hath an husband that believeth not, and if he be pleased to dwell with her, let her not leave him. . . For what knowest thou, O wife, whether thou shalt save thy husband?"

To be sure, it would have been far better had you prayed for your husband *before* your marriage, asking God to save his soul *before* you married him. Then you would have been obeying His will fully; and surely He answers prayer. But having gone contrary to His will in the first place, you can only ask forgiveness, and continue to pray for your husband's salvation. And our God is the God of forgiving love, as well as the God who hears and answers prayer. Doubtless you have made your own path harder by not obeying fully in the first place; but "His grace is sufficient" for every need!

Question: What is the difference between water baptism and the baptism of the Holy Spirit?
Answer: *Water baptism* is a baptism unto Christ's death. In my baptism I confess that I have died to the old life as a man in Adam under the dominion of sin.

The Holy Spirit does not baptize unto death, but into the one new body, which is the church. The Holy Spirit baptizes into the mystical body of Christ. (See I Cor. 12:12, 13.)

Question: What do you understand the Scriptures to teach in regard to the mode of baptism?

Answer: Rom. 6:4 teaches that baptism is a symbol of our identification with Christ in His death and resurrection. "Therefore we are buried with him by baptism into death: that like as Christ was raised up from the dead by the glory of the Father, even so we also should walk in newness of life." When a believer submits himself to baptism, he is proclaiming his faith in Christ's death, burial, and resurrection as the means by which he is saved.

As to the mode, John 3:23, as well as other passages, give us some light. There we read: "And John also was baptizing in Ænon near to Salim, because there was much water there." There is no doubt that John baptized by immersion, else there would have been no need of "much water." The word "baptize" means to "dip" or "plunge"; and that can be performed only where there is "much water."

Acts 8:36-38 is another passage that suggests "much water"; "And as they went on their way, they came unto a certain water; and the eunuch said, See, here is water; what doth hinder me to be baptized? And Philip said, If thou believest with all thine heart, thou mayest. And he answered and said, I believe that Jesus Christ is the Son of God. And he commanded the chariot to stand still: and they went down both into the water, both Philip and the eunuch; and he baptized him."

I could sprinkle a hundred people with a cupful of water, and it would not be necessary to "go down into the water" to do that. Immersion certainly sets forth beautifully the great truths baptism illustrates — death, burial, and resurrection. However, we must ever bear in mind that water baptism has nothing to do with salvation. The only water baptism known to

Scripture is the immersion of a person *after* he has already believed unto salvation.

Question: How would you show one who believes in baptismal regeneration the error of his teaching?

Answer: By pointing out the dozens of references in the Bible that tell us plainly how to be saved—by faith in the shed blood of the Lord Jesus Christ. Some of these are: John 1:29; 3:16, 36; 5:24; Acts 16:31. There are hundreds of passages which definitely state that faith in the Lamb of God, and faith in Him alone, saves the soul. The thief on the cross had no time to be baptized; yet the Lord Jesus promised that he would go with him to paradise.

Of course, we should obey the Lord's command by being baptized. But this ordinance is a testimony before men, angels, and demons, that we are trusting the blood of Christ; it is not essential to salvation. It follows salvation. Therefore, to claim that it is essential to salvation, is to limit the efficacy of Calvary's cross.

Question: Do not Mark 16:16; John 3:5; and Acts 2:38 teach that baptism in water is necessary to salvation?

Answer: No, or else the dying thief on the cross would not have entered paradise. Please note the second clause of Mark 16:16. This text does *not* say, "He that is *not baptized* shall be damned (or condemned)"; but only, "He that *believeth* not."

Christ and His apostles plainly taught that baptism with water is an ordinance to be obeyed, as an outward testimony of an inward change of heart; but they did not teach that one must be baptized in order to be saved.

Moreover, Acts 10:43, 44, 47 state that Cornelius and his household received the Holy Spirit *before* they were baptized; and the indwelling of the Holy Spirit is a mark of sonship:

"And because ye are sons, God hath sent forth the Spirit of His Son into your hearts, crying, Abba, Father" (Gal. 4:6).

You ask about John 3:5: "Except a man be born of water and of the Spirit, he cannot enter into the kingdom of God." This verse has no reference to baptism. It does refer, as in other passages of Scripture, to *"the washing of water by the word"* of God. The Lord Jesus said to His disciples, "Now ye are clean *through the word* which I have spoken unto you" (John 15:3); and again He prayed, saying, "Sanctify them through thy truth; thy *word* is truth" (John 17:17).

Paul, writing to the Ephesians, said that "Christ loved the church, and gave himself for it; that he might sanctify and cleanse it with *the washing of water by the word*" (Eph. 5:25, 26). And to Titus he said plainly: "Not by works of righteousness which we have done, but according to his mercy he saved us, by *the washing of regeneration,* and renewing of the Holy Ghose" (Titus 3:5).

Peter, likewise, wrote, saying that we are "born again, not of corruptible seed, but of incorruptible, *by the word of God,* which liveth and abideth for ever" (I Pet. 1:23).

This is the meaning of John 3:5 — as many other Scriptures prove. The sinner is born again through the quickening, cleansing power of the Holy Spirit, as He applies the living Word of God to the unregenerate heart. These are God's only two agencies in regenerating the sinful soul — the Spirit of God and the Word of God.

Then the ordinance of baptism follows, in obedience to our Lord's command, and as a testimony to the world of new life in Christ Jesus.

Question: Why do you not baptize infants and very young children?

Answer: Because it is my firm conviction that baptism follows conversion. I am happy to *dedicate* infants and young children to the Lord, in the Lord's house or in the home. In fact, it seems to me that every Christian parent *should* dedicate his child to God, both as an act of devotion to Him and as a safeguard to the child.

But dedication is not baptism. Dedication is the act of the parent, in which he presents his child to God and assumes responsibility for the training of that child for Him. Baptism, however, is the act of the believer himself, in which he confesses faith in the Lord Jesus who died for our sins and rose again for our justification.

Question: What is meant by being "baptized for the dead" (I Cor. 15:29)?

Answer: This is an important question; for the Mormon doctrine is built upon an erroneous interpretation of this text. The Mormons claim that baptism is absolutely essential to salvation; and that if one should die unbaptized, a friend here on earth could be baptized as his proxy, the credit for this act being applied to the man dead. This is the Mormon's interpretation of the text, "baptized for the dead."

Of course, there is not a vestige of Scripture in Corinthians or in any other part of the Bible to substantiate such a perversion of the truth of God's Word.

Paul's argument all through I Cor. 15 is that Christ is risen from the dead; and because He lives, we too shall live. The resurrection of Christ is the foundation stone of Christianity. Without it our faith is vain, and we are still in our sins. In the resurrection of Christ God demonstrated the sufficiency and the efficacy of the redemption price that our Lord paid when He died on Calvary.

Baptism is a picture of our association with Christ in His death and resurrection. It speaks not only of death, but also of our being risen with Him. But if Christ is not risen from the dead, as some evidently contended, then, as Paul asked, "What shall they do which are baptized for the dead, if the dead rise not at all? why are they then baptized for the dead?" (I Cor. 15:29). In other words, if Christ be not risen from the dead, then we have been baptized unto a dead man, and of what significance or value could that be? Baptism speaks of resurrection, as well as of death; but if Christ be not risen, the ordinance of baptism loses all of its significance; for then we should have been baptized for (i.e., "unto") the dead (or "a dead man"), which would have no meaning at all.

The whole trend of the argument Paul follows in I Cor. 15 makes it conclusive that this is what Paul is talking about! for he says in verse 20: "But now *is* Christ risen from the dead, and become the firstfruits of them that slept."

Question: How could the disciples do greater works than Christ, as He said in John 14:12?

Answer: The disciples were to do greater works than Christ because the Holy Spirit, whom Christ said He would send, was not to be confined by a body to one place. He could so energize believers everywhere that the Gospel could spread far more rapidly and more widely than when proclaimed individually by the Lord Himself, and supported by His mighty works. This power was not in the disciples, but in the promised Comforter. The first fulfillment of this promise is seen in Acts 2, in the mighty power that accompanied Peter's preaching.

Again, someone has suggested the added thought that soul-winning is the greatest work in all the world, greater even than feeding the multitudes and healing the sick. While our Lord's miracles led many to trust in Him, yet they were also the credentials of His deity in a very special sense. To us is given the greatest of all privileges — that of pointing never-dying souls to Him, the only Saviour from sin. And this is the greatest of all works a human being can do; greater than healing the sick; greater than feeding the five thousand with loaves and fishes; greater even than raising the dead. James closes his epistle with these significant words: "He which converteth the sinner from the error of his way shall save a soul from death, and shall hide a multitude of sins." Yet we ever need to remember that it is "not by might, nor by power, but by my Spirit, saith the Lord of hosts" (Zech. 4:6).

Question: Should a Christian sue for slander?

Answer: It all depends upon what you mean by slander. If you are suffering at the hands of others *for Christ's sake,* because you are a Christian, then you are to take the same kindly and patiently.

If, however, your personal character is being attacked, that is another thing; and courts and prisons were established for slanderers. Let us remember, though, that "prayer changes things"; and I am convinced that Christians could accomplish far more through prayer than they do, when it comes to such matters, without taking them to court.

Question: Please explain Eph. 4:26, "Be ye angry, and sin not: let not the sun go down upon your wrath."

Answer: There is such a thing as righteous indignation; and this is what the inspired writer had in mind. When we see an injustice done or a sin committed against God and man, it would be a sin not to be angry. The Lord Jesus was righteously indignant when the money changers made His "Father's house a den of thieves." But when we are angry because of personal wrongs, we sin and dishonor God. These we should accept as opportunities of showing to the world that Christ is real, and that He enables us to live joyously and victoriously over personal injustice.

However, we must guard against all malice and hatred and display of temper, which is anger. These surely are not becoming in a Christian; nor do they cause his testimony to count for Christ.

Question: What does the Bible teach concerning woman's ministry and women preachers? Does God call women to preach the Gospel?

Answer: In discussing the subject of woman's ministry in the church, we need to recognize the breadth of Scripture, as well as its clearly defined limitations in regard to the subject, lest we become one-sided. God has a wonderful and a remarkable ministry for women. There are by far more women doing the work of the Lord today in the world than there are men. Missionary women will often go where men will not, and they seem never to be discouraged. I have more requests from women for tracts and Gospel literature than I have from men. God has used and is using women in a remarkable way.

However, God has placed a ban on woman's taking the place of authority: "Let the woman learn in silence with all subjection. But I suffer not a woman to teach, nor to usurp authority over the man, but to be in silence" (I Tim. 2:11, 12). And having given this command, God went on to tell His reason for so doing: "For Adam was first formed, then Eve. And Adam was not deceived, but the woman being deceived was in the transgression" (I Tim. 2:13, 14).

The devil, when he brought sin into the world, did not go to the man; he went to the woman. The man had the place of authority, and no doubt Adam was placed there in such a position that he was able to withstand Satan. When Adam took the fruit of the tree of knowledge of good and evil, he was not deceived. He knew what he was doing. Adam sinned against light; consequently, Adam was in the deeper transgression. The devil did not deceive Adam. When the woman took the fruit, Satan deceived her, saying, in substance: "You will know more than you know now. God knows you will benefit by eating the fruit, so perhaps He did not say that you should not eat it." Eve was deceived. But when she brought the fruit to Adam, he knew what he was doing; and to please her, he took part of the fruit.

For that reason God has put woman in the place of subjection. This is a type of Christ and the church, the greatest type given in the Bible of the bride and the Bridegroom, Christ and the church. Moreover, if God demands that the woman be subject to the man, He also demands that the man be ready to die for the woman. This is greater still. Why? Because "Christ also loved the church, and gave himself for it" (Eph. 5:25-32).

The place of authority is given to the man; and when the woman steps out of the place of subjection into the place of authority, the end is confusion. We have already seen what God has said about it in I Tim. 2:11-14. Another similar passage is found in I Cor. 14:34: "Let your women keep silence in the churches: for it is not permitted unto them to speak; but they are commanded to be under obedience, as also saith the law." Those verses make clear what the woman's place in the assembly is; when the congregation is gathered together for worship in a scriptural way, the woman's place is one of silence, so far as the ministry is concerned. She recognizes the headship of the man, because it speaks of Christ, who is the Head of the church. *It is not a matter of superiority or of inferiority; it is a matter of order.*

On the other hand, conditions do prevail in the church that are not governed by these Scripture passages. For instance, teaching a Bible class and evangelizing sinners do not constitute the assembly, which is the organized church. I Cor. 11:5 declares that a woman may prophesy; that is, "forth-tell," or "tell forth" the message of salvation to sinners. But the place of woman today as pastors of churches, exercising authority over the men, even in the worship hour of the assembly, is one of the signs of the last days.

Question: Is it right for Christians to send their boys to a military academy? And should Christians maintain such a school?

Answer: Military academies for boys do not specialize in the science of war, in spite of the association connected with the name. They offer the regular curriculum found in any school, together with rigid training in discipline.

Whether such a school has an advantage over others depends largely upon who is guiding its policies.

Question: Jude 21 says, "Keep yourselves in the love of God." How is this done?

Answer: We keep ourselves in the love of God by obedience. This is shown in John 15:10: "If ye keep my commandments, ye shall abide in my love; even as I have kept my Father's commandments, and abide in his love."

The commandment the Lord Jesus refers to is that we "love one another." Many believers, because they harbor malice, resentment, and ill-will toward other believers, miss fellowship with Christ, and lose a consciousness of His presence. How this command needs to be pressed upon the conscience of Christians today!

To keep ourselves in the love of God, also includes Bible reading, prayer, the stewardship of life and possessions—our whole Christian testimony.

Question: What is the meaning of Luke 21:19, "In your patience possess ye your souls"?

Answer: The Lord is speaking of the tribulation that is to precede His return to the earth, and is giving instruction to the Jewish remnant in regard to life and conduct in that day. Among other things, He exhorts them to faithful, patient continuance in His Word, which will give rest to their souls, even in an hour such as that. It is a lesson many of God's people need to learn in this dispensation of the grace of God.

Question: Is there such a thing as dying before one's time? Did not Paul refer to this in one of his letters? My twin sister died a few weeks ago, leaving three little children, all under nine years of age. Her husband is a minister, but does not believe the old fashioned faith that my sister believed. Can you give me some light on this subject?

Answer: You evidently have in mind what Paul wrote to the Corinthian Christians, but it does not necessarily apply to your sister's case. Corinth was a very wicked, corrupt city; and some of the early Christians, not long out of heathenism, were not giving a good testimony before the world. For example, some were abusing the sacred ordinance of the Lord's Supper, evidently making it a time of eating and drinking "unworthily." (See 1 Cor. 11:27-34.) Therefore, Paul wrote to them, saying: *"For this cause many are weak and sickly among you, and many sleep* (that is, die). *For if we would judge ourselves, we should not be judged. But when we are judged, we are chastened of the Lord, that we should not be condemned with the world. Wherefore, my brethren, when ye come together to eat, tarry one for another. And if any man hunger, let him eat at home;* that ye come not together unto condemnation."

However, Paul did *not* say that those who had died because of this practice were lost. Their souls were saved if they believed on the name of the Lord Jesus; but when they did not give a good testimony to Him, God took them home to heaven, out of the way, as it were, lest they be "condemned with the world." They will suffer loss at the judgment seat of Christ, when rewards are given to Christians for service rendered for Christ. But this is not a question of salvation; that is determined once for all by one's faith in the crucified and risen Lord Jesus. Yet these verses teach us a solemn lesson on faithfully witnessing to Christ.

As for your sister's case, this may not apply at all. Often we can not understand the providences of God; and this is one of the things we have to leave with Him. In another group of questions in this series you will find a discussion of why God's children suffer. Possibly you will there find the answer to your question.

Question: What is meant by the last clause of I Cor. 5:10?

Answer: The apostle, in this entire chapter, is exhorting Christians to live a life separated from the godless world. Therefore, he says in verses 9 and 10: "I wrote unto you in an epistle not to company with fornicators: yet not altogether with the fornicators of this world, or with the covetous, or extortioners, or with idolaters; for then must ye needs go out of the world." Then he adds in the following verses, "But . . . if any that is called a *brother* (i.e., a Christian) be a fornicator . . . put away from among yourselves that wicked person."

This is but another way of saying that, as Christians, living in a sinful world, we must of necessity come in contact with ungodly and immoral men; but it ought not to be so in the church. In the world of business, for example, we must have dealings with the ungodly. Otherwise, "we must needs go out of •the world." God does not intend that we should go into monastic seclusion. Nor does He always take us home to heaven as soon as we are saved. We can not help what the ungodly do. But when it comes to a matter of church-discipline and personal purity and keeping company with professing Christians whose lives dishonor the name of Christ, then God says we must put them away from us.

Question: Can a Christian commit suicide?

Answer: A Christian might be mentally unbalanced and take his life when he is not in his right mind; but I can not believe that a Christian could deliberately, in his right senses, commit suicide. Mental derangement is a disease of the mind; and God will surely, in His wisdom and justice, not hold a person responsible who is mentally sick to the extent that he has lost his reason. On the other hand, many who do not know Christ do deliberately plan suicide. Of course, they will be held responsible for rejecting Christ as their Saviour, as well as for taking their own lives.

Therefore, if a born again soul loses his reason and takes his life, then he goes to heaven; he belongs to Christ. If, however, a man rejects Christ, he is a lost soul, whether he plans deliberately to commit suicide, or whether, in a moment of insanity, he takes his life. Always one's eternal salvation or his eternal condemnation is determined by his answer to the question: "What then will ye do with Jesus, which is called Christ?"

Question: How may I know the will of God for my life?

Answer: Whole volumes have been written on this vital subject. Let me outline a few brief ways which are considered fundamental by Bible-loving Christians in determining the will of God:

1. By the prayerful, consistent study of His Word.

2. By definite, earnest prayer.

3. By doing well the thing at hand to do, trusting God to open doors or to close doors according to His will.

4. By taking into consideration the responsibilities and duties God has placed in your path. These may hinder your going to the foreign field, for instance. Or the lack of these may indicate a call to go.

5. By heeding an urgent desire to respond to God's call to some field in foreign lands or in the homeland. This may be the result of listening to another tell of the need for the Gospel message.

6. By asking the prayers and counsel of a godly saint, who may be able to advise, and who certainly can pray.

7. By being willing — yes, glad — to follow the Lord, wherever He may lead.

There are many precious promises of definite leading for the child of God who seeks His will. We can quote only one and give a few references here:

"I will instruct thee and teach thee in the way which thou shalt go: I will guide thee with mine eye" (Psa. 32:8). See also Exod. 33:14; Deut. 31;6; Josh. 1:9; Psa. 37:3-5; Isa. 30:21; 41:10; Matt. 18:19; Rom. 8:28.

Question: Will you please explain how Christians will be punished for wrong doing?

Answer: One answer to your question is found in I Cor. 11:30-32. Some of the Corinthians were carnal Christians. Among other sins, they were making the Lord's Supper a time of eating and drinking. Therefore, Paul wrote to them, saying: "For this cause many are weak and sickly among you, and many sleep. For if we would judge ourselves, we should not be judged. But when we are judged, we are chastened of the Lord, that we should not be condemned with the world." In other words, if Christians fail to give a testimony to the world of the power of Christ; if they are a hindrance to the spread of the Gospel, sometimes God had to take them out of the way. Their souls are saved, but their works following salvation are not worthy of reward.

That leads us to say also that one way a Christian is "punished," to quote your question, is by the very fact that in heaven he will not receive certain rewards for service rendered. He will "suffer loss" at the judgment seat of Christ, even though he himself shall be saved. (See I Cor. 3:11-15.)

Again, if a born-again soul does not obey God, he loses the great joy of fellowship with his Lord. The child who disobeys his parent does not lose his sonship; but so long as he rebels, he is out of fellowship with the parent. So it is with the child of God. He does not lose his sonship, but he does lose the joy of his salvation until he gets right with God, confesses his sin, and seeks to do His will.

To return to the subject of chastening, you need not be reminded of the fact that this may take many and varied forms. The word, literally, means "child-training." As a parent should train a child through discipline, so also our Heavenly Father often has to "child-train" us. We are so slow to learn! And sometimes — not always — He has to allow sorrow and suffering to bring us back to the place of utter trust and dependence upon him. Read Heb. 12:3-11 for God's Word on this matter. "Whom the Lord loveth he chasteneth . . . But if ye be without chastisement, whereof all are partakers, then are ye bastards, and not sons." If a man lives in sin and is not chastened, even though he may *profess* to be a Christian, according to this from God's Word, that man is not a son; he is a bastard, and a hypocrite.

Question: Why are some of God's most devoted saints called upon to suffer greatly in this life?

Answer: A number of scriptural reasons might be given to show why Christians suffer affliction. In another place we have discussed why God sometimes has to chasten, or "child-train," us; therefore, we shall not say more about that here. But why do those who live in close fellowship with the Lord sometimes know the depths of sorrow? Here are some of the outline facts; space will not permit full discussion:

1. *"Tribulation worketh patience"* (Rom. 5:3; cf. James 1:3). Trials may embitter those who do not love God; but they burn up the dross in the Christian, as he lets his all-wise Father mold and shape his life. With Job, the tested one may say, "When he hath tried me, I shall come forth as gold" (Job 23:10). "Though he slay me, yet will I trust him" (Job 13:15).

2. *Sometimes God permits one of His saints to be an example to an ungodly world of the sufficiency of God's grace.* Such was Job—an example before Satan, angels, men and demons. And his example has encouraged thousands to trust God, even when they could not understand why they were called to suffer. Jod did not know of Satan's accusation to God; yet his faith did not waver.

3. *"The God of all comfort . . . comforteth us in all our tribulation, that we may be able to comfort them which are in any trouble, by the comfort wherewith we ourselves are comforted of God"* (II Cor. 1:3, 4). Nothing gives one a more sympathetic understanding of the need of those in sorrow than does sorrow itself. It is a training school for those who would serve others in distress.

4. *"That I may know him, and the power of his resurrection, and the fellowship of his suffering"*—this was the prayer of the Apostle Paul—that he might know the fellowship of His suffering. And Paul proved that God's grace was sufficient for every trial! (Phil. 3:10; II Cor. 12:9). Moreover, he learned

that God's "strength is made perfect in weakness." Therefore, Paul could rejoice in trials. They made him know Christ better by throwing him back on faith; and he was willing to pay the price.

5. *Tribulation teaches the Christian to set his affections on things above, "where Christ sitteth on the right hand of God"* (Col. 3:1-2). It teaches him that "here have we no continuing city, but we seek one to come . . . a city which hath foundations, whose builder and maker is God" (Heb. 13:14; 11:10).

Other Scriptures might be quoted, but these give us some of the precious lessons to be learned through the furnace of affliction. And let us not forget our Lord's parting word to His disciples: "In the world ye shall have tribulation: but be of good cheer; I have overcome the world" (John 16:33).

Question: What is sanctification, if it is not holiness or sinless perfection?

Answer: "Sanctification" and "saint" are kindred words, and imply separation from the godless world. We are set apart for God; that is sanctification.

Sanctification, however, is two-fold: One aspect of the term has to do with our standing before God; the other, with our state. Sanctification as to our standing before God is brought about by the blood of Christ, and is eternal, complete, once for all. "We are sanctified through the offering of the body of Christ once for all" (Heb. 10:10).

Sanctification as to our state and daily walk is another thing. This is brought about through the operation of the Word of God, as we read it and allow it to judge our walk and ways. Christ said in His prayer for His disciples, "Sanctify them through thy truth: thy word is truth" ((John 17:17). And Paul wrote of the same thing in Eph. 5:25, 26: "Christ also loved the church, and gave himself for it; that he might sanctify and cleanse it with the washing of water by the word." As we read the holy Scriptures, meditate upon them, love them, and seek to live by them, we are being separated from the things that would defile. This is sanctification in respect to our life and walk.

We have become afraid of the term, because those who teach sinless perfection in this life have appropriated it and perverted its scriptural meaning. But that should not cause us to give up the word or its message to us. It is the Christian's duty and privilege to be sanctified, though he can never claim sinless perfection this side of heaven. Then, "when he shall appear, we shall be like him" in glory—free from sin and its power.

Question: Does Matt. 5:48 teach sinless perfection in this life?

Answer: Matt. 5:48 reads as follows: "Be ye therefore perfect, even as your Father which is in heaven is perfect." The word "perfect" here and in other similar New Testament passages means the mature and complete Christian experience. It means that "the babe in Christ" should "grow in grace, and in the knowledge of our Lord and Saviour Jesus Christ," giving an ever-increasing evidence to the world of His saving and keeping power. Nowhere in the Bible are we taught that we can become sinless in this life. Yet we are constantly exhorted to grow more and more like Him who is "altogether lovely." Only when we get to heaven shall we be freed from the very presence of sin.

Question: What is the meaning of Heb. 12:14? Does this verse not teach sinless perfection — "Without holiness no man shall see the Lord"?

Answer: This verse would teach sinless perfection if it had been quoted correctly. Read it again carefully: "Follow peace with all men, and holiness, without which no man shall see the Lord." If a man is truly regenerated, he will "follow after holiness." That is, he will pursue it. If, however, he follows after sin, and pursues sin and uncleanness, this is evidence that he is a hypocrite, no matter how loud his profession may be.

Question: How could Saul of Tarsus make Christians blaspheme?

Answer: You doubtless refer to Acts 26:11, which reads, in the Authorized Version, "I punished them oft in every synagogue, and compelled them to blaspheme." If you will read this verse in the Revised Version, you will find the more accurate translation, which gives these words an entirely different meaning: "And punishing them oftentimes in all the synagogues, *I strove to make them blaspheme.*"

This does not say that Paul *succeeded* in making Christians blaspheme. It is a fact of history that hundreds of saints have suffered torture and death rather than deny the Lord who bought them.

Question: Is worry a sin?

Answer: Yes, fretting and worrying indicate a lack of faith in an all-wise and loving Father in heaven. And that is a sin. I Peter 5:7 is reassuring, if only we would heed it, "casting all" our "cares upon him," remembering that "he careth" for us. Many other passages also tell us not to worry, among which some of the most definite are: Matt. 6:25-34; Phil. 4:6, 7, 19.

Question: What are the conditions to answered prayer?

Answer: Let me merely outline briefly some of the conditions to answer prayer:

1. *We must pray to the Father in the name of the Son,* even as our Lord said: "Whatsoever ye shall ask in my name, that will I do, that the Father may be glorified in the Son. If ye shall ask anything in my name, I will do it" (John 14:13, 14; cf. John 16:24).

2. *We must pray for God's glory, not for selfish ends,* "that the Father may be glorified in the Son" (John 14:13).

3. *We must pray according to God's will.* "We know not what we should pray for as we ought: but the Spirit himself maketh intercession for us . . . according to the will of God" (Rom. 8:26, 27). "And this is the confidence that we have in him, that, if we ask anything according to his will, he heareth us: and if we know that he hear us, whatsoever we ask, we know that we have the petitions that we desired of him" (I John 5:14, 15).

4. *We must pray in faith, believing that God will answer.* "And all things, whatsoever ye shall ask in prayer, believing, ye shall receive" (Matt. 21:22). "According to your faith be it unto you" (Matt. 9:29).

5. *We must abide in Him*: "If ye abide in me, and my words abide in you, ye shall ask what ye will, and it shall be done unto you" (John 15:7). "And whatsoever we ask, we receive of him, because we keep his commandments, and do those things that are pleasing in his sight" (I John 3:22).

6. *We must pray "with thanksgiving,"* praising God for our salvation and for His providences. (See Phil. 4:6.) Prayer and praise should ever go hand in hand.

Many other Scriptures might be given on this subject.

Question: Why are our prayers not always answered, even after many years?

Answer: Two things might be said in answer to your question:

1. God tells us in James 4:2: "Ye ask, and receive not, because ye ask amiss, that ye may consume it upon your lusts (or pleasures)." If we pray for selfish purposes, then we need not expect God to answer our prayers.

2. We must remember that, when we pray according to God's will, He either gives us what we ask, or He gives us something better. His ways are not our ways; and He makes no mistakes. There are many things about God's ways with us that we shall not fully understand until we get to heaven; but we know that we can safely pray, then leave the issues with Him.

We must not grow discouraged. We must "pray without ceasing." "The effectual fervent prayer of a righteous man availeth much." (See I Thess. 5:17; James 5:16.)

Question: Should we pray for the unsaved?

Answer: By all means! We find in the Bible a number of such prayers. The Lord has set an example in Luke 23:34 where He prayed for His own murderers. Stephen also prayed for those who stoned him.

We are exhorted in I Tim. 2:1 to make "supplication, prayers, intercessions, and giving of thanks . . . for all men." Paul connects this exhortation with the definite, all-inclusive truth of verse 4 in this same chapter, saying that "God our Saviour . . . will have all men to be saved, and to come unto the knowledge of the truth." "All men" surely includes the unconverted.

Indeed, the Christian who does not spend much time in prayer for lost souls is selfish, unconcerned about eternal issues, lacking in love to God and to his fellowmen.

Moreover, there is no greater joy than that of soul-winning. "He that winneth souls is wise . . . And they that be wise shall shine as the brightness of the firmament; and they that turn many to righteousness as the stars for ever and ever" (Prov. 11:30; Daniel 12:3). And how can a mere mortal point a human soul to the living God, except through prayer and utter dependence upon Him?

X

AFTER DEATH—WHAT?

Question: If we love God in this life, shall we be angels in heaven?

Answer: No! Decidedly, no! The angels were created angels. We were created human beings. These represent two entirely different orders of God's creatures. Angels are spirit-beings; we are flesh and blood. And in the resurrection, we shall be "flesh and bone," even as the risen Christ was in His glorified body. (See Luke 24:39.) The holy angels are our servants, "ministering spirits" unto us who are the "heirs of salvation" (Heb. 1:14). We are sons, members of the household of God.

Our Lord Jesus, when He became a Man, was made for a little time "lower than the angels . . . That he might taste death for every man," and "lead many sons unto glory" to a position higher than the angels—"heirs of God and joint-heirs with Christ" (Heb. 2:5-18; Rom. 8:17). "What a wonderful Saviour!"

Question: What did Paul mean by "the third heaven" and "paradise" in II Cor. 12:2, 4?

Answer: Paradise and heaven are now one and the same place. Paul said, in the passage you quote, that he was "caught up to the third heaven." Then he added that he was "caught up into paradise," evidently referring to the same event.

There are three heavens mentioned in the Bible: First, where the birds and clouds are; hence "the birds of the heaven." Second, there is the realm of the sun, moon and stars; hence "the stars of the heaven." And third, heaven is God's dwelling place. This is the meaning of I Kings 8:27:

"But will God indeed dwell on the earth? behold, the heaven and heaven of heavens cannot contain thee." This is where Paul was "caught up." It is now identical with paradise. However, before the resurrection and ascension of Christ, paradise was a waiting place for the spirits of the redeemed, a part of Sheol or Hades. (For further discussion of this important subject, see the next question).

Question: Do the terms "paradise" and "heaven" refer to the same place?

Answer: Since the resurrection and ascension of Christ, paradise and heaven have been identical. Paul wrote in II Cor. 12:2 that he was "caught up to the third heaven." Then in verse 4 of the same chapter, referring to the same event, he said that he was "caught up into paradise."

Paradise and heaven, however, were not the same before the resurrection and ascension of Christ. The Lord Jesus said to the thief on the cross, "To day shalt thou be with me in paradise" (Luke 23:43). Yet after His resurrection and before His ascension, He said to Mary, "Touch me not: for I am not yet ascended to my Father" (John 20:17). If He had not ascended to the Father, He could not yet have returned to heaven. He *had* gone to paradise. [Between this appearance to Mary and later appearances to His disciples, the risen Lord evidently did ascend to His Father; for we read that "they came and held him by the feet" (Matt. 28:9; cf. Luke 24:39). But that is another story, beside the point here.]

At His ascension Christ took paradise up to heaven; for paradise was the intermediate state of the souls of the Old Testament saints, including the repentant thief who died on the cross.

To understand clearly what the Bible teaches on this question, one need only compare several portions of Scripture. This we did in some detail a few months ago, in our radio Bible study on "God's Plan of the Ages." The question under consideration is discussed on pages 102-109 of the printed lectures on this series, excerpts from which are reprinted here:

1. *The Old Testament saints went to paradise.* None of the Old Testament saints went directly to heaven when they died. Their bodies, of course, went into the grave and are still awaiting the resurrection; but their spirits went to a place called paradise, to the place where the Lord Jesus went while His body lay in the tomb, to the place where the repentant thief on the cross went when he died. (See Luke 23:43.) And paradise was then a part of Sheol, or Hades.

To prove this point, let us turn the pages of our Bible back to a remarkable prophecy, written by David as he was inspired by the Holy Spirit of God. It is found in Psalm 16:8-11, and foretells the resurrection of the Lord Jesus from the dead. Both Peter and Paul quote this prophecy to prove the resurrection of Christ. (See Acts 2:25-31; 13:32-37.)

If you happen to be reading from the King James or Authorized Version, you will be perplexed as to the meaning of Psalm 16:10 and Acts 2:27: "Thou wilt not leave my soul in hell." These words were spoken by the Son of God to His Father in heaven, as the following statement makes clear: "Neither wilt thou suffer thine Holy One to see corruption." We know that Jesus' body did not "see corruption," for it arose from the dead. But did His soul go to "hell" during the three days and three nights following the crucifixion? The answer is, emphatically, "No." And the explanation of that verse is this: The original Hebrew word used in Psalm 16:10 is not "hell," but "Sheol"; while the original Greek word used in Acts 2:27 is not "hell," but "Hades." The Revised Version so translates them, accurately so. "Sheol" and "Hades," therefore, refer to the same place, and are simply the names given by the two different languages, Hebrew and Greek, for "the place of the departed spirits." (Always the Greek word for "the lake of fire" is "Gehenna.")

From the time of Adam until the ascension of Christ, Sheol was divided into two realms or compartments: (1) Paradise; and (2) an awful prison, a place of torment. Between the two there was "a great gulf fixed." (See Luke 16:26). The exact location of Sheol we do not know; but the Lord Jesus said that, as Jonah was three days and three nights in the great fish, so should "the Son of man be three days and three nights *in the heart of the earth*" (Matt. 12:40). And Paul in Eph. 4:9 wrote: "He also descended first *into the lower part of the earth*." Jesus went to paradise, we know, according to Luke 23:43. Paradise was one of the two realms of Sheol. But further than this, God has not revealed the location of Sheol. Certainly it is the place of death.

Turn now to the story of Luke 16:19-31. This is not a parable, as some would have us believe. The Lord Jesus did not use personal names in His parables; and here He speaks of Lazarus, Abraham and Moses. Moreover, He said: "There *was* a certain rich man. . . And there *was* a certain beggar named Lazarus." The one beheld the other, yet they were in the different realms of Sheol. They conversed with each other; yet one was in a place of enjoyment, comfort, and peace; the other, in a place of remorse, sin and torment. Between them there was "a great gulf fixed."

2. Christ "led a multitude of captives captive." With His ascension, Christ took paradise up with Him to heaven; so that since then paradise and heaven have been identical, as already stated in answer to your question. Thus paradise, before the ascension of Christ, was *a waiting place* for the redeemed until "the way into the holiest of all," even heaven itself, should be opened by the finished work of Christ on Calvary.

For the Scripture on this marvelous truth, read Psalm 68:18 and Eph. 4:7-10, where the prophecy is given, later to be quoted and explained by Paul, in the light of what the Lord Jesus had by that time accomplished when He "led a multitude of captives captive" (R.V.)

3. *The New Testament saints "absent from the body" are "present with the Lord"* (II Cor. 5:8). Paul wrote to the Philippians, saying that he had "a desire to depart, and to be *with Christ"* (Phil. 1:23). And where is Christ? At the right hand of the Father. (See Acts 7:56; Heb. 1:3; 8:1; 12:2; Col. 3:1; Mark 16:19.)

The spirits of the Christless dead still go to Hades, where they await the great white throne judgment. Their final destination, after sentence has been reaffirmed at the great white throne, will be Gehenna. This is the teaching of Rev. 20:11-15.

Question: "What is the difference between "Hades" in Luke 16:23 and "Gehenna" in Rev. 20:11-15?

Answer: Hades is the abode of the Christless dead, where they await the great white throne judgment. It is not purgatory; nor is it a place of second chance. It is a waiting place. "Gehenna" is the lake of fire, the "second death," the final doom of the lost.

Question: What is meant by the terms: "The first resurrection" and "the second resurrection"? I was taught that there would be one great judgment day, at a general resurrection, when the "sheep" and the "goats" would be separated the one from the other.

Answer: Between the first and the second resurrections there will be a period of a thousand years, when our Lord will reign upon the earth. But before we consider these separately, let us remember the following fundamental truths:

(1) The sins of the believer on Christ Jesus *have been judged* at Calvary's cross; and he "shall not come into judgment, but is passed from death unto life" (John 5:24, (R.V.).

(2) The believer's works *will be judged* at "the judgment seat of Christ" when the church is translated. (See Rom. 14:10; II Cor. 5:10; I Cor. 3:11-15.) This judgment will be to determine the rewards to be given to the redeemed in that day, and has nothing to do with salvation from sin. The Lord Jesus accomplished a *finished* work on the cross for all who will accept the *free gift* of His redemption.

(3) The wicked dead—all who shall have rejected Christ —will stand before "the great white throne," where the books will be opened, and it will be proved to them that their names are not written in "the Lamb's book of life." (See Rev. 20:11-15.) There they will be judged, and punishment will be meted out to them, also "according to their works." In other words, there will be degrees of reward in heaven and degrees of punishment in hell, according to the light and opportunity we have had.

(4) The nations will be judged at the return of Christ in glory: Some, to enter into His millennial kingdom; others, to go into everlasting punishment. These are the "sheep" and the "goats" referred to in Matt. 25:31-46. But you will note that in the presence of the returning King, the Lord Jesus, will be gathered *"all nations"* (verse 32); that the reward to the blessed will be that they will *"inherit the kingdom"* (verse 34); and that the reward will be given to those who have been kind to Christ's *"brethren"* (verse 40). It seems very clear that this judgment, immediately following the great tribulation, which is "the time of Jacob's trouble," will be to determine how the *nations* shall have treated God's chosen people, Israel, Christ's *brethren* according to the flesh, during that time of trouble. Then His covenant with Abraham will be literally fulfilled: "I will bless them that bless thee, and curse him that curseth thee" (Gen. 12:3).

"The First resurrection," to return now to your question, is also called "the resurrection of life" and "the resurrection of the just" (Luke 14:14; John 5:29). In this last named verse the second resurrection is called "the resurrection of condemnation," R.V. Now turn to Rev. 20:4-15, where the two resurrections are contrasted in no uncertain terms, and where we read that between the two there will be the period of a thousand years, when Christ shall reign on the earth. All New Testament teaching dovetails with the passages to which we have just referred.

The first resurrection will take place when the church is translated, forever to be with Christ. (See I Thess. 4:13-18; I Cor. 15:51-53; Phil. 3:20, 21; I John 3:2, and many other passages.)

Immediately afterwards, the seventieth week of Daniel's prophecy will run its course on earth, during which brief period a number of startling events will come to pass: The revelation of the Antichrist (II Thess. 2:1-12); the revival of the Roman Empire under his sway; the great tribulation, ending with the battle of Armageddon. To bring to a close this darkest period in the world's history; and to deliver His people, Israel, the Lord Jesus will return from heaven with His saints to set up His kingdom and to reign on earth a thousand years. (See Rev. 19:11-16 and many other passages of Scripture concerning the millennial kingdom.)

We have discussed in another question the fact that the martyrs of the tribulation period will share in the first resurrection.

To sum all we have said, the first resurrection will take place *before* the millennium, when Christ comes for the church. The bodies of the righteous dead will be raised and re-united with their spirits, which ever since death shall have been in paradise during Old Testament times and "with Christ" since

His ascension into heaven. The living saints will be changed "in a moment, and in the twinkling of an eye." and all these shall be "forever with the Lord"—body and spirit—glorified—like Him who died on Calvary for sinners!

"The second resurrection," to summarize again, will take place *after* the millennium, when the wicked dead will be raised, judged, and cast into the lake of fire. It is a solemn thought that, while paradise is no longer in Sheol, yet that awful prison, the place of torment, is still inhabited by the wicked dead of all ages. It is a solemn thought that one day, at "the great white throne" judgment, that compartment, too, will be empty.   In that day "death and Hades" will deliver up their dead, and will be cast into the lake of fire. (See Rev. 20:13, 14; compare Matt. 5:22, 29, 30, and other references.) The Greek word for "hell" in these passages is "Gehenna," and refers to the lake of fire.

In Rev. 20:13 the word "death" refers to the grave, and speaks of the bodies of the wicked dead; whereas the word "Hades" here refers to the present abode of the spirits of the wicked dead of all ages, as we have already seen. So it is that this verse plainly says that soul and body of the wicked will be re-united, judged, and cast into the lake of fire—why? Because those who stand before "the great white throne" will have rejected the atoning work of Christ on the cross.

My friend, one day we shall all stand before Christ, "the Judge of all the earth." "The Father . . . hath committed all judgment unto the Son" (John 5:22, 25-29). Shall we be "forever with the Lord"? Or shall we be forever "in utter darkness"? The answer to these questions will be determined by our answer to another question, the most vital in all of God's universe. "What shall I do then with Jesus which is called Christ?" (Matt. 27:22).

Question: What is the meaning of the Lord's word in John 11:25, 26, "I am the resurrection and the life: he that believeth in me, though he were dead, yet shall be live: and

whosoever liveth and believeth in me shall never die"? Did the Lord refer to the dead in Him who shall be raised, and the living who shall be translated at His coming for the church?

Answer: I think so. The Lord Jesus here made an illusion to the translation of the living and the resurrection of the saints as outlined in I Thess. 4:16-18. Accordingly, these words might be paraphrased as follows: "He that believeth in me, though he were dead (though he should die before Christ's return for the church), yet shall he live ('the dead in Christ shall rise first') : and whosoever liveth (until Jesus comes) and believeth in me shall never die (but shall be changed 'in a moment, and in the twinkling of an eye')."

However, through Paul the Lord set forth the details in regard to this event. The great truth concerning the translation of the church was not made clear until after the formation of the church at Pentecost; and to Paul this was made known by special revelation.

But referring again to the meaning of John 11:25, 26, I should like to add this fact: There is the fundamental, underlying truth that every Christian holds, whether premillennial or postmillennial, that whosoever "believeth" on the risen Lord Jesus, in every age, shall inherit everlasting life. And I think this passage has this deep, spiritual meaning bound up in it.

Question: Please explain Rev. 20:5, "This is the first resurrection." If the dead are raised prior to the tribulation, how could this be the first resurrection?

Answer: Rev. 20:5 refers to the tribulation saints, who are included, in God's reckoning, in the first resurrection; i.e., the resurrection of believers on the Lord Jesus Christ. The translation of the church before the tribulation, and the resur-

rection of the tribulation saints at the close of the tribulation—
these constitute the "first resurrection," called in Luke 14:13, 14
"the resurrection of the just" and in John 5:29 "the resurrection of life."

Question: Do the saved go immediately to heaven when they die?

Answer: The Scriptures teach positively that a true child
of God goes immediately to heaven at the time of physical dis-
solution of body and soul. II Cor. 5:8 gives us that assurance:
"We are confident, I say, and willing rather to be absent from
the body, and to be present with the Lord." (Cf. Phil. 1:23
and other passages of Scripture.)

Luke 16:22 tells us that the angels receive the spirits of
the departing saints—a comforting thought, that they take our
spirits home to heaven and the presence of God. They are our
"ministers," you know, "ministering spirits, sent forth to minister for them who shall be heirs of salvation" (Heb. 1:14).
They guard us here on earth, and take us to heaven when we
die. "The angel of the Lord encampeth round about them that
fear him, and delivereth them" (Psa. 34:7). "For he shall
give his angels charge over thee, to keep thee in all thy ways.
They shall bear thee up in their hands, lest thou dash thy foot
against a stone" (Psa. 91:11).

Question: Shall we recognize our loved ones in heaven?

Answer: We know One whom we are going to recognize
in heaven. The divine truth concerning this blessed reality and
glorious experience is found in I John 3:2: "Beloved, now
are we the sons of God, and it doth not yet appear what we
shall be: but we know that, when he shall appear, we shall
be like him; for we shall see him as he is." Here we learn that
we are going to be like Christ, and that we shall see Him as
He is.

Some have used the transfiguration experience of Christ, as recorded in Matt: 17:1-13; Mark 9:2-13; Luke 9:26-38, as proof that we shall recognize one another when we reach heaven in our glorified bodies. The argument is that the three disciples on the mount of transfiguration recognized Moses and Elijah. Now Moses represented the dead in Christ who shall be raised; Elijah represented those who will remain until the rapture and be called away to heaven without dying. Surely there seems to be some support here for this teaching.

Others quote I Cor. 13:12: "For now we see through a glass, darkly; but then face to face: now I know in part; but then shall I know even as also I am known." Their argument is that this Scripture teaches that we shall know one another when we are in our glorified bodies.

There are many questions that are asked in this connection; but where the Scriptures are silent, we must be silent. One question frequently raised is this: "If we are conscious of the presence of our loved ones who are enjoying the glory and bliss of heaven, shall we be conscious of the absence of those of our friends and relatives who are suffering the sorrows of the second death?" And again, we hear the question: "If a saved individual leaves this earth as a babe or a little child, will that individual have the body of an adult in the resurrection?"

While these questions last named are not answered in the Bible, yet we do know that "sorrow and sighing will flee away . . . and God shall wipe away all tears." We like to think that God has need for little children in heaven; and that we shall see them there as little ones with their glorified bodies. Yet we would not substitute our personal wishes, guesses, or ideas for the Word of God. And we may be assured that, if it will add to our bliss to recognize our loved ones in heaven, most certainly our Heavenly Father will permit us to do so.

Question: How can there be degrees of reward for saints in heaven? Would that not be a source of envy and strife? Of course, these things can not be, in heaven.

Answer: The Bible teaches that there are degrees of reward in heaven. (See I Cor. 3:11-15.) The Bible also teaches that there will be no envy in heaven. Nothing shall enter there that would defile. We do not have to harmonize these things.

However, even with our finite minds, we can readily see that just as some have a greater spiritual understanding—shall I say capacity for the things of God?—just as some let Christ take their whole lives now on earth, even so will their capacity for the enjoyment of heaven be greater. The little child who loves the Lord is as happy as can be; but surely the older we grow and the more we have fellowship with Christ, the greater our love for Him.

I like to think of our rewards in heaven as something that shall be "to the praise of his glory," something that will mean even greater service for Christ throughout all eternity, rather than think of rewards as something for our own glory. I like to think of the crowns awaiting the Christian in this light—all to show forth the praises of Him who hath called us out of darkness into His marvelous light. To me, this settles all such questions as the one you ask.

Again, our Lord's words in Luke 12:48 should cause us to think seriously of our responsibility in giving out the Gospel: "Unto whomsoever much is given, of him shall be much required."

Question: Please explain I Cor. 15:50, "Flesh and blood cannot inherit the kingdom of God." Is this not a denial of the resurrection of the physical body? Does not the statement in I Cor. 15:44 also deny that our resurrection bodies

will be material? "There is a natural body, and there is a spiritual body."

Answer: Not at all. The first verse you quote, which mentions "flesh and blood," refers to our bodies as they now are, as natural, corruptible, mortal bodies. Our resurrection bodies will be like the resurrection body of Christ. (See I John 3:2; Phil. 3:20, 21.) His body was material, but it was "flesh and bones" (Luke 24:39). Christ's resurrection body did not have one drop of blood in it, for He had shed His blood on Calvary as a sin offering. The life of the *flesh* is in the blood" (Lev. 17:11). But our spiritual bodies will be, like Christ's, of "flesh and bones," glorified, immortal, incorruptible. That our Lord's body was real, even as ours will be real, is seen in His words, "Handle me, and see; for a spirit hath not flesh and bones, as ye see me have. And when He had thus spoken, he shewed them his *hands* and his *feet*" (Luke 24:39, 40.) There they saw the marks of Calvary, even as Thomas also saw, in his risen Lord, the nail prints and the riven side. (See John 20:24-29.)

The statement in I Cor. 15:44 means that our material resurrection bodies will be governed by our spirits. A natural body governs the spirit; a spiritual body is governed by the spirit. Hence we shall know no limitations, such as the laws of gravitation. Christ passed through walls and closed doors, even with a body of flesh and bone. And we shall be able to do likewise.

Question: What is the meaning of Rom. 8:10: "And if Christ be in you, the body is dead because of sin, but the Spirit is life because of righteousness"?

Answer. It means that our redemption at present is only partial. My spirit has been quickened, but not my body. The body is yet to be quickened, when Christ comes to translate the church. Then He will "change our vile body, that it may be fashioned like unto his glorious body, according to the working whereby he is able even to subdue all things unto himself" Phil. 3:21). When that takes place, our redemption will be complete—body, as well as soul.

Question: In what body will the wicked dead be raised to stand before the great white throne? We know that the Christian's body is sown a material body, and raised a glorified body, like Christ's. But what of the wicked dead?

Answer: The Spirit of God describes the resurrection body of the believer, but is strangely silent in regard to the nature of the resurrection body of an unbeliever. All we know is that the body of the unbeliever will come forth from the grave at the resurrection of the unjust, will stand before the great white throne, and will there be judged. Read John 5:29; Rev. 20:11-15.

Question: If the wicked dead do not go immediately to the lake of fire, why did the rich man of Luke 16:24 say that he was "tormented in this flame"?

Answer: In Rev. 20:13, 14 we read that at the great white throne, where the wicked will be judged, "death and hades delivered up the dead which were in them. . . And death and hades were cast into the lake of fire." This part of the vision which John saw is yet future, as the text plainly states. As we have tried to set forth in answer to preceding questions, "death" here speaks of the grave; "hades," in this instance, of the abode of the wicked dead while waiting for the great white throne judgment. (We have seen that paradise was taken out of hades when Christ ascended on high, and led "a multitude of captives captive.")

Now it is also very clear that the rich man of Luke 16 was "in torment," in conscious suffering. The reference to the "flame" indicates how terrible are the consequences of sin.

When the Lord Jesus Christ calls the wicked dead from their graves; when their spirits are delivered up from hades, bodies and souls re-united forever, will be cast into the lake of fire, from which no one ever returns. In the Greek this is called "Gehenna."

Question: If the rich man of Luke 16:19-31 was in Hades as a disembodied spirit, how could it be said that he lifted up his "eyes, being in torments"? How could be speak of the "finger" of Lazarus, who was in paradise; and of his own "tongue"?

Answer: The spirit has a form, just as the body has a form. And the form of the spirit is, in all probability, the form of the body. It is true, the dead, whether in Christ or out of Christ, are disembodied spirits. The Scriptures, however, imply that, while they are without a body, yet they do not *miss* the body. In other words, they are not conscious of disembodiment. This is implied in II Cor. 12:2. There Paul tells us that he was caught up into the third heaven; whether in the body or out of the body, he could not tell. If he was out of the body at the time of that experience, he was not conscious of it. This sheds a great deal of light upon the present disembodiment of the dead; and this is the explanation of the rich man's speaking of his "tongue" and of Lazarus' "finger." It explains also the Scripture reference to the rich man's "eyes," in the passage to which we refer.

Question: I have heard it said that men will be judged only for their works. Will you please give Scripture to prove that they will be judged for their sins?

Answer: Surely they will be judged according to their works, but their sins are included in their works. If sins are not works—bad works—what are they? In Rev. 20:11-15 we read of the judgment of the wicked before the great white throne.

There they *will* be judged "according to their works." Some will be held more responsible than others, because they will have rejected more light than others. Some "shall be beaten with many stripes," while others "shall be beaten with few stripes" (Luke 12:47, 48). But read on to the last verse of the twentieth chapter of Revelation; there the statement is clear and definite: "And whosoever was not found written *in the book of life* was cast into the lake of fire." How does one get his name written in the Lamb's book of life? By believing on Him, the "Lamb slain from the foundation of the world," by accepting His atoning work on the cross for cleansing from sin.

Every Scripture passage that sets forth the Lord Jesus as the only *Way* to God—and there are many such passages—every one of these leaves man without excuse before our just and holy God. "He that believeth on the Son hath everlasting life: and he that believeth not the Son shall not see life; but the wrath of God abideth on him" (John 3:36). (See also John 5:24; 1:29; 3:16; Rom. 3:23; 6:23; Acts 16:31; and dozens of similar verses.)

XI

UNFULFILLED PROPHECY

Question: Please explain I Cor. 15:52. Does it not teach that the church will go through the tribulation, even to the last of the trumpet judgments described in Rev. 8:11?

Answer: I Cor. 15:52 has nothing to do with the trumpet judgments of Rev. 8:11. It describes the first resurrection and the translation of the church, which take place *before* the Antichrist is revealed on earth. Note the words, addressed to *"Christians*: "We shall not all sleep, but we shall all be changed, in a moment, in the twinkling of an eye, at the last trump: for the trumpet shall sound, and the dead shall be raised incorruptible, and we shall be changed" (I Cor. 15:51, 52). Compare this passage with I Thess. 4:13-18, which refers to the same event, and calls the "trumpet" the "trump of God."

The seven trumpet judgments of Revelation are sounded by *angels;* "the trump of *God"* will call the church home. Perhaps it will be just the word "Come," even as we read in Rev. 4:1 the message to John, "Come up hither." This call to John is prophetic of the call of the church when the Lord translates His bride. Everything from Rev. 4:1 on to the end of the book has to do with events which will take place *after* the rapture of the church, including the seven trumpet judgments.

Question: Does Heb. 9:28 teach the doctrine of a partial rapture at the coming of Christ for the church? Some hold that it does: "Unto them that look for him shall he appear the second time without sin (that is, apart from sin) unto salvation." Will only those who "look for him" be translated?

Answer: This verse does not teach a partial rapture, nor does any other passage teach such a doctrine. I Cor. 15:23 distinctly says, "Christ the firstfruits; afterward they that are Christ's at his coming." The expression "they that are Christ's at his coming" includes every child of God.

As for the text you quote, if you will read the whole chapter, you will see that the apostle is expounding the meaning of the Jewish tabernacle service. The position of the people before the door of the tabernacle, waiting for the high priest to come out, is the *position* of every believer, whether he understands it or not. Every believer is waiting for the Lord to return. He may not understand dispensational truth; he may know very little about the Lord's second coming; but positionally he is waiting for the Lord to appear "the second time apart from sin unto salvation"—salvation of the body for the church; national salvation for Israel.

Question: Some say that the church will be translated at the end of the first three and one-half years of the seventieth week of Daniel, which is just before the tribulation period. Others say that the church will not be translated until after the tribulation, but will go through it. Please explain.

Answer: The church will be raptured before the seventieth week of Daniel begins. II Thes. 2:7, 8 is one of the clearest passages that proves this fact. The Antichrist will not be revealed until the Holy Spirit's restraining influence in the church is taken "out of the way." And, of course, the Antichrist is to be the ruling personage of the seventieth week of Daniel's prophecy.

The church began on the Day of Pentecost (Acts 2), and is now in the process of being formed. One day, perhaps sooner than men realize, the last member will be added to the body of Christ, which is His church. This is called by Paul in Rom.

11:25 "the fulness of the Gentiles," which expression may be freely translated, "the full number of the Gentiles." When the church is complete, then God will call it home to heaven; and not until then will the seventieth week of Daniel begin to run its course.

Question: Will the unsaved living on earth know it when Christ translates the church?

Answer: There is nothing in the Scripture to indicate that they will know what has taken place. Certainly they will miss loved ones and friends. To the godless world, the translation of the church will doubtless be as a "seven-days' wonder." Then the Antichrist will be revealed; and his actions will so occupy the minds of unregenerate men that many will soon forget what shall have transpired in the rapture of the church—so blinded will they be by Satan.

However, let it be remembered that there will be the martyred remnant of believers during the tribulation period, those who will accept the message of the 144,000 Jews, God's messengers on earth during that dark time.

Question: "When shall these things be?" How can it be that a retired minister, who claims to have studied the Bible for fifty years, says that, as he sees it, not enough prophecy has been fulfilled for the Lord to come during our lifetime?

Answer: Possibly your friend has in mind the revelation of Christ before the world as King of kings and Lord of Lords. If so, he is correct. Certain things must take place before that event, such as the translation of the church, the revelation of the man of sin, and his brief reign on the earth, the great tribulation, and the Battle of Armageddon.

There are no prophecies, however, to be fulfilled before the translation of the church as described in I Thess. 4:13-18.

Signs do not have reference to the church, but to Israel only. We are not looking for "signs." We are listening for a "sound." (See I Cor. 15:52; I Thess. 4:16.) The coming of the Lord for the church is always imminent. Hence the oft-repeated exhortation to be "ready" for His coming.

Question: Will the great tribulation begin immediately after the church is translated?

Answer: No; it will take place during the last three and one-half years of Daniel's "seventieth week" (a period of seven years). As soon as the church is translated, and the restraining influence of the Holy Spirit working in the church is taken away, then shall "that wicked one be revealed," who is the Antichrist. (See II Thess. 2:7-10.) He will seem to the ungodly world to be a great peacemaker. To the Jews he will pretend to be their Messiah. He will confirm a covenant with them, and will receive allegiance from them *until* he sets up his image, in "the holy place" of the restored Jewish temple, to be worshipped. Daniel calls this "the abomination of desolation"; and Christ quotes Daniel, using these very words concerning this event that is to be. An "abomination" to a devout Jew is idolatry; and the believing remnant of Israel will spurn the pretentions of the false Messiah. Then the Antichrist and all the hosts of Satan will turn upon Israel, persecute her; and that will be "the great tribulation," of which our Lord spoke. (Compare Dan. 9:27 with Matt. 24:15 and following verses.)

The great tribulation will terminate with the return of Christ in glory to deliver His earthly people.

Question: What is meant by the "thousand three hundred and five and thirty days" of Dan. 12:12?

Answer: There are three time periods in Dan. 12:
....*The first* is in verse 7, where the length of the tribulation period is given: "a time (one year), times (two years), and an

half (one-half year)." This represents three and one-half years, and is the length of the tribulation period, equivalent to 1260 days.

The second period is in verse 11: "And from the time that the daily sacrifice shall be taken away, and the abomination that maketh desolate set up, there shall be a thousand two hundred and ninety days." Here we find thirty days added to the 1260 of the tribulation period. During those extra 30 days, certain events will take place after the return of Christ to the earth, such as the judgment of the living nations, and the binding of Satan.

The third period is in verse 12: "Blessed is he that waiteth, and cometh to the thousand three hundred and five and thirty days" (1335). Here is a still longer period, concerning which God says, "Blessed is he that . . . cometh" thereunto. Why? Because he will then be in the millennium, with all tribulation past.

Question: To what period in Egyptian history does the desolation of forty years belong, as prophesied in the twenty-ninth chapter of Ezekiel?

Answer: It is difficult to locate historically the forty years of Egypt's desolation. Some claim that this prophecy refers to a period after the millennium, but to my mind the passage found in Ezekiel 29:13-16 makes it clear that the forty years referred to have already passed. For thousands of years Egypt has been "the basest of kingdoms"; and before the rise of the old Roman Empire, she must have known forty years of terrible judgment.

Question: My pastor says that the doctrine of the premillennial coming of Christ to the earth is dangerous and fanatical. He told his people not to use the Scofield Reference Bible for this reason. What shall I do about it?

Answer: Your pastor may be orthodox, fundamental, and true to the Word of God in other doctrines; if so, he is a real Christian. But my advice to you would be to "search the scriptures" for yourself. They speak for themselves; and no doctrine is more emphasized in the New Testament than is this one of our Lord's return to set up His own kingdom; yes, and in the Old Testament prophecies, as well, concerning His promises to Israel.

It is to be regretted that many of the false cults have incorporated some of this truth in their creeds; but every time, you will note, they have perverted this precious truth. Should their error rob us of our "blessed hope"? Assuredly not. Satan is ever alert. He takes Scripture and perverts it, seeking to bring to naught any great work of God. And this is definitely true concerning the doctrine of our Lord's return.

As for the Scofield Reference Bible, it has been used of God to bless multitudes; and it will continue to be used by Him, critics to the contrary. In recent months an attack on this edition of the King James Version has been let loose; but no good can come of such an attack. In the first place, the ministers who are opposing it have made statements that are untrue, possibly having gone on hearsay. They have maintained that Dr. Scofield was not qualified to perform his task. They fail to acknowledge that, even before his conversion, he was a brilliant lawyer, a man of scholarship. They fail to state that he sat at the feet of one of the greatest theologians of any day, the late Rev. James H. Brookes, D.D., of St. Louis, Mo. They are either wilfully or ignorantly overlooking the fact that the consulting editors of this edition of the Bible, whose names appear on the opening pages, are men of profound scholarship, unquestioned orthodoxy, and great usefulness to the church of Christ in leading sinners to the Saviour. More might be said upon this subject, but suffice it to say that millions of the Scofield Reference Bible have been scattered over the earth; and will yet be used to the blessing of multitudes. If I were you, I should use it. God will bless you in such a study of His Word.

Question: Will you please explain Matt. 10:23, where Christ said to his Disciples, "Ye shall not have gone over the cities of Israel, till the Son of man be come"?

Answer: In this chapter our Lord was not only giving the disciples instructions for their immediate work of witnessing; but He was also, as in the twenty-fourth and twenty-fifth chapters of Matthew, looking on down the future, even to the time of His return to the earth in glory. The verse about which you ask was spoken concerning this yet future event, and refers to the *unfinished* testimony to the nation of Israel, when the 144,000 witnesses of Revelation will proclaim once again the message, "The Kingdom of heaven is at hand."

Question: Please explain Matt. 24:34, "Verily I say unto you, This generation shall not pass, till all these things be fulfilled."

Answer: The Greek word used for "generation" means "race, kind, family, stock, breed." Matthew 24 and 25 refer to the end of the age, and this verse must not be taken out of its context.

Question: Who are the 144,000 of Rev. 7:4-8; 14:1-5?

Answer: They will be converted Jews who will be God's witnesses in the earth during the seventieth week of Daniel, preaching "the gospel of the kingdom," pointing many to the coming of the King. This will be after the translation of the church. It is noteworthy that Israel is being prepared for this ministry, in that there are Jews in every land, speaking every language. When God's hour strikes, they will go out in zeal, proclaiming the crucified and risen Lord Jesus as their Messiah and coming King.

Different cults have claimed to be the 144,000. But what is more ridiculous, in view of the fact that the very names of the tribes of Israel are given in Rev. 7:4-8? There will be 12,000 from each of the twelve tribes. And they will be Israelites, not some godless, Christ-rejecting cult of satanic origin!

Moreover, their ministry is *still future* — all of Revelation from Rev. 4:1 to the end of the book is future. How, then, can these false cults today pretend to be the 144,000? They have no scriptural ground for such a claim.

Question: Who will the "two witnesses" of Rev. 11:3-12 be?

Answer: The Bible does not tell us definitely, and there is a difference of opinion as to who these will be. Some think they will be a group of the redeemed, witnessing in the power of Moses and Elijah. Others think they will probably be Moses and Elijah themselves. We are inclined to believe the latter, although we can not be dogmatic, where God has not told us definitely.

Our reasons for believing the "two witnesses" will be Moses and Elijah are these:

1. Moses died and was buried by God upon Mount Nebo: "and no man knoweth of his sepulchre unto this day" (Deut. 34:5, 6). Satan contended with Michael over "the body of Moses" (Jude 9). Elijah went to heaven without dying. Did God thus preserve the bodies of these two, representing the law and the prophets, that they might be His witnesses to Israel, as well as to all the world, during the darkest period of all history? Surely their message would bear weight with Israel in that dark hour!

2. The miracles which they will do, as foretold in Rev. 11:3-12, are like unto the miracles performed by God through Moses and Elijah when they were on earth.

3. Mal. 4:5 tells God's people, Israel, some significant words: "Behold, I will send you Elijah the prophet before the coming of the great and dreadful day of the Lord." Christ verified this prophecy (Matt. 17:11).

Question: Please explain Matt. 12:43-45: "When the unclean spirit is gone out of a man, he walketh through dry places, seeking rest, and findeth none. Then he saith, I will return into my house from whence I came out; and when he is come, he findeth it empty, swept and garnished. Then goeth he, and taketh with himself seven other spirits more wicked than himself, and they enter in and dwell there: and the last state of that man is worse than the first. Even so shall it be also unto this wicked generation.

Answer: All kinds of interpretations and applications have been made of this prediction. It is very clear, however, that there is but one explanation, and that is in respect to the *unbelieving generation*. Note how verse 45 closes, "Even so shall it be unto this wicked generation." The word "generation" is certainly to be understood in the sense of "race." (Compare the footnote in the Scofield Reference Bible on Matt. 24:34 for the meaning of the Greek word used here.)

The "unclean spirit" in Israel in Old Testament times was idolatry. In the time of Christ, it had left the nation; for the captivities had brought God's people to see the folly and sin of idolatry. Even now Judaism is swept clean of that evil spirit, and boasts of reform. But it will not be so forever. The unclean spirit will return and bring "seven others" with him. It will take possession of the house again, and the last state will be worse than the first.

Because Israel, as a nation, has rejected her Messiah, the Lord Jesus, she is still in spiritual blindness. And when she makes a covenant with the Antichrist, during the seventieth week of Daniel's prophecy, then she will be allowing the return of the demon, with seven other spirits, as it were. The Antichrist will try to force all the world to worship his image. That will be idolatry in its last, bold form. Israel will see that the Antichrist is a false Messiah; will break her covenant with him; and will, consequently, have to go through the great tribulation. Only the return of the Lord in glory will save His chosen people, Israel, from annihilation from the earth. The Antichrist and his forces will seek the utter destruction of God's people, but the Lord will come and save them.

Question: What is your understanding of Rev. 16:13, 14? "And I saw three unclean spirits like frogs come out of the mouth of the dragon, and out of the mouth of the beast, and out of the mouth of the false prophet. For they are the spirits of demons (R.V.), working miracles, which go forth unto the kings of the earth and of the whole world, to gather them to the battle of that great day of God Almighty." What are these spirits like frogs, and are they in the world today?

Answer: They are evidently evil systems of teaching, because they emanate from the MOUTH of the dragon, and of the beast, and of the false prophet. They will go forth, permeate the masses, and bring about a world-crisis, ending in Armageddon. We are not to set "times and seasons" for the Lord's return; but we are to discern "the signs of the times." And the systems might well be foreshadowed by some of the godless forces in the world today.

To say that these "unclean spirits" are in the world today, would be to set dates, approximately; and we must guard against that, which is expressly forbidden by Christ Himself.

At the same time, Satan's tactics do not change much; and his purpose has ever been to seek to bring to naught God's great plan of redemption. His is ever an attack upon Christ and upon God's people. So that in a real sense, his systems of teaching have been in the world, in one form or another, ever since the fall of man.

Question: Please explain Matt. 24:19: "Woe unto them that are with child, and to them that give suck in those days!"

Answer: Matthew 24 tells of the great tribulation period on the earth, "the time of Jacob's trouble"; and the Lord is speaking in verse 19 of the distress that those will be in who are with child in those days. To a certain degree the same thing is true in any war zone in any age; but how much more it will be in that day when there shall be trouble, such as never was, "no, nor ever shall be"!

Question: Is there anything in the Bible about the Cities of Petra?

Answer: They are not mentioned by name; neither is there a direct proof that they are referred to in the Bible. But many students of prophecy wonder if they may prove to be a place of refuge for persecuted Israel during the great tribulation. In Dan. 11:41 we read that Moab "shall escape out of his (the Antichrist's) hand." In His message to the disciples concerning this "time of Jacob's trouble," the Lord warned them that those who will be living in that day in the land of Judea will have to "flee into the mountains." And in the same chapter He said, "Except those days should be shortened, there should no flesh be saved." It will be a time of terrible bloodshed and suffering and persecution. Israel will need a place of refuge!

Again, in Isaiah 26:20 we read a verse that is suggestive of how God will protect the faithful remnant of His people, Israel, in that day: "Come, my people, enter thou into thy chambers, and shut thy doors about thee: hide thyself as it were for a little moment, until the indignation be overpast."

Putting all these references, and many others about the tribulation period, together, it seems clear that there will be a place of refuge for a remnant of Israel in that day. Since the land of Moab will escape out of the hand of the Antichrist, possibly that is the land which will harbor God's persecuted people from the satanic wrath of the kings of the earth for "a little while." Then the Lord Himself shall come in glory to put down sin and to rule over restored Israel.

They tell us that the late Rev. W. E. Blackstone, D.D., was so convinced that this would be the hiding place for Israel, that he spent hundreds of dollars, placing New Testaments in the crannies of the rocks of the Cities of Petra, so that in that coming day of stress the Hebrew people might read for themselves of their Messiah, when their hearts are ready to turn to Him. Could it be that God put it into the heart of this dear saint, so to prepare for that hour?

About 1934 or 1935 "The National Geographic Magazine" had in its February issue a leading article, telling of the marvels of these ancient cities—long undiscovered by generations now living, yet marvelously preserved in the sides of the rocks of this natural hiding place from the outside world.

Question: What is the meaning of Ezekiel 37, which tells of the vision of the valley of dry bones?

Answer: Verses 11-14 of this chapter explain the vision which God gave to Ezekiel. The whole passage speaks of the *national* resurrection of Israel. They have long been buried, as a nation, in the many countries of the world; but even now we see the beginning of the restoration of this ancient people in their own land. The remarkable progress of the nation of

Israel during the past few years is one of the most significant "signs of the times," all of which point to the return of Christ to the earth to reign. When He does come, then Ezekiel 37 will be literally fulfilled; and Israel will be restored to her own covenant rights, established in her own land.

Question: What is the meaning of Rev. 9:6, "And in those days shall men seek death, and shall not find it; and shall desire to die, and death shall flee from them?

Answer: Rev. 9 is a part of the description of the great tribulation. The record of the trumpet judgments, of which this verse is a part, is descriptive of the terrible judgment that will come upon apostate Christendom when the "great delusion" of II Thess. 2:11 is on. So great will be the mental and spiritual agony that some apostates will attempt to commit suicide to escape those days, but God will not allow them to do so. Let us be thankful that, when those days are running their course, the true church will have been translated to heaven.

Question: What is the meaning of Matt. 24:28, "Wheresoever the carcase is, there will the eagles be gathered together"?

Answer: The carcase represents the corrupt and apostate part of the Jewish nation; the eagles are symbols of God's judgment.

Of course, at the battle of Armageddon, the Gentile nations will also be gathered, many of whom will also go into everlasting condemnation. But Matthew 24 was spoken to the disciples concerning *Israel* during the tribulation period, and at the return of Christ in glory.

Question: Where will Armageddon be fought, and what armies will be the contestants?

Answer: Armageddon is a large plain of triangular shape a few miles from Jerusalem; about fourteen miles on the north, bounded by the hills of Galilee; about eighteen or twenty miles to the east, bounded by the hills below Nazareth; and about twenty miles on the southwest, bounded by the highlands of Samaria. Here is a vast plain, in a hilly country, very suitable for the maneuvering of large armies. Many a battle has been fought upon this plain. It is called in the Old Testament the valley of Megiddo, the plain of Jezreel, and the plain of Esdraelon. While many battles have already been fought upon that plain, yet in Revelation we read of the greatest battle of all, yet in the future. It will end with the most decisive victory of all history. The Antichrist, the king of the north (Russia), and the sunrising kings will meet on this battlefield.

In Rev. 19:19 we have Armageddon described: "And I saw the beast, and the kings of the earth, and their armies, gathered together to make war against him that sat on the horse, and against his army." The battle will be over in a moment; for the Lord will slay His enemies by the "sharp sword" that shall proceed out of His mouth. (See Rev. 19:15.) The victory will accomplish the deliverance of God's earthly people, the believing remnant of the Jews.

Question: Please explain Dan: 12:2: "And many of them that sleep in the dust of the earth shall awake, some to everlasting life, and some to shame and everlasting contempt." What resurrection is referred to in these verses?

Answer: These words could well be applied to the two resurrections, explained elsewhere in this series of studies: The first resurrection, to take place before the thousand years' reign of Christ, when the believers will be raised; and the second resurrection, to take place after the reign of Christ on earth, when the wicked dead shall stand before the great white throne.

But my understanding is that this verse in Dan: 12:2 refers to the *national* resurrection of Israel; for the prophet is addressing Israel in the preceding verse, speaking of the great tribulation period, also referred to by our Lord in Matthew 24. If so, then Daniel here refers to Israel's *national* resurrection, not to the physical resurrection from the dead.

Certainly Israel has long been buried, *nationally,* among the nations of the earth. But one day she will awake. (See Ezek. 37.) God has repeatedly stated that the national idea will awaken in Israel — and does this not seem to be literally true today? Some will awaken to everlasting life, because they will repudiate the claims of the Antichrist. Some will awaken to shame and everlasting contempt, because they will become a part of the apostasy, worshipping the Antichrist.

Question: Why will the nations fight for the possession of Palestine? For years it has been nothing but a waste, of no value commercially, or in any other way.

Answer: The question you ask would have been difficult to answer some twenty years ago, but not so today. Palestine is anything but a "waste, of no value commercially." In fact, it is acknowledged to be the richest land in the world. The Dead Sea is a vast chemical reservoir. Its riches alone are greater than the combined wealth of all the nations, to say nothing of other portions of this land of promise.

Dr. Thomas A. Norton, of New York City, editor of "Chemicals," gives the following estimate of the wealth of the Dead Sea:

Mineral	*Tons*	*Value*
Potash	1,300,000,000	$ 70,000,000,000
Bromine	853,000,000	260,000,000,000
Salt	11,900,000,000	27,500,000,000
Gypsum	81,000,000	120,000,000
Calcium Chloride	6,000,000,000	85,000,000,000
Magnesium Chloride	22,000,000,000	825,000,000,000
		$1,267,620,000,000

In rebuilding Palestine, the Israeli are using these minerals to enrich the land and to turn desolate places into watered gardens, vineyards, and fruitful groves. A recent issue of a Los Angeles newspaper stated that, through experimental farming, oranges weighing a pound each have been produced in this fruitful land. This has been made possible by the minerals of the Dead Sea, which are used to enrich the soil — and there is enough to fertilize the whole of Palestine.

It is this vast wealth that will bring Russia from the north "to take a spoil." (Read Ezek. 38:10-12.)

Question: Is it not a plain fact that the European countries are already lining up, seemingly in readiness for the Antichrist, the tribulation period, and the battle of Armageddon?

Answer: We can see how easily a confederacy of nations could be formed by the peoples occupying the territory of the old Roman Empire. Once many ridiculed the prophetic Word of God, saying that such a thing was impossible; but what student of history today would be so bold?

The return of the Jew to the land of Palestine is the most startling sign today, and this makes all other events very significant. The prophets foretold that Israel would return to her own land—not all of the nation, but part of the people; and that they would go back in unbelief.

Another remarkable circumstance in world events is the situation in the East. The "kings of the east," literally, "the kings that come from the sunrising" (Rev. 16:12), will play a significant part in world events in the last days. During the last half-century the Orient has been compared to a waking giant, being roused from a long slumber. The time will come when East and West and North and South will meet on the plains of Megiddo, for the last great war. Palestine is the geographical and political center of the world, and has always been in the mind of God. The Bible says so, in Deut. 32:8: "When the Most High divided to the nations their inheritance, when he separated the sons of Adam, he set the bounds of the people according to the number of the children of Israel."

Increased lawlessness in the earth and apostasy in professing Christendom are two other striking "signs of the times." Yet we must be careful not to set dates; for our Lord expressly told us not to do that. He did give us these "signs" whereby we might know that His coming draweth nigh, that we might be ready for His coming.

Question: What did Christ mean by "the abomination of desoration, spoken of by Daniel the prophet" (Matt. 24:15)?

Answer: Both Daniel and our Lord referred to the image of the beast, which he will set up "in the holy place" during the "seventieth week of Daniel." It will be an idol, an image of himself; and he will require all the world to worship him, or be martyred. An idol, to a devout Hebrew, is an abomination and certainly it is to God. When Israel realizes by this act of the Antichrist that he is a false Messiah, the believing part of the nation will refuse him recognition. He in turn will persecute Israel; and this will be the beginning of the great tribulation, to which our Lord referred in Matt. 24.

Question: What is meant by "the mark of the beast" (Rev. 13:16, 17)?

Answer: These two verses, together with the one just preceding them, plainly indicate that all those who refuse to worship the Antichrist and his image in that coming day will have to starve. They will not be able to buy or sell without in some way, called here receiving "the mark of the beast," letting the world know that they give allegiance and worship unto him.

Thank God! There will be many who will prefer martyr-dom to worshipping Satan's masterpiece in the earth. God never leaves Himself without a witness in the world.

Question: I recently heard a Bible teacher state that the Antichrist will be the re-incarnation of Judas Iscariot. He supported his argument by linking John 17:12, where Judas is called "the son of perdition," with II Thess. 2:3, where the Antichrist is described in the same words. Please explain.

Answer: I do not think these two verses necessarily refer to the same person. It is speculation to say that Judas will be the Antichrist.

Question: What is meant by "MYSTERY, BABYLON THE GREAT" as described in Rev. 17, 18?

Answer: This is a description of apostate Christendom during the reign of the Antichrist. After the true church is translated, professing Christendom will be united in one great body. All true believers will by that time be "with the Lord." But those who are Christian only in name will form a religious confederacy, called in Rev. 17:5 "THE MOTHER OF HAR-LOTS," in contrast with the true bride of Christ, which is the church. For a time this false system will make a great show of their godless, Christ-less profession. They will be in league with the Antichrist, the beast. Then he will turn on this "mother of harlots" and devour her, as described in these chapters of Revelation.

For a full discussion of this subject, see our radio studies in the book of Revelation. The lectures on these two chapters are also printed in booklet form, entitled "The Scarlet Woman—Her Final Apostasy, Fall, and Desolation."

Question: My pastor says that God has fulfilled His promises to the Jew, and that, when He speaks of Israel in the New Testament, He means "spiritual Israel," or all who love Him. What is the correct view in this matter?

Answer: One of the best answers to this question is the Jew himself. If any other people had been persecuted, martyred, hated, as has Israel, that people would have been annihilated or assimilated among other nations of the world ages ago. But what do we see before our very eyes today? Russian Jews, Spanish Jews, German Jews, Austrian Jews, English Jews,, American Jews — everywhere, in every nation, the sons of Israel are a separate people. And God alone is responsible for keeping His chosen people a separate nation. Why? Because He promised to do it. He promised to give Israel a King, even Jesus; and His Word cannot be broken. The Jew has been rightly called "the miracle of the ages." Why people can be so blind as not to see it, is but one of the tokens of Satan's power over unregenerate men, as well as those who do not accept the Scriptures for what they say. Romans 11 states clearly that God will again deal with Israel as a nation.

Now I realize that many devout Christians, postmillennialists, do *spiritualize* these promises of God, made to Abraham and his children. But let me say, in all kindness, that I think they are missing some of the most precious and comforting truths in all the Bible when they try to explain away the "promise of his coming" to bring order out of chaos, and to fulfill His covenant with Israel. We must learn rightly to divide the Word of truth.

Question: Do you believe the Jewish temple will literally be re-built where the Mosque of Omar now stands?

Answer: The prophetic Scriptures plainly teach that the Jewish temple will stand on the site where the Mosque of Omar now is. There have already been three temples: Solomon's, Zerubbabel's, and Herod's. Then there is to be a temple during the tribulation, in which the Antichrist will set up the "abomination of desolation," which is his own image, to be worshipped. Whether the present building on the temple-site, which is the Mosque of Omar, will be converted into a Jewish temple for the period of the reign of the Antichrist; or whether the Mosque of Omar will be destroyed, and the temple built on that site, I do not know. But Jewish worship will be restored on that spot. Arab and Jew, both descendants of Abraham, have contended through the years for Abraham's land; but God will give it unto the children of Isaac, even as He has promised in His Word.

The fifth temple will be the millennial temple, and is described in Ezek. 40-44.

Question: Does Rom. 11:26 teach that every Jew will be saved? "And so all Israel shall be saved: as it is written, There shall come out of Sion a Deliverer, and shall turn away ungodliness from Jacob."

Answer: No, Paul was referring to the *national* restoration of Israel, when Christ returns in glory to establish His millennial kingdom. In that age, as in every age, every man who is regenerated, whether Jew or Gentile, must be born again by a personal faith in the death of Christ as an atonement for his sin.

Many Jews will become apostate and accept the claims of the Antichrist. These Daniel describes in Dan. 12:2 as those who "shall awake . . . to shame and everlasting contempt."

Question: How have "all families of the earth been blessed" in the descendants of Abraham?

Answer: Christ was a Jew "according to the flesh"; and unto the Jews were "committed the oracles of God" (Rom.

3:2). So that Christ and the Bible came through the nation of Israel to bless the whole world.

During the reign of Christ on earth this promise of God to Abraham will be fulfilled completely. Then the Gentile nation will seek the God of Israel; and through His chosen people blessing will flow to all families of the earth.

Question: Will it be literally true that "the lion and the lamb shall lie down together" in Christ's kingdom on earth, or is this figurative?

Answer: Yes, we believe that it will be literally true. All ferocity will be taken away from the beasts of the field; there will be peace in the animal kingdom, as well as among men. "They shall not hurt nor destroy in all my holy mountain: for the earth shall be full of the knowledge of the Lord, as the waters cover the sea" (Isa. 11:9). These words from God, as well as many other passages, tell us what to expect when Jesus reigns in righteousness. Read all of this eleventh chapter of Isaiah to see the beautiful prophecy.

There were no thorns in Eden; and in that coming day, "instead of the thorn shall come up the fir tree, and instead of the brier shall come up the myrtle tree" (Isa. 35:1). The nations of the earth shall "beat their swords into plowshares, and their spears into pruninghooks: nation shall not lift up sword against nation, neither shall they learn war any more" (Isa. 2:4).

"The creation (R.V) itself also shall be delivered from the bondage of corruption into the glorious liberty of the children of god" (Rom. 8:21).

Question: If the millennium sees a converted world, how can Satan find a host to rebel against God at the close of the thousand years, as described in Rev. 20:7-9?

Answer: In reply to your question, let me quote from pages 191, 192 of our former radio studies on "God's Plan of the Ages":

The world *will* be converted at the *beginning* of the millennium. But children will be born into the world during the earthly reign of Christ, though the curse of Gen. 3:16 will be lifted. Three times in the eleventh chapter of Isaiah (in verses 6 and 8) we read that there will be little children in the Kingdom Age. And Zech. 8:5 tells us "that the streets of the city shall be full of boys and girls playing in the streets thereof." Just as it is necessary in this age for the children of godly parents to be converted, to accept Christ as a personal Saviour, so it will be during the reign of Christ on earth. And just as today many children of Christian parents are Gospel-hardened, so in the coming day many will be glory-hardened.

All will have to *obey* the King of kings, for He will rule "with a rod of iron." But some will render feigned obedience. Acts of rebellion against Him will be dealt with speedily, but voluntary heart-allegience will be required of the redeemed citizens of the kingdom of Christ. In every age it is the cross of Calvary's Lamb which must be accepted or rejected by the sinner! The moment Satan is "loosed out of his prison" after the millennium, all those who have rendered feigned allegiance to the King will enter into the last great rebellion against the God of heaven . . . Apart from the grace of God, even the millennium will not change man's nature. Nothing but the blood of Calvary's Lamb can change the sinful nature of a human soul—not even the glorious, perfect environment of Christ's own millennial reign.

Question. What is meant by the words, "Gog and Magog," in Rev. 20:8?

Answer: Ezek. 38:2 answers your question: "Gog, the land of Magog, the chief prince of Meshech and Tubal"—these words plainly refer to "the northern (European) powers, headed up by Russia . . . 'Gog' is the prince; 'Magog' his land. The reference to Meshech and Tubal (Moscow and Tobolsk) is a clear mark of identification" (quoted from the footnote on Ezek. 38:2, the Scofield Reference Bible).

These people of Russia evidently will be the leaders of the last rebellion against God, as the passage in Revelation plainly asserts.

Question: What will become of the Jewish nation after the millennium? Where will they dwell?

Answer: They will be in the new earth. Read carefully Isa. 66:22, "For as the new heavens and the new earth, which I will make, shall remain before me, saith the Lord, so shall your seed and your name remain."

National distinction among saved Gentile nations will pass, but Israel will remain the memorial nation.

XII

ROMAN CATHOLICISM

As an introduction to this chapter, which deals with questions relating to Roman Catholic doctrine, let me say that I am so glad to learn that many Catholics are following these radio messages. Some have written, expressing deep gratitude for help received. I am grateful to God for the privilege of helping these friends.

Again, I should like to add that, while the discussion to follow indicates definitely that I do not hold certain tenets of this church; yet I do believe that many Roman Catholics have been in years past and are today saved people. Every man who accepts Jesus as the only begotten Son of God, who believes in His atoning work on Calvary's cross and His bodily resurrection for our justification, is saved. Paul and Silas said to the Philippian jailer, "Believe on the Lord Jesus Christ, and thou shalt be saved" (Acts 16:31); and abundant scriptural proof can be offered for this fact.

Let me say also that, while I am sure that many individuals in the Roman Catholic Church are born again by the Holy Spirit; yet I do believe that the *system* is filled with much that is contrary to the teaching of the Bible, and dishonoring to God. We who live in so-called Christian lands can not begin to realize the evils that have been tolerated—and even propagated—by this system. But our country has the open Bible; and where the people have the Word of God, there is always more and more light. It was not so in the Dark Ages, when the papacy dominated much of the world. It is not so today in Latin America and other Roman Catholic countries that might be named. There the people are forbidden to have the Bible in their own tongue: the priesthood is often corrupt; and a Roman Catholic in this country would blush with shame at the doctrines and practice of the clergy.

One final word: After the true church is translated, all Christendom, both Catholic and Protestant, will unite in one final, godless attempt for world-power. But these will be Christian only in name; all real Christians, both Catholic and Protestant, will by that time be "with the Lord."

Question: Was the Roman Catholic Church the first Christian Church?

Answer: First, we call your attention to the statement in Acts 2:10, which tells us that among the "Jews, devout men, out of every nation under heaven" (Acts 2:5), there were *"strangers from Rome, Jews and proselytes."* Again, in Paul's Epistle to the Romans we read these words: "Salute Andronicus and Junia, my kinsmen, and my fellowprisoners, who are of note among the apostles, who also were in Christ before me" (Rom. 16:7). Here we learn that there were some believers in Rome who were "in Christ" before Paul was saved. Thus we know that there was a church in Rome some years before Paul wrote the Epistle to the Romans.

But there was an assembly in the city of Jerusalem, and there was one in Samaria *before* there was an assembly of New Testament saints in Rome. In this sense, therefore, the church at Rome was not the first New Testament church.

The claim is made by the Roman Catholic Church that Peter was the first bishop of Rome, and that the present pope, recognized by the Roman Catholics as the head of the church, holds this office by right of apostolic succession. In refutation of this claim, let us state that there is only one case of apostolic succession in the Scriptures. In Acts 1 we learn that Matthias took the place of Judas, in fulfillment of prophecy. In the case of James, the recognized leader of the church in Jerusalem (see Acts 15), no successor was chosen following his death, recorded in Acts 12:1, 2.

The Apostle Paul did not succeed any of the twelve apostles. His special apostleship to the Gentiles is mentioned in Rom. 11:13, wherein he magnifies his Christ-given apostleship. If you will read carefully Gal. 2:1-9, you will learn that the Apostle Paul did not receive his apostolic authority from Peter or from the eleven; but directly from God; and that the twelve disciples had no jurisdiction over him when he made known the truth concerning the church, which is the body of Christ. This truth was given to Paul by special revelation from God. In a very peculiar sense Paul—not Peter—was the Lord's "chosen vessel" to reveal the calling, program and destiny of the church, or body of Christ. Not one of the twelve apostles used the word "body" in referring to the church, so far as we have any record in the Bible. In Gal. 2:1-9 we learn that Peter and his associates sat at the feet of Paul, and learned the Lords' program for the church in this age of grace.

While it may be claimed that, historically, the Roman Catholic Church is the oldest of the *denominations* of Christendom today; yet it can easily be proved by comparing the teachings of the Roman Catholic Church with the Roman Catholic Bible that they are not the true Bible church of Christ.

Let us take, for instance, Paul's epistle to the Romans. That epistle was written to the assembly of saints, or the church, or churches, at Rome. It was written about 60 A.D. It was dictated by the infallible Holy Spirit. It should, therefore, be accepted by men who claim to be Christians, as the infallible Word of God, the divine instruction governing the Christian church.

In that epistle every statement concerning salvation by grace, and by grace alone, is contrary to the doctrine of salvation as taught and practiced by the Roman Catholics. Neither in the Epistle to the Romans nor in any other writing of Paul or any of the apostles is there a single imitation that there were any archbishops, cardinals, popes, or a special order of priests in the body of Christ. The entire papal system and priesthood in the Roman Catholic Church are altogether unscriptural. This is true also concerning the confessional and forgiveness of sins as practiced by the priests in Roman Catholicism. Their school of cardinals, prelates, and religious dignitaries is altogether contrary to the plain teaching of the Word of God. And this is also true concerning their peculiar doctrine of the holy eucharist.

There is not one line of Scripture in any of the writings of the apostles in support of the false teaching of Roman Catholicism concerning the special ministry of Mary, the mother of the Lord Jesus; the worship of saints; purgatory; or penances. All their teaching concerning salvation by works, prayer for the dead, and the canonization of saints is unscriptural.

All of these erroneous teachings of Roman Catholicism are found in the *footnotes* and *interpretations* of their Roman Catholic Bible, *not in their Bible itself*. This is fundamental! (As we shall see in the following questions and answers, the Catholic Bible is not greatly different from our Protestant Bible, except for the Apocryphal Books, which we do not consider inspired by God.)

As to whether or not a Roman Catholic can be saved, let me say that, to my certain knowledge, many members of this church believe in the virgin birth of Christ, His eternal deity, and His shed blood as an atonement for the soul. Therefore, I do not hesitate to say that a Roman Catholic who believes these truths is born again, even though he may be spiritually blinded regarding other precious doctrines of the Christian faith.

(Specific questions referred to above are treated separately in the following pages.)

Question: Why are the Apocryphal Books included in the Roman Catholic Bible, yet excluded from the Protestant Bible?

Answer: There are a number of reasons why the Apocryphal Books are not recognized by the Protestant Church as being inspired by the Holy Spirit:

1. They do not claim divine authority.

2. Some of these books disclaim such authority, as seen in II Maccabees 11:23, 15:38.

3. They contradict facts that are found in the Scriptures that we know are inspired. Compare Baruch 1:2 with Jer. 23:6, 7.

4. The Jews never received them as inspired. Orthodox Jews would rather forfeit their lives than falsify any portion of the Old Testament of sacred Scripture. And they never accepted the Apocryphal Books as being anything more than the work of man.

5. The Lord Jesus and His apostles never quoted from them.

6. The Roman Catholic Church rejected them until 1545; therefore, can not claim apostolic authority for them. These books were accepted at this late date because of a fanciful support that is found in them for the doctrine of purgatory.

Some of the Apocryphal Books are historical; some are fanciful. A careful reading of them will convince one taught by the Holy Spirit that they were not divinely inspired.

Question: I have before me a very kind letter from a Roman Catholic listener who, having read our printed radio message on Rev. 17, 18, asks the following question: Does not the angel's statement to Mary, "Blessed art thou among women" (Luke 1:28), justify us in exalting the mother of our Lord?

Answer: In saying, "Blessed art thou among women," the angel said no more than had been said of many other women in the Bible. It is written in Judges 5:24 concerning "Jael the wife of Heber the Kenite" that she should be "blessed *above* women," whereas it is said of Mary, "blessed art thou *among* women." There is, therefore, more reason for exalting Jael than Mary, according to the meaning of the term.

The same word "blessed" is used 41 times in the New Testament, and often in the Old Testament. For example, we read: "Blessed is he whose transgression is forgiven, whose sin is covered" (Psa. 32:1). "Blessed is he that considereth the poor" (Psa. 41:1). Dozens of similar verses might be quoted. The word "blessed" simply means "happy." Mary was "happy" in being chosen as the mother of her Saviour; and she naturally rejoiced in the thought that all generations would call her happy.

Mary herself denied the doctrine of the immaculate conception when she said in Luke 1:47, "My spirit hath rejoiced in God *my Saviour.*" The name "Saviour" implies sin, as seen in the angel's words to Joseph: "Thou shalt call his name Jesus: for he shall save his people from their sins" (Matt. 1:21).

Again, Mary exults in the *mercy* of God: "His mercy is on them that fear him from generation to generation" (Luke 1:50). From the context it is evident that she includes herself among the recipients of his mercy. Mercy implies sin. Where there is no sin, there is no need of mercy. Mary was a good woman, but she did not claim to be sinless.

Question: Why not pray to the Virgin Mary and to other departed Saints? Why are Protestants so opposed to the Roman Catholic practice of praying to the Virgin Mary and to other departed saints? Protestants ask their Christian friends to pray for them here. I have heard you request your radio audience to pray for you personally. Why not, then, ask the departed saints to pray for you? If their prayers availed

while they were here on earth, surely they would have efficacy if offered in the presence of God.

Answer: My friend, in stating your questions, you have answered it. You ask, "Why not request the *departed* saints to pray for you?" Just simply because they are "departed." How can I ask them, seeing they have departed? I can request my radio audience to pray for me because they are on earth, and near enough to hear the request. But Mary and the other saints of past generations are "departed."

The real Mary was never omnipresent, omniscient, or omnipotent. And though she is now in heaven, yet she does not possess these attributes, which belong only to God. Millions of Roman Catholics scattered all over the earth pray to her at the same time. How can she hear them, unless she can be everywhere at once? If she is omnipresent, then she must be divine; for omnipresence is an attribute of deity. And both Roman Catholic and Protestant Churches deny that she is divine. Then she is not omnipresent. And to pray to her is but a waste of time. Moreover, to say that God takes the prayers of His people and presents them to Mary, is to make Him her petitioner, thus putting Him in a subordinate position.

The fact is, my friend, you might as well kneel down in the streets of Los Angeles and pray to King George in Buckingham Palace as to pray to Joseph, Peter, Paul, or any other saint in the calendar. Going to heaven does not make the saints omnipresent.

And let me say just here that *every Christian is a saint,* meaning a separated one, set apart by God from the Christ-rejecting world, unto Himself. Paul addressed his letter to the Romans to the "saints" at Rome; and he constantly referred to his fellow-Christians, *then living,* as saints. Now to be sure, some Christians are more saintly, in the common use of the term, than others ; but as one has expressed it, "The word 'saint' is the family name of every one of God's born-again children." There is nothing in the Bible to authorize the canonizing of a Christian after he is dead. One is a saint the moment he puts his faith in the Lord Jesus. And the term indicates what God expects of His children—separation from the things that would defile, through a close walk with him in a godless world.

Mary confessed her need of a Saviour. She made a statement to Elizabeth, the mother of John the Baptist, which forever settles the question as to whether or not a Christian should pray to her. To Elizabeth she said, in the beautiful Magnificat, "My soul doth magnify the Lord, and my spirit hath rejoiced in God my Saviour" (Luke 1:46, 47). Here is the definite statement that Mary was a sinner, needing a Saviour—a beautiful character, to be sure, but born again by faith in the atoning work of the eternal Son of God.

Mary prayed with the disciples and the other women in the upper room. The last reference to Mary in the Bible is found in Acts 1:14, where she was with the disciples and the other women in the upper room, praying and waiting for the promise of the Holy Spirit, in accordance with the express command of the risen Christ. Not only was she obedient to Him here, but she made no claim to superiority. She is listed as just one with the other believers on the Lord Jesus, praying to the Father in the name of the Son, even as He had commanded.

There is not the slightest suggestion in all the Word of God that we are to pray to Mary. If God had intended that we pray to her, would He not have said so in His Word? Moreover, to kneel down before her image is nothing short of idolatry, as I see it.

Again, if God had intended her to have the exalted position given her by the Roman Catholic Church, would He not have given more prominence to her in the book of Acts and in the epistles? I repeat—Acts 1:15 is the last reference to her in the Bible! The record of the virgin birth of Christ, found in Old Testament prophecy and in the Gospels; indeed, permeating all the New Testament—this is exceedingly important. We acknowledge that the mother of our Lord, according to the flesh, was "blessed among women." But it is highly significant that, after the story of His nativity and boyhood, there are few references to Mary in all the New Testament. And in none is there the least inference that she is given a position more exalted than that of any other believer on Jesus.

My friend, if you feel that you need a saint to pray for you, find a man or woman of God here on earth. Tell that one your need. And you may be sure that you will have one who can intercede for you.

There is . . . one Mediator between God and men, the man Christ Jesus" (I Tim. 2:5). Best of all, my friend, go directly to your Great High Priest, the Lord Jesus Christ. He "ever liveth to make intercession" for His blood-bought children. Read all of the Epistle to the Hebrews for a marvelous presentation of the person and work of our Great High Priest. The following passages are especially clear: Rom. 8:34; Col. 3:1; Heb. 2:17, 18; 4:14-16; 6:20; 7:24-28; 9:24; 10:19-22.

Question: Is it true that Jesus had half-brothers, sons of Joseph and Mary? I have heard this denied.

Answer: Yes, after Jesus was born in Bethlehem, Joseph and Mary had sons and daughters. In Matt. 14:55, 56 we read: "Is not this the carpenter's son? if not his mother called Mary? and his brethren, James, and Joses, and Simon, and Judas? And his sisters, are they not all with us?" (Cf. Mark 6:3; Matt. 12:46; John 2:12; Acts 1:14; I Cor. 9:5; Gal. 1:19.)

The denial that Mary had other children originated with Roman Catholic teaching that she was sinless; this is called the

access into the Holiest of All, even heaven itself; for there our Great High Priest is "seated at the right hand of the Father," to plead the cause of His blood-bought children. Read the seventeenth chapter of John to see how He prays for us, even as He did in that marvelous intercessory prayer, uttered before He went to the cross.

There is a great difference between a *priest* and a *preacher* in the Bible. The preacher presents God to man; the priest presents man to God. "There is one God, and *one mediator* between God and men, the man Christ Jesus" (I Tim. 2:5).

The preachers in the Catholic Church are giving to their people "another gospel" (Gal. 1:8, 9); that is, a mixture of ritualism, Judaism, and the gospel of grace.

Question: Do these passages teach "priestly absolution" as held by the Roman Catholic Church: Matt. 16:19; 18:18; John 20:23? What did Christ mean when He said, "Whose soever sins ye remit, they are remitted unto them; and whose soever sins ye retain, they are retained"?

Answer: There is no such thing in Christianity as priestly absolution. There was priestly absolution in Judaism, as in Leviticus; but this does not belong to the Christian Church or to Christianity. In this age of grace, *all* of God's children are priests — women as well as men. (See I Pet. 2:9; Rev. 1:6.) And no other priesthood exists in Christianity.

To "remit sin" is to declare sin forgiven on the basis of faith in the Lord Jesus. We find Peter declaring remission of sins in the household of Cornelius: "To him (Jesus) give all the prophets witness, that through his name whosoever believeth in him shall have remission of sins" (Acts 10:43).

To a man who has taken Christ as his Saviour, we bring God's message and "declare sins forgiven." To the man who spurns Christ, we bring God's message that his sins are retained, and that he is "in the gall of bitterness, and in the bond of iniquity" (Acts 8:23).

Both Peter and Paul forbade anyone to worship them. even to fall down before them in reverence. There is not the slightest intimation in any Scripture that either Peter or Paul or any other apostle permitted sinner or saint to confess sins to them as is done according to the so-called doctrine of "priestly absolution."

Every believer, in his dealings with men, declares sins forgiven or unforgiven according to what the inquirer does with Christ. The text has no other meaning.

Question: Why do Protestants say that the Roman Catholic mass is not scriptural? I am a Roman Catholic, and I listen regularly to the eleven o'clock broadcast. In many ways your teaching is in agreement with what I believe. But you speak of the bread and wine of the Lord's Supper as representing the body and blood of our Lord. Christ Himself said, "This is my blood . . . this is my body." Why is it that the Protestants do not accept the word of the Lord as being literally true? In the Catholic mass we are taught that the bread and wine become the literal body and blood of Jesus, even as He Himself affirmed.

Answer: There are several reasons why the Protestant Church does not accept the Roman Catholic interpretation of these words:

1. When our Lord instituted this memorial, He sat at the table with His disciples in His physical body. The blood, the life of the body, flowed through His veins. And yet He took the bread in His hands and said, "Take, eat; this is my body, which is broken for you: this do in remembrance of me" (I Cor. 11:24). That bread remained bread. He was sitting there before them; they could look upon Him, could feel and touch

His hands. His body was unchanged. He must have been speaking figuratively, because He said, "This is my body, which *is* broken for you." And yet at that moment Christ's body had not been broken, had not been crucified.

And when He took the cup and said, "This cup is the new covenant in my blood, which *is* shed for you" (Luke 22:20), that which was in the cup did not undergo any change. It did not actually become the blood of our Lord; for His blood was still flowing in His veins, soon to be poured out for our sins upon Calvary's Cross.

2. The word "is" as used by the Lord here is found all through the Bible to mean "represent." When our Lord said, "This is my body," He said, according to the custom of the language used, "This represents my body."

Go back to Gen. 41:26, where you read, "The seven good kine *are* seven years; and the seven good ears *are* seven years: the dream is one." Will anyone claim that the seven good cows and the seven good ears were literally seven years of 365 days each, which had not yet come to pass? All admit that they *represented* seven years.

Again, Daniel said to Nebuchadnezzar, "Thou *art* this head of gold" (Dan. 2:38). Did Daniel mean to say that the king standing before him was really gold? Of course, such an interpretation would be foolish, and Nebuchadnezzar was *represented* by the head of gold.

In Rev. 1:20 we find the words, "The seven stars *are* the angels of the seven churches: and the seven candlesticks which thou sawest *are* the seven churches." Has anyone ever risen to claim that these words are to be taken literally? They are symbolic, of course.

The Lord Jesus said more than once. "I *am* the bread of life." (Read the sixth chapter of John.) Now to follow the Roman Catholic interpretation, we must declare that Jesus, who said this, was not flesh and bone and muscle and hair; but that He was literally bread.

Such illustrations of this point could be added by the dozens. My friend, the Lord's presence is not in the bread and wine. Our Lord's presence is not in the elements, in some mysterious way, so that they are not symbols. Not at all. We eat and drink the body and blood of our Lord Jesus Christ when by faith we recognize His presence with us, and when by meditation upon His Word we feed our souls upon Him who once died for our sins upon the cross. Our Lord said, "Where two or three are gathered together in my name, *there am I in the midst of them*" (Matt. 18:20)—*not in the midst of the elements, but in the midst of His people!*

Question: Do the verses in John 6:53-58 not refer to the Lord's Supper? And do we not eat His flesh and drink His blood when we take the bread and the wine of the communion?

Answer: These words say, in part: "Except ye eat the flesh of the Son of man, and drink his blood, ye have no life in you. Whoso eateth my flesh and drinketh my blood, hath eternal life; and I will raise him up at the last day."

This passage has no reference whatsoever to the Lord's Supper. Christ explained His own words, leaving no doubt as to their meaning. In verse 52 of this same chapter it is recorded that the Jews "strove among themselves, saying, How can this man give us his flesh to eat?" And in verse 63 our Lord answers this question: "It is the Spirit that quickeneth; the flesh profiteth nothing: the words that I speak unto you, they are spirit, and they are life." Therefore, to "eat the flesh" and to "drink the blood" of the Lord Jesus—this figurative language simply means that we are to receive His Word into our hearts by the power of the Holy Spirit.

The Word of God is constantly compared to food, as the following examples prove:

At the close of the forty days of temptation, the Lord Jesus said to Satan: "Man shall not live by bread alone, but by every word that proceedeth out of the mouth of God" (Matt. 4:4).

Jeremiah said: "O Lord . . . Thy words were found, and I did eat them; and thy word was unto me the joy and rejoicing of mine heart" (Jer. 15:16).

Job also said, "I have esteemed the words of his mouth more than my necessary food" (Job 23:12).

Again, David in Psalm 119:103 wrote, saying, "How sweet are thy words unto my taste! yea, sweeter than honey to my mouth!"

Thus you see, my friend, that you eat the flesh of the Lamb and drink His Blood when you receive the words of Jesus daily into your heart by faith; when you have His wonderful Book with its thousands of promises made *real, living, powerful, energetic* in your heart by the power of the Holy Spirit. This is especially true when you meditate upon those portions of the Word that present Christ as the One who died for your sins— when you receive Him into your heart as Saviour and Lord.

John 6:53-58 has no reference at all to the Lord's Supper.

Question: From what passage of Scripture do the Roman Catholics get their idea of purgatory?

Answer: The Roman Catholics take I Cor. 3:15 as the basis for their doctrine concerning purgatory: "But he himself shall be saved, but so as through fire" (R.V.). But we know that neither this verse nor any other verse in the Word of God teaches such doctrine; for there is no such state or place as purgatory. The whole body of Scripture, including the direct teaching of the Lord Jesus, makes it very plain that there is no second chance after death. What we do with Jesus *in this life* determines our eternal state.

What I Cor. 3:15 does teach is clearly set forth by the entire passage from which the sentence quoted above is taken. And every careful student knows that the only way to interpret any statement is to take it in its true setting. This chapter — and this verse — both tell us that the believer's *works* will be tested before the "judgment seat of Christ," for the giving of eternal rewards for service rendered for the Lord.

This is a figurative expression, "yet so as through fire." Our works, done in the name of Christ, will have to stand the searching test of His all-seeing eye. And as fire burns up the dross, so only that which is done from an honest heart, for His glory, shall abide.

Paul is addressing those, in this passage, who have built upon the "foundation, which is the Lord Jesus Christ"; such as these are *already* saved. But some Christians "build" more God-honoring works upon that foundation than do others. Surely the Apostle Paul should receive a greater reward than should the repentant thief on the cross. Only those works which are built upon that one foundation — after we are born again — will be rewarded; and the thief on the cross had no time to serve his Lord after he was saved. Yet he himself was saved; he went with Christ to paradise.

Suppose you were awakened in the middle of the night with a cry of, "Fire, fire!" Suppose you had just time enough to escape from your burning house with your life, but you saw your house and all your valuables burned to ashes. You yourself would be saved, yet saved "so as through fire."

There will be many believers at the judgment seat of Christ who will see the greater part of the fruit of their Christian service burned up as useless. Their souls will be saved; their salvation will be left to them because they trusted in Jesus; but their works will be as "wood, hay, stubble." The Lord will say to such as these, "My child, I can give thee no reward for *that*." If we build hospitals and give alms and do acts of kindness "to be seen of men," even though we do these things in the name of Christ, then we receive our reward here on earth, in the praise of men. What further reward need we expect? That is what the passage means.

Read the chapter carefully, my friend, and you will see that Paul is not discussing salvation of the soul, but rewards for service. It is the believer's "work" that shall be revealed; and our salvation is "not of works, lest any man should boast" (Eph. 2:9).

The doctrine of purgatory is of a piece with the evil practise of the sale of indulgencies in Europe during the Dark Ages, when the Roman Catholic Church led deluded souls to believe that they could *buy* immunity from punishment. And it is a well known fact that, even today, in those Catholic countries where the Bible is kept from the people, many miserably poor people *pay* the priests to pray for their dead. Catholicism in America would blush with shame at some of the things done in these veritably heathen lands. And we need go only to Latin America to find such practises.

XIII

FALSE RELIGIOUS IN PROFESSING CHRISTENDOM

Question: Are Christian Scientists Christian?

Answer: Christian Science is the religion of Mrs. Mary Baker Glover-Patterson-Eddy. The textbook is "Science and Health" with a "Key to the Scriptures." In that textbook Mrs. Eddy claims that she discovered this religion in 1866, and gave it the name "Christian Science."

She had been a disciple of Mr. Quinby of Portland, Maine, who had received instruction from Mesmer. Mr. Quinby practiced what is known as Mesmerism. Mrs. Eddy was also associated with Mrs. Annie Lee, who was a teacher of Shakerism. Christian Science is a mixture of Pantheism, Unitarianism, Quinbyism, Shakerism, Theosophy, and some other things. *It is neither scientific nor Christian.*

Mrs. Eddy claimed that her religion, or "science," agrees with the Bible. Yet in her writings she called God the Father "a principle"; Christ the Son "an idea"; and the Holy Spirit "divine science." Her teachings deny the Bible story of creation and redemption; salvation by grace through faith in the shed blood of the Lord Jesus Christ; His bodily resurrection. According to this cult, sin, sickness, and death are the unrealities of human conclusions; man is spiritual and co-existent with God; and if we live after death, we must have lived before birth. Mrs. Eddy denied the personality, even the existence, of Satan. She taught that the sea represents God, and that Christ is as one drop of water in the sea. In line with Pantheism, she taught that all that is good is God, and God is all good.

Inasmuch as there are multitudes of redeemed sinners who, spiritually speaking, do not know their right hands from their left, there are undoubtedly some of them that have been caught in this satanic delusion, and still have enough faith in the shed blood of the Lord Jesus to be saved. But no one can be an intelligent Christian—intelligent concerning the plain teaching of the Bible—and accept and follow the teachings of Christian Science. No one can be saved who *believes* the teachings of Christian Science.

Question: What is the Unity School of Christianity?

Answer: The Unity School of Christianity is like Christian Science, New Thought, and Theosophy, in that it denies the blood atonement of Jesus Christ. It was founded about forty-two years ago by Mrs. Myrtle Fillmore. We might summarize its contradiction of the Word of God in six denials of the "faith" once for all delivered unto the saints." These are as follows:

1. *Unity denies that the Bible is uniquely inspired.* In the magazine, "Unity," published February, 1929, page 152, Mrs. Fillmore says: "Beginning with the very first chapter of Genesis, the Bible is an allegory." "Everybody can be inspired; if we think that inspiration ceased with Jesus, or with Paul and the apostles, we hinder the stream of God-thought from flowing to us; and we get no direct revelation."

2. *Unity denies sin and the personality of Satan.* In "Unity" (No. 5, page 503) there is the statement: "There is no sin, sickness, or death." In "Lessons in Truth," page 185, there is the statement: "God is good, and God is all; therefore, I refuse to believe in the reality of the devil or evil in any of its forms."

3. *Unity denies that salvation is by grace through faith in the Lord Jesus Christ.* It teaches that we achieve perfection by a realization that we are God through constant affirmation. Master and mind are one, says Unity. We all have a God-mind. Followers of Unity know nothing about the blood of Christ, and attempt to find salvation by the denial of the reality of sin and

by the constant affirmation, "I am good, and therefore I am God."

4. *Unity denies that Jesus is the Christ any more than any man.* According to Unity, it is the privilege of every man to be everything that Jesus was. In the booklet, "Christian Healing," page 172, there is the statement: "He became the Word of God incarnate because He fulfilled all the requirements of the law. But this is the privilege of every man." Such statements as these are to be found all through the writings of Unity.

5. *Unity denies that death is universal, and teaches that Unity disciples may never die.*

6. *Unity also denies a real heaven, and teaches reincarnation.*

Question: What are the errors taught by Jehovah's Witnesses, who under Judge Rutherford, are carrying on the work which was begun by Pastor Charles T. Russell?

Answer: In the first place, the Russellites, or Rutherford-ites, are Unitarians. They say that the doctrine of the Trinity was well suited to the Dark Ages, which, according to Pastor Russell, produced it. Therefore, they deny the deity and personality of the Holy Spirit.

They also deny the eternal deity of Jesus Christ, the Son of God. They teach that He was *a* god, but not *the* God. They teach that, before His incarnation, He was none other than the Archangel Michael. Thus they make our Lord a *created* angel, not the Creator. They teach that Jesus was a human being during His earthly ministry, but that in His incarnation He was not the spiritual being He was before. They teach that at the Cross His humanity was annihilated, that after His death His body was either secretly taken away by God or "dissolved into gases." They teach that man is not saved by God's grace through faith in the Lord Jesus Christ alone, but by doing good works.

Pastor Russell taught that Jesus Christ returned in October, 1874, and went into hiding with some of His disciples, and that in October, 1914, He was to be manifested with the living disciples known as "the true wheat." The number of these disciples was to be 144,000. (He took this number from the reference in the book of Revelation to the 144,000 Israelites.)

Pastor Russell worked out a millennial dawn and kingdom-salvation program, because he could not understand what God would do with the heathen who had never heard the Gospel, and therefore, could not be held responsible for accepting or rejecting it. Pastor Russell taught, and most of his disciples still teach, that the time of Christ's manifestation is to be determined by multiplying 360 years by 7 (or 2520 years) to the year that the Jews were taken away by the king of Babylon, about 600 B.C. They said that during the kingdom reign of Christ on earth the heathen and others who have died are to be brought back to the earth and given an opportunity to hear the kingdom message.

Jehovah's Witnesses teach soul-sleep, and are bitterly opposed to any and all orthodox teachings concerning hell and the lake of fire.

According to the plain teaching of the Word of God, no one can be saved who believes what is taught by Jehovah's Witnesses concerning the Lord Jesus Christ, to say nothing of other error in this system. Therefore, we would warn our readers against it as a dangerous and pernicious perversion of the truth of God.

Question: What is the teaching of the Mormons?

Answer: The Mormon Church was organized in 1830 by Joseph Smith, and in the same year "The Book of Mormon" was published. At the center of this movement, with its apostleship and priesthood, stood the Mormon head, Joseph Smith. He claimed for himself nothing less than that he was God's mouthpiece, standing as God to give laws to the people.

Their text book is "The Book of Mormon"; and the movement claims that this book—not the Bible—is the voice of truth for this age.

The errors of Mormonism are legion. The system teaches that there are many gods; and as far as this earth is concerned, Adam is our father and the only god with whom we have to do. Mormonism says that Jesus was the Son of Adam-God and Mary. (It claims that Jesus was married at Cana to Mary and Martha and other Mary's; and that, therefore, He could "see His seed" before the crucifixion.) It teaches that Joseph Smith is a descendant of Christ; that the Holy Spirit is but an influence, not a Person; that salvation must be worked out by the individual himself through the forms and ritual of the Mormon Church. It holds that baptism by immersion is absolutely necessary for salvation; and that, if one dies without baptism, a friend on earth may be baptized as his proxy. This is the interpretation that Mormonism gives to I Cor. 15:29 (discussed in this series under the topic, "Baptized for the dead"). Mormonism teaches that all who are not Latter-Day Saints; that is, members of this movement, will be damned.

The Gospel of the grace of God through faith in the Lord Jesus Christ is unknown in Mormonism.

Question: What is Spiritism?

Answer: Spiritism is the theory that the spirits of the dead do communicate and hold intercourse with those who are still upon the earth. We know that Spiritism is not of God, for the following reasons:

1. It is absolutely forbidden in the Scriptures. See Deut. 18:19-21; Lev. 19:31; Isa. 8:19-22; I Chron. 10:13, 14.

2. The spirits of the dead in Christ are with the Lord, and do not return to the earth. See II Sam. 12:23. Phil. 1:23; II Cor. 5:8.

3. The spirits of the Christless dead could not return to the earth, even if they so desired. Read carefully Luke 16:19-31. The rich man desired Abraham to send Lazarus back to earth to warn his brethren. Abraham stated that this was not necessary, because his brothers had the writings of Moses and the prophets. But why did he not return *himself* to warn his brethren, if the dead really return to the earth? He could not return because there was *"a great gulf fixed."* The rich man could not pass over to where Lazarus was, let alone leave his prison and return to earth.

The only explanation of Spiritism, therefore, is that those who appear in seances are demons who impersonate our loved ones. Paul says in Eph. 6:11, 12: "Put on the whole armour of God, that ye may be able to stand against the wiles of the devil. For we wrestle not against flesh and blood, but against principalities, against powers, against the rulers of the darkness of this world, against spiritual wickedness in high places."

Let us also remember that God smote Saul because he dabbled with Spiritism. (See I Chron. 10:13, 14.)

Question: Anglo-Israelism declares that Jesus Christ was an Israelite, but not a Jew. Was Jesus a Jew?

Answer: Of course, the Lord Jesus was a Jew, "arcording to the flesh." Anglo-Israelism is noted for its fancies and fallacies. It is about the only false religion I know that has no truth in it whatsoever. Many of the cults have some truth, mixed with much error, usually robbing the Lord Jesus of His deity and atoning work on Calvary. But Anglo-Israelism is fanciful.

There is abundant Scripture to prove that Jesus was a Jew. The two genealogical records, found in Matthew and Luke prove it; that is, that He came through the tribe of Judah—and the word "Jew" comes from "Judah." (It is often used, however, to refer to all Israel.) Heb. 7:14 tells us also: "It is evident that our Lord sprang out of Judah."

Again the woman at Jacob's well addressed Christ as a Jew, and He not only accepted her statement as true—He did not deny it—but He also called Himself a Jew. Note these words from their conversation: "How is it that thou, *being a Jew, askest* drink of me, which am a woman of Samaria? For the Jews have no dealings with the Samaritans" (John 4:9). And our Lord's statement to her is conclusive: "Ye worship ye know not what: *we* know what we worship: for salvation is of the *Jews.*"

At the trial and crucifixion of Jesus Pilate said to the *Jews,* "Behold your King!" (John 19:14). And the inscription was written over the cross, "JESUS OF NAZARETH, THE KING OF THE JEWS."

It is both futile and foolish to try to prove that Jesus was not a Jew. All history, both secular and sacred, furnish irrefutable evidence that He came from the tribe of Judah. Moreover, God foretold that He would; and "the word of God can not be broken"! (See Gen. 49:10 for the direct prophecy.) Yet other prophecies of the Old Testament, quoted in the New tell us that He came through the house of David; and David was of the tribe of Judah. (Compare II Sam. 7:12-16 with Rom. 1:3; the genealogies; and other references in the Acts and in all the New Testament.)

For further discussion of this subject, write for our former radio studies, entitled, "Anglo-Israelism—True or False?"

Question: Am I an Israelite? A Seventh Day Adventist friend and an Anglo-Israelite friend both tell me that I am. The former bases her contention on Rom. 9:4-8; the latter, on the number thirteen. Both declare that there will be no restora-

tion of the Jews. I always understood that being born again made one a Christian, but does it make a Gentile a spiritual Israelite?

Answer: No Gentile ever becomes an Israelite. Two of the most outstanding vagaries of the present day are Anglo-Israelism and Seventh Day Adventism. If you do not possess a copy of our radio booklet on "Anglo-Israelism — True or False," I shall be glad to send you one. As for Seventh Day Adventism, I recommend that you read "Ought Christians to Keep the Sabbath?" by the late Rev. R. A. Torrey, D.D. Both these books will answer your questions more fully than space will permit here.

Let me say, however, that the Bible speaks of some who are "of the synagogue of Satan" (Rev. 3:9); and the system you name belongs to this class, *because they make light of and frustrate the grace of God.*

Now concerning the text you quote, remember that we are "Abraham's children" according to "the promise." "The promise" is in Christ; and having accepted Him, we become the *spiritual* children of Abraham. But, mark you, it is "the promise," and not "the covenant" that Paul mentions. "The covenant" has to do with an *earthly people* and an *earthly land,* the land of Palestine. We Gentiles may claim none of the things that have to do with the Abrahamic covenant, or with the earthly people—Israel. The trouble with those who hold these teachings which you name, is that they do not distinguish between the "promise" made to Abraham of the Saviour for the whole world and the "covenant" made with him concerning the earthly people, Israel. *And Israel is not the church,* though the church is composed of Jews and Gentiles. Read carefully Gen. 15:18; it concerns the land of Palestine: "In the same day the Lord made a *covenant* with Abram, saying, Unto thy seed have I given this land, from the river of Egypt unto the great river, the river Euphrates."

Question: What is the Seventh Day Adventist organization, and what is erroneous in its teaching?

Answer: Seventh Day Adventism originated from the movement of William Miller, who was born in 1782 in Massachusetts. In 1833 in Low Hampton, N. Y., he began to preach that the end of the world was at hand. He set the date, October 10, 1843, for this event. Thousands turned to this cry of warning, and in ten years perhaps 100,000 people became Adventists. When Miller's prophecy failed, he set another date— 1844. The failure of the second prophecy demolished the follies of the Miller Movement; and out of the fragments, Seventh Day Adventism was construed under the high priestess, Ellen G. White.

The errors of Seventh Day Adventism are many. The doctrine of salvation by works is believed by this cult, denying salvation by grace. According to Seventh Day Adventism, the keeping of the law is absolutely necessary; and believers who fail in observing the Sabbath (Saturday) are lost. If one does not keep the Sabbath, even though he believes in the Lord Jesus, he has "the mark of the beast," and will be annihilated when Christ comes. The system teaches that "the seal of God" is found in keeping the Saturday-Sabbath; while "the mark of the beast" is evidenced by keeping the first day of the week.

Seventh Day Adventism teaches that its members are the 144,000 of the book of Revelation. It holds the doctrines of soul-sleep and the annihilation of the wicked. It places the writings of Ellen G. White side by side with the Bible as being alike fully inspired. In this, as well as in other ways, it is like Mormonism, Christian Science, and Russellism, all of which deny the sufficiency of God's revelation through His Word, and add writings of men to be the inspired Word of God.

Question: What is the "I Am" movement, and who founded it?

Answer: In answering this question, we are not referring to the "I Am" movement of "Father Divine," the colored preacher of New York, but to the "I Am" movement of the Ballards of Chicago. This cult, called "The Philosophy of Life," was started several years ago by Mr. and Mrs. G. W. Ballard. These two, together with their son, Donald Ballard, claim to be the accredited messengers of the ascended master, Saint Germain. They claim that Saint Germain is an ascended master of the seventh ray, and that Jesus is an ascended master of the sixth ray. They have much to say about the cosmic rays, the cosmic laws, and the divine director.

Their affirmations and prayers are to the "Mighty I Am Presence" above, clothed in what they call an electronic body. They claim that the light comes from this "Mighty I Am Presence" to the "mighty I am presence" in the flesh-bodies here on earth. Their god is "light, wisdom, and power," or "love, intelligence, and energy."

The Ballards claim to have constant contact with and revelations from the ascended master, Saint Germain. They claim that both Saint Germain and Jesus send them messages from above, in which their disciples are instructed to follow the teachings of the Ballards, to buy their books, and not to listen to anything that is contrary to their teaching.

This is one of the most diabolic, blasphemous delusions ever given out by Satan. There are thousands of intelligent-looking, well-dressed men and women in this movement, which now claims several hundred thousand adherents. They promise their followers health and wealth and a philosophy by which they can reach perfection and ascension. They claim that Saint Germain was Samuel, and that afterwards, in a different body, he was in conference with the Lord Jesus while He was on earth. The Ballards have written several messages, claiming that they were from Jesus with the full endorsement of Saint Germain.

It is claimed that Mr. Ballard was the faithful centurion of Luke 7, and later on was George Washington.

With them doubt, fear, and error are negatives, and must be consumed by a violent flame that surrounds the flesh-body of the disciple here on earth. They deny the Bible record of creation, redemption, and immortality. To them Christ is unknown as an atoning Saviour. He is a Way-shower, as in Christian Science. They claim that Christ became the power of God by repeating such formulas as: "I AM THAT I AM," "I am spirit," "I am life," "I am Christ," "I have all power," "I know no sin." Could anything be more blasphemous than this false teaching? Moreover, these apostates claim that, if men today follow Christ in these declarations, they, too, will become Christs!

This cult is a mixture of Christian Science, Unity, Theosophy, and Spiritism. It is both unscriptural and anti-Christian. It is a shadow of "the strong delusion" which will prevail upon the earth during the reign of the Antichrist. (See II Thess. 2:11.)

Question: Some ministers claim that every one, even the devil, will be saved when Christ gives the kingdom back to the Father after His millennial reign on earth. These ministers base this teaching on Phil. 2:9-11, where we read "that every knee shall bow" before God. If that is so, why was Christ's great sacrifice necessary, if after a few years' punishment, we all are to be saved anyway?

Answer: What some ministers believe and what the Bible teaches are two different things, although it is to be regretted that it should be so.

There is a difference between *reconciliation* and *subjugation*. It is true that "God also hath exalted him (Jesus), and given him a name which is above every name: that at the name of Jesus every knee should bow, of things in heaven, and things in earth, and things under the earth; and that every tongue should confess that Jesus Christ is Lord, to the glory of God the Father" (Phil. 2:9-11). Paul here is speaking of *subjugation;* therefore the three realms are named: Things in heaven; things in earth, and things under the earth. Even Satan and his demons *know* that Jesus Christ is Lord; but the day will come when they will have to *confess* it before all of God's universe. The words here give no intimation, however, of a saving faith on the part of the unregenerate; nor does any portion of Scripture. On the contrary, many passages might be cited, to prove just the opposite. Rev. 20:10 is enough to prove what will become of Satan, the Antichrist, and all his followers: "And the devil that deceived them was cast into the lake of fire and brimstone, where the beast and the false prophet are, *and shall be tormented day and night for ever and ever.*"

What Phil. 2:9-11 does teach is that men and angels and demons, even Satan, will bow the knee before Jesus of Nazareth, acknowledging Him as King of kings and Lord of lords. This passage is a wonderful proof of the deity of Christ. But when it comes to a matter of love and heart-allegiance, even salvation, that is another matter entirely. Read Col. 1:20: "Having made peace through the blood of his cross, by him to *reconcile all things unto himself* . . . whether they be things in earth, or things in heaven . . ."—here you will note that nothing is said of *reconciling* things under the earth, although the things under the earth *will be subjugated to Christ.*

Question: What are we to understand by Eccl. 12:7: "Then shall the dust return to the earth as it was: and the spirit shall return unto God who gave it"? Does this passage not teach that the spirits of all—saved and lost—return to God at death?

Answer: This verse is understood when read in the light of the last verse of the same chapter, as well as in the light of all Scripture: "For God shall bring every good work into judgment, with every secret thing, whether it be good, or whether it be evil" (Eccl. 12:14).

The spirits of all men, both saved and lost, return to God *to give an account.* This is the same teaching as that set forth in John 5:28, 29. The teachings concerning the judgments and the distinction between the judgment seat of Christ for believers and the great white throne judgment for unbelievers, are given in the epistles and in Revelation. Discussion of these topics is found under questions in this series dealing with the rewards of believers and the judgments. Therefore, we shall not repeat them here.

Question: What is modernism, and what is meant when a minister is declared to be a modernist?

Answer: Modernism is the substitution of human philosophy for divine revelation. Really, the word "modernism" is a misnomer. Its true title should be "ancientism"; for it asks the old question raised by Satan in the Garden of Eden, "Hath God said?"

Modernism denies the inspiration of the Bible, the Virgin Birth and the deity of Christ, the fall of man, and the atonement of Jesus Christ. It also denied the physical resurrection of Christ; and, of course, laughs at the doctrine of His second coming. Modernism is as anti-christian as are Christian Science and Theosophy. It is the worst blight on Christendom today.

A modernist preacher is one who believes in modernism.

Question: Do you not think it is unchristian to be forever finding fault with the so-called modernists? Many of them are doing much good in the world, and are living exemplary lives

Answer: There is a difference between fault-finding and earnestly contending "for the faith once for all delivered unto the saints" (Jude 3). Certainly we must be kind, holding the truth in love. But we must not fail to warn men to flee from the wrath to come. Perhaps the following outline facts will suffice to show why we feel impelled to point out the unbelief in the so-called modernistic camp; yet let it be remembered that these false teachings are not modern. They were being taught when our Lord was on earth.

1. This school of theology teaches that the Bible *contains* the Word of God, but is not the infallible, verbally inspired, eternal Word of God.

2. It robs our Lord Jesus of His eternal deity, seeking to destroy all faith in His Virgin Birth, His miracles, His bodily resurrection, and His coming again.

3. It denies the efficacy of Calvary's Cross, substituting man's own efforts—self-righteousness—as a means of salvation. This can never be done. Good works are important, but they are the fruit of salvation, never the means of salvation.

These are just some of the most dangerous of the teachings being proclaimed from many pulpits of evangelical churches in Protestantism today. The men who teach such doctrines would be more honest with God and with their congregations if they would come out in the open and take their stand against Christ and His Word. Perhaps they are self-deceived; we know they are deceived by Satan. And we dare not keep silence so long as such doctrine is being sounded forth in the name of our blessed Lord.

XIV

MISCELLANEOUS QUESTIONS

Question: What is the difference between the cherubim and the seraphim?

Answer: The cherubim are not identical with the seraphim. There are different ranks and orders in the angelic hosts; and the cherubim and seraphim are but two of these. The cherubim appear to have to do with the holiness of God as outraged by sin. The seraphim have to do with the uncleanness in the people of God. (See Isa. 6:18.)

Question: How do you explain Paul's experience as described in II Cor. 12:19?

Answer: When Paul was "caught up to the third heaven . . . into paradise," that experience was doubtless a part of God's special revelation to him. To Paul was given the special revelation concerning the church, which had hitherto not been revealed. Some Bible students think this experience of II Cor. 12 may have occurred when Paul was stoned at Lystra, and left for dead. (See Acts 14:19.) Whether at that time, or on some other occasion, Paul was certainly given a glimpse of heaven, that he might be prepared for his great ministry.

However, such experiences are not given to God's people today. We must ever remember that at the time of Paul's experience the Bible was in the process of formation, and God's revelation was not then complete. But we have the full revelation of God as found in His Word; and are called to walk by faith, not by sight.

Question: Does the world with its wealth belong to God or to Satan?

Answer: The world and all it contains belong to God. "The earth is the Lord's, and the fulness thereof (Psalm 24:1). However, the devil and his people *possess* much of it. There is a difference between ownership and possession. I own my umbrella, but someone else possesses it. Christ will one day come and take possession, and the uttermost parts of the earth will be included in His kingdom. "He shall have dominion also from sea to sea, and from the river unto the ends of the earth" (Psalm 72:8).

Question: What do you understand the phrase, "The fear of the Lord," to mean? I do not like to think of being afraid of God.

Answer: This is an Old Testament expression, meaning "reverential trust." You are right; we need not be, and we should not be, afraid of God, if we have trusted His atoning work on Calvary for our salvation. In His death and resurrection, our Lord Jesus took away even "the fear of death" (Heb. 2:14, 15); and death is Satan's most powerful weapon.

Adam and Eve were afraid of God because they had sinned. But God clothed them with "coats of skins," having shed the blood of the animal sacrifice, in order to obtain a garment for His sinning creatures to wear as they stood in His holy presence. Even so, no man can stand before a holy God dressed in his own good works, or by his own righteous acts. He must be clothed in "the righteousness of Christ." But having received this covering for his sins, he is no longer afraid of God; he is not afraid of death or the grave. He knows that, in Christ, he is victor over death and the grave. Yea; he longs for the "appearing" of his Saviour; longs to see Him and be with Him—forever. There is no fear of God to the born-again soul; rather, there is a consciousness of love and trust and worship and praise.

Question: What was the difference between the Jewish temple and the synagogue?

Answer: These buildings differed in that the temple was the only place where sacrifices could be offered; whereas the synagogue was merely a place for reading and prayer.

Question. I am a member of a Protestant Church, but I do not accept the miracles recorded in the Bible. My intellect will not permit me to do so. Why do you insist upon a belief in such doctrines as the Virgin Birth of Christ and His bodily resurrection as essential to salvation? I think I am as about as good as most Christians who profess to believe these things.

Answer: Let me seek to answer your question by two passages of Scripture; there are many other passages which might be used. In the first place, *"the natural man* (the unsaved man) *receiveth not the things of the Spirit of God*: for they are foolishness unto him: neither can he know them, because they are spiritually discerned (that is, by the power of the Holy Spirit)." (See I Cor. 2:14; compare I Cor. 1:17-2:16. In this entire passage we find a contrast between "man's wisdom" and "the wisdom which cometh from above.") My friend, the Christian faith is based upon the supernatural, from beginning to end, and makes no attempt to satisfy man's *intellect;* rather it satisfies the *heart.* There is no place for rationalism. *"The preaching of the cross is to them that perish foolishness; but unto us which are saved it is the power of God."*

In the second place, let me exhort you, in the words of the Lord Jesus, "Ye must be born again . . . Except a man be born again, he cannot see the kingdom of God" (John 3:3, 7). Read all of the third chapter of John, in which Christ told Nicodemus that the sinner must let the Holy Spirit of God regenerate the heart, giving him new life in Christ, before he can be saved—

much less *grasp spiritual truth!* Do not make a god of your intellect, my unsaved friend. Go to Calvary's Cross, and "behold the Lamb of God, which taketh away the sin of the world." (John 1:29).

One other word; we are not saved by our own goodness." "Not by works of righteousness which *we* have done, but according to *his mercy* he saved us, by the washing of regeneration, and renewing of the Holy Ghost" (Titus 3:5). Good works should *follow salvation;* but they can never be the *means* of salvation. "All have sinned, and come short of the glory of God" (Rom. 3:23). Let no man trust in his own self-righteousness to make him fit for the presence of a holy God; for "all our righteousnesses are as filthy rags" in His sight. (See Isa. 64:6.)

Question: Can a murderer be saved?

Answer: Yes, the repentant thief on the cross was a murderer and a robber; and yet Christ said to him, "Today shalt thou be with me in paradise" (Luke 23:43). David was a murderer, but he was forgiven.

Murder is a terrible sin; but we must be careful not to limit the power and the grace of God. And we must be careful not to put a difference between the self-righteous, moral man and the sinner who acknowledges his wrong. Sin is sin before God; and "all have sinned, and come short of the glory of God" (Rom. 3:23). All must be born again.

Question: Why send missionaries to other countries? They have their religions. Are they not good enough?

Answer: "There is none other name under heaven given among men, whereby we must be saved" (Acts 4:1). But note the first clause of this verse particularly: "Neither is there salvation in any other!" Peter had just been preaching Christ crucified, and Christ risen from the dead when he uttered these striking words before the Jewish Sanhedrin. And literally dozens of similar passages might be quoted.

It is not enough to be sincere; the Mohammedan is zealously sincere—rabidly sincere, even to the point of the sword. It is not enough to pray; the pagan prays to his false gods—gods of wood and stone. It is not enough to have a moral code; the Confucianist has long had a moral code, but his soul is lost unless he believes in the Lord Jesus Christ, the only Saviour from sin.

The so-called "modernist"—though his creed is far from modern—asks just such a question as this; for he does not believe the shed blood of Christ necessary as an atonement for the soul. He is trusting in his own self-rigteheousness, which, God says, is as "filthy rags" in His holy sight. He is self-deceived. Good works and environment can never wash away the sinner's stain of sin. "Nothing but the blood of Jesus" can make the heart "whiter than snow." That is why we *must* send the Gospel to the ends of the earth, if we care for men's eternal salvation— if we want to obey our Lord's explicit command.

Question: Are infants and young children who die saved?

Answer: Yes, all infants, including stillborn babies, and young children who have not reached the age of accountability at death, go immediately into the presence of God. Christ died for "the world"; and His atonement provides for these. "Of such is the kingdom of heaven" (Mark 10:14).

Question: A friend of mine says that every Jew who lived and died before the crucifixion of Christ was saved, because Christ's atonement wiped out all their sins. If so, would this not apply to all nations, as well as to Jews?

Answer: Yes, it would if the statement of your friend were true. But it is not true. The Lord said to the Jews of His time, "If ye believe not that I am he, ye shall die in your sins" (John 8:24). And again, "Whither I go, ye cannot come" (John 8:22). The Old Testament Scriptures abound with the teaching that being a descendant of Abraham will avail nothing, apart from Abraham's faith in a coming Redeemer. God has had one plan of salvation from the beginning. People who were saved during the Old Testament days were saved by looking forward to Christ's death, and by trusting in that foreseen sacrifice. In this dispensation, we look back and are saved through faith in the sacrifice of Christ already accomplished.

Question: Does I Tim. 2:15 teach that, if a mother dies in child-bearing, she will be saved, whether she believes in Christ or not? "Notwithstanding she shall be saved in childbearing, if they continue in faith and charity and holiness and sobriety."

Answer: In the first place, nothing is said here of her *death* in childbearing.

In the second place, the Revised Version renders the more accurate translation: "She shall be saved (or *preserved*) *through* childbearing."

And finally, the context makes the meaning clear. Paul had been speaking of how the serpent deceived Eve in the Garden of Eden, and of woman's consequent position of subordination to the man—not inferiority to him. Therefore, Paul, said, that the woman should "keep silence" in the public assembly of Christian worship. (This question is discussed in another place in this series.) Having referred to God's declaration of woman's position, Paul draws this conclusion as to her place in the church.

Now God's own words to Eve are found in Gen. 3:16: "Unto the woman he said, I will greatly multiply thy sorrow and thy conception; in sorrow thou shalt bring forth children; and thy desire shall be to thy husband, and he shall rule over thee." Having restated this *order,* as set forth by God in the Garden of Eden, Paul then shows that, in spite of Eve's sin; in spite of her "sorrow" as a result of her sin; yet God will *preserve* the woman *through* her sorrow, especially when she manifests faith and love and a life of separation from the godless world.

There is nothing in this verse to intimate that a woman is saved *because* of childbearing. On the contrary, all Scripture teaches that no one can be saved except by a personal faith in the atoning work of Christ on the cross.

Question: I was recently on a jury to try a man for murder. Although I was convinced that the man was guilty, yet I voted against capital punishment, because I could not see such a course to be in harmony with Christian principles. Was I right?

Answer: No; you were not. You were very wrong. You were very seriously wrong. The law of capital punishment was not a part of the Jewish law at all. It antedated the Law of Moses by 1,000 years. It was one of God's fundamental, governmental laws, as recorded in Gen. 9:6, "Whoso sheddeth man's blood, by man shall his blood be shed: for in the image of God made he man." The law has never been modified or abrogated. Moreover, it is plainly reiterated in the thirteenth chapter of Romans, where God is speaking of the responsibility of *rulers.* The state not only has a right to put a murderer to death; it has no right to let him live. God put government in the world to restrain sin. In His sight it is a terrible thing to take a life. To be sure, it is the civil government's right to execute the extreme penalty; most certainly not the right of the mob. But God will hold governments responsible for the administration of justice in the world. Every civil officer is "the minister of God to thee for good . . . for he beareth not the sword in vain" (Rom. 13:4).

My friend, you must not confuse the rules for Christian conduct with God's charter of earthly government. The attempt to abolish capital punishment is man's professing to know more about earthly government that the Creator Himself.

On pages 51, 52 of our studies in "God's Plan of the Ages" we discussed this subject at some length. Let me quote two paragraphs from this, especially for an illustration which seems to clarify the issue:

"God's Word does not deny the murderer pardon from sin. It is right that we should pray for the salvation of the condemned man, and seek to lead him to Christ. David was a murderer and he was forgiven. But a sentimental setting aside of God's governmental law has led to a great crime wave in our country today. Human life is cheap; the murderer often escapes justice; whereas in his execution he makes known the enormity of murder and the value of human life.

"Some years ago Governor Pollock of Pennsylvania refused pardon to a young man who was sentenced to die for deliberately planned murder: In this Mr. Pollock was acting as *a governor*. Shortly before the execution, this high official, acting as *a Christian,* sat in that young man's cell and talked to him about his soul. He said to the condemned youth that, while he could not escape man's law, yet there was One who had come to take his place *before God.* 'You can not escape the law of Pennsylvania,' he explained, 'for there is none to die for you. But so far as your relationship to God is concerned, you *may* escape; for Christ died in your stead.' Do you see, my friend, that Governor Pollock was talking as *a governor* and as *a Christian?* He was obeying God's fundamental law in administering justice, at the same time pointing the sinner to the

Saviour who is both just and the justifier of him who believes in His shed blood as an atonement for sin."

Question: What is the difference between soul and spirit?

Answer: Gen. 2:7 reads as follows: "And the Lord God formed man of the dust of the ground (that was his *body*), and breathed into his nostrils the breath of life (his *spirit*); and man became a living *soul*."

The Rev. William L. Pettingill, D.D., has aptly explained the difference between body, soul, and spirit in these words:

1. "Man has a body. In this he is like all of the creation of God throughout the animal and vegetable world. The brutes have living bodies, and so do the trees and plants.

2. "Man has a soul. In this he is unlike the trees and plants, but he is like the lower animals. The soul is the seat of the emotions, the passions, the feelings, the desires, the likes and dislikes, the affections, and the will. All these things we have in common with the beasts.

3. "Man has a spirit. In this he is unique among God's creatures. 'The spirit of man is the candle of Jehovah' (Prov. 20:27), and it is this that is set aglow when man is born again; and then God's Spirit testifies with man's spirit that he is a child of God. God cannot be known by the body; nor by the soul, but only by the spirit. And even the human spirit is incapable of finding out anything about God or of knowing God except by revelation of the Spirit of God."

Two verses from the New Testament state clearly that there is a difference between soul and spirit:

Paul wrote, saying to the Thessalonians, "I pray God your whole spirit and soul and body be preserved blameless unto the coming of our Lord Jesus Christ" (I Thess. 5:23).

"The word of God is quick (or living), and powerful, and sharper than any two-edged sword, piercing even to the dividing asunder of *soul* and *spirit,* and of the joints and marrow, and is a discerner of the thoughts and intents of the heart" (Heb. 4:12).

Let me quote from our studies on "God's Plan of the Ages," pages 23, 24: "With the possession of a spirit, man became God-conscious, which fact determines an impassable gulf between the most sinful, the most degraded man and the highest form of animal life.

"Some time ago a noted professor took a chimpanzee into his home, that it might be a close companion with his own boy. As we might suppose, he did this in order to study the animal carefully. Later he declared that the chimpanzee acted in many ways as intelligently as his boy; for among other things he learned certain customs of table etiquette. He could use a knife, a fork, a spoon, even a table napkin. The professor thus endeavored to show how closely related the animal kingdom is to man. Now all that he said about the formation of certain habits may be true; but there is one thing the boy could do that the ape could never do, no matter what his training or development might be. The ape could never reverently look up into the face of God and say, 'My Father.' It requires *"God-likeness* to do that. It requires the possession of a spirit. And only to man did God give this likeness to Himself when He created him and 'breathed into his nostrils the breath of life." Man was not left to be guarded by instinct, as in the case of the brute creation. To him God gave the intelligence to understand His will and His requirements."

Question: Jude 12 speaks of apostates in the last days as "twice dead." How can a man be twice dead?

Answer: In the first place, this passage is highly figurative. Apostates are likened unto "hidden rocks . . . shepherds without fear . . . clouds without water . . . autumn trees without fruit, twice dead, plucked up by the roots . . . wild waves of the sea . . . wandering stars." Therefore, on the face of it, one does not need to attempt to give a literal meaning to these words. Such is never the case in any literature. Yet the meaning is unmistakable, and all the more impressive by these comparisons.

However, there is a two-fold description of the man who is unregenerated; that is, he is "twice dead," as it were, for these two reasons, either one of which would mean that his is a lost soul: (1) He is "dead in trespasses and sins," never having been regenerated (Eph. 2:1); and (2) he is dead in a false religion, trusting in a false sense of security. Such a condition is described in Rev. 3:1, "Thou hast a name that thou livest, and art dead." John here is speaking of unregenerate church members. It is sad to see people who think that a certain ritualism, or church attendance, or alms-giving, or self-righteousness can make them fit for the presence of a holy God. "Nothing but the blood of Jesus" can take away the sins of the unregenerate heart!

Question: What is meant in Eph. 6:12 by "spiritual wickedness"? How can any wickedness be "spiritual"?

Answer: The apostle is not using the word "spiritual" to mean something to be desired, pertaining to the Holy Spirit; but rather, to describe the power of Satan and his hosts. The devil is a fallen angel. (See Isa. 14:12-17; Ezek. 28:12-18.) And as such, he is a spirit-being. Man is "flesh and blood," and therefore unequally matched against his adversary, Satan, who is far more powerful than he. As human beings "we wrestle not against flesh and blood (other human beings), but against principalities, against powers, against the rulers of the darkness of this world, against spiritual wickedness in high places" (Eph. 6:12).

If we were left to struggle with Satan in our own strength, we should inevitably fight a losing battle. But "thanks be to God!" He has given us His own all-powerful, indwelling Holy Spirit; and in His strength "we are more than conquerors through Him that loved us" (Rom. 8:37).

The host of spiritual beings in the army of Satan and under the direction of Satan is what Paul has in mind in Eph. 6:12. Hence the exhortation which follows, to put on the "whole armour of God."

Question: What is meant by "the holy Catholic church" in "The Apostles' Creed"?

Answer: These words mean the church universal, and pertain to all Christendom, not the Roman Catholic or Greek Catholic Churches. This definition is given in any good dictionary.

Question: Please explain these words from "The Apostles' Creed" which say that our Lord "descended into hell."

Answer: The word "hell" here was used in the same sense as that of the King James Version of our English Bible in such passages as Psa. 16:10; Acts 2:27. These two references give the prophecy and the fulfillment of the promise of God the Father to Christ the Son, that His soul would not be left in "Sheol" or "Hades." For a full explanation of the meaning of these terms, see the index to this series. But here suffice it to say that the literal translation of the word is not "hell," but "Sheol" or "Hades," meaning the place of the dead. Our Lord most assuredly did not go to hell, which is the lake of fire, called in the Greek "Gehenna." He did go to paradise, which was then a part of "Hades." It was the place where the departed spirits of the righteous dead awaited His bodily resurrection and ascension before being taken up into the very presence of God. Paradise was certainly a place of bliss. (See "Paradise.")

Question: Since all secular history centers about the birth of Christ—B.C. and A.D., why do men not realize that He is God and the only Saviour?

Answer: We wonder, "Why?" And yet Satan has blinded their eyes to this silent testimony to the deity of our Lord. Every unsaved man, even the infidel, must unconsciously bear witness to the recognition given Christ every time he dates a letter or a check or a legal document. The poet was taught with wisdom from above when he wrote:

> "In the cross of Christ I glory,
>   Towering o'er the wrecks of time!"

Question: Was the wine the Lord made at the marriage in Cana of Galilee fermented?

Answer: Luke 1:15 sheds light upon the question you ask. This verse concerns John the Baptist, and it reads: "For he shall be great in the sight of the Lord, and shall drink neither wine nor strong drink."

You have a difference here between "wine" and "strong drink." The wine would be unfermented; the strong drink fermented. Some may take issue with this explanation; and I do not profess to know just what the wine at the marriage feast was like. This I do know, that our sinless Saviour, who throughout His inspired Word warns against the use of intoxicating liquor, would have no part in creating a thing that would cause one of His creatures to sin!

Moreover, He states plainly through Paul in Rom. 14:21 what the Christian's attitude should be toward doubtful things: "It is good neither to eat flesh, nor to drink wine, nor anything whereby thy brother stumbleth, or is offended, or is made weak." We should abstain, not only from wine, but also from anything that causes the weak brother to stumble.

Question: Please explain Matt. 17:10-13, especially verses 12, 13, where we read: "Elias is come already . . . Then the disciples understood that he spake unto them of John the Baptist."

Answer: Let me quote from Dr. C. I. Scofield: "All the passages must be construed together (Matt. 11:14; Mark 9:11-13; Luke 1:17; Mal. 3:1; 4:5, 6). (1) Christ confirms the specific and still unfulfilled prophecy of Mal. 4:5, 6: 'Elias shall truly first come and restore all things.' Here, as in Malachi, the prediction fulfilled in John the Baptist, and that yet to be fulfilled in Elijah, are kept distinct. (2) But John the Baptist has come already, and with a ministry so completely in the spirit and power of Elijah's future ministry (Luke 1:17) that in an adumbrative and typical sense it could be said: 'Elias is come already.' Cf. Matt. 10:40; Phm. 12, 17, where the same thought of identification, while yet preserving personal distinction, occurs."

Question: Please explain Matt. 16:28: "Verily I say unto you, There be some standing here, which shall not taste of death, till they see the Son of man coming in his kingdom."

Answer: These words of our Lord foretold His transfiguration, which was witnessed by Peter, James, and John "after six days." These three saw Christ transfigured—a foreview of His coming glory, when He will be manifested before all the world as King of kings and Lord of lords. The transfiguration scene is described immediately after these words, in chapter 17.

Question: When were the disciples converted? Before or after Christ died? If before, why did they not understand when He told them that He was to be crucified?

Answer: They were converted before Christ died, some through the preaching of John the Baptist when he said, "Behold the Lamb of God, which taketh away the sin of the world"

(John 1:29). Then, too, Christ told them to rejoice because their names were "written in heaven" (Luke 10:20).

There are several reasons why they did not understand when He told them He was to be crucified:

1. The human mind is very dull and slow to grasp spiritual things, and the disciples were no exception.

2. They were ignorant of the Scriptures. They were so eager for Christ to set up His kingdom on earth that they over-looked the numerous prophecies that pointed on to the cross, hoping rather for the immediate fulfillment of the even more numerous promises of the reigning Messiah—all found in their Old Testament Scriptures. The New Testament, of course, was not then written. (Compare Luke 24:25-27, 44, 45; I Pet. 1: 10, 11.)

3. Again, their personal love for the Lord made them shudder at the thought of His being crucified.

However, at the close of His public ministry the disciples did seem to understand, in a measure, because in Matt. 24:1-3 we find them asking questions in regard to His return to the earth.

When the Holy Spirit came on the Day of Pentecost, their eyes were fully opened; and they preached salvation through faith in Christ's death and resurrection.

Question: Which apostle took the place of Judas—Matthias or Paul?

Answer: Matthias. I Cor. 15:5 answers this question definitely. Here Paul says that the risen Lord was seen "of the twelve." This certainly included Matthias, because Judas had already hanged himself; and Paul goes on to state in verse eight of the same chapter: "And last of all he was seen of me also, as of one born out of due time."

Those who say that Paul took the place of Judas do not under-stand the peculiar character of Paul's apostleship. He was the minister to the Gentiles in a special sense (Acts 9:15; Rom. 1:5; 11:13; Eph. 3:8); whereas the twelve are connected particularly with the twelve tribes of Israel.

Moreover, there is nothing to indicate that the choice of Matthias (Acts 1:21-26) was contrary to the will of God.

Question: Does the Bible tell us how Peter died?

Answer: In John 21:18, 19 the risen Lord said to Peter: "Verily, verily, I say unto thee, When thou wast young, thou girdest thyself, and walkedst whither thou wouldest: but when thou shalt be old, thou shalt stretch forth thy hands (this suggests crucifixion), and another shall gird thee, and carry thee whither thou wouldest not. This spake he, signifying by what death he should glorify God."

This is all the Bible tells of how Peter died. Tradition says that he was crucified with his head down, for he felt unworthy to be crucified as was his Lord. But that is only tradition. It may or may not have been so.

Question: Please explain Matt. 10:34-36: "Think not that I am come to send peace on earth: I came not to send peace, but a sword. For I am come to set a man at variance against his father, and the daughter against her mother, and the daughter in law against her mother in law. And a man's foes shall be they of his own household."

Answer: The Lord Jesus has been giving the disciples instructions for their ministry. Among other things He said that they might expect persecution and hypocrisy and unbelief. Having given them the important statement concerning the necessity of confessing Him before men, He then went on to utter the words quoted above, about which you ask. Taking the passage in its entire setting, and in connection with all Scripture, the meaning is plain: To accept Christ as a personal Saviour from sin often alienates one's closest relatives. And experience has proved this to be true hundreds of times. Often a Christian has more fellowship and understanding with other Christians not in his own household than he can have with his own sister or brother or father or mother, simply because the bond in Christ is even more binding and real than are blood-ties.

Our Lord in all His teachings made it very plain that the church and the preaching of the Gospel will not "bring in the kingdom." They will not usher in "peace on earth." He Himself will do that; and He leaves His witnesses on earth now to lead men to Himself, making them members of His body, which is His church. That is His purpose for this age.

In keeping with the entire message of this chapter, He then added: "He that loveth father or mother more than me is not worthy of me; and he that loveth son or daughter more than me is not worthy of me" (verse 37). If it is a choice between loved ones and the One "altogether lovely," my friend, then you must take Christ. I have known a number of consecrated Christians who have even had to leave loved ones and home for Christ's sake. That is what He meant when He said, "I came not to send peace, but a sword." He will one day be acknowledged by all the world as the "Prince of Peace," but now He is calling out from the world "a people for his name."

Question: What is the difference, if any, between "the kingdom of heaven" and "the kingdom of God"?

Answer: There is a difference in the Word of God between "the kingdom of God" and "the kingdom of heaven." I find very often, especially among postmillennial ministers, that they pray publicly, asking God to "bring in the kingdom," meaning thereby that God will hasten the day when the church will convert the world, and all the world will know Christ. My friends, the church has nothing to do with bringing in the kingdom of Christ, except as she evangelizes the world, wins souls to Him, Christians, who are making up the body of Christ, His bride. When that body is complete; when the seventieth week of Daniel has run its course, then He Himself will bring in His own kingdom, when He returns personally to earth—not to find a converted world, but rather to find the nations of the earth in open rebellion against Him.

"The kingdom of God" is anywhere where God reigns, whether it is in your heart and life, or in some other life; whether it is in the worship of the holy angels; whether it is in heaven or on earth. Of course, the angels that fell through sin are not in the kingdom of God. It is an inclusive term, and applies to every place, everywhere, in heaven and in earth, where God is obeyed. That is God's kingdom; it is where He reigns. An unsaved man is not in that kingdom. He is doing his own will; and will never be in that kingdom until he is born again. That is why the Lord Jesus said to Nicodemus, "Verily, verily, I say unto thee, Except a man be born again, he cannot see the kingdom of God" (John 3:3).

But with "the kingdom of heaven" we have nothing to do. It is Christ's personal rule on earth. The term "the kingdom of heaven" is confined to the book of Matthew alone; and Matthew wrote particularly for the Jews, proving that Jesus of Nazareth is their Messiah and promised King. It is the same kingdom as that described in Dan. 2:44, "And in the days of these kings shall the God of heaven set up a kingdom which shall never be destroyed." "These kings" in this verse refer to the ten kings of the revived Roman Empire, who will give allegiance to the beast during the seventieth week of Daniel. They are pictured by the ten toes of Daniel's vision, on which the smiting stone will fall, breaking them to pieces. That smiting stone is a picture of Christ, the "stone cut out without hands," which, according to Daniel's version, "became a great mountain, and filled the whole earth." When the Lord Jesus returns, not only will He break in pieces all the godless kingdoms of the earth; but He will also rule "from sea to sea, and from the river unto the ends of the earth" (Psa. 72:8). Then will "the kingdom of heaven" be set up *on earth;* it is synonymous with Messiah's kingdom.

Question: Please explain I Pet. 4:6, "For this cause was the gospel preached also to them that are dead, that they might be judged according to men in the flesh, but live according to God in the spirit."

Answer: The answer which the Rev. William L. Pettingill, D.D., gives to this question is as terse as any I have seen. He says of this text:

"You notice it doesn't say the men who *were* dead. It says it was preached to them that *are* dead. The meaning is that those that are now dead had the Gospel preached to them while they were yet living. The third chapter of I Peter has something on practically the same subject, verses 18, 19, and 20: 'For Christ also hath once suffered for sins, the just for the unjust, that he might bring us to God, being put to death in the flesh, but quickened by the Spirit: by which also he went and preached unto the spirits in prison; which sometime were disobedient, when once the longsuffering of God waited in the days of Noah, while the ark was a preparing, wherein few, that is, eight souls were saved by water.' The answer is that Christ went in His Spirit—the Spirit of Christ, the Spirit of God—the Holy Spirit, and preached through Noah in the days before the flood to those who now are spirits in prison. It does not mean that He has gone to them since they entered the prison and preached there to them. There is mystery about these passages, but this seems to be the true explanation."

Question: Do you believe that the sun actually stood still in the midst of the heavens in the days of Joshua? (See Joshua 10:12, 13.)

Answer: Scientifically, no. To all appearances, yes. We must ever remember that the Bible uses the language of appearance, even as the language of appearance is the language of the masses today. Our newspapers record each morning the actual time the sun rises and sets. Scientifically we know that the sun does not rise or set. Our newspaper editors know that fact, but they use the language of appearance because there is no other language that better transfers to others the thought they have in mind.

It is the language of appearance that the Word of God uses; for the Bible is a universal Book, and the Holy Spirit in describing Joshua's action uses the language that people can understand.

Question: Please explain Matt. 15:26, where the Lord Jesus said to the Syrophenician woman, "It is not meet to take the children's bread, and cast it to the dogs."

Answer: Dr. Scofield gives an excellent explanation of this entire incident in a few words: "For the first time the rejected Son of David ministers to a Gentile. It is a precursive fulfillment of Matt. 12:18. Addressed by a Gentile as Son of David, He makes no reply, for a Gentile has no claim upon Him in that character . . . Addressing Him as 'Lord,' she obtained an immediate answer. See Rom. 10:12, 13."

Question: Please explain the words of John the Baptist in John 3:29, "He that hath the bride is the bridegroom; but the friend of the bridegroom, which standeth and heareth him, rejoiceth greatly because of the bridegroom's voice: this my joy therefore is increased."

Answer: In this statement we have the difference between the relationship of the Old and the New Testament saints to Christ. John the Baptist, who represents the Old Testament saints, said that he was glad to *know* the Bridegroom. John was not a part of the bride, which is the church. He died before the Day of Pentecost, when the church had its beginning. However, John said, in substance, "I am glad just to *know* the Bridegroom." As for the bride, she *has* the Bridegroom. In this John showed his great humility, even as he also said, "He must increase, but I must decrease" (John 3:30).

Topical Index

TOPICAL INDEX

Chapter I—THE BIBLE

Chapter II—THE TRIUNE GOD

Chapter V—THE SOVEREIGNTY OF GOD

Chapter VI—LAW AND GRACE

Chapter VII—THE ETERNAL SECURITY OF THE BELIEVER

Chapter VIII—THE BAPTISM OF THE HOLY SPIRIT
THE TONGUES MOVEMENT
DIVINE HEALING

Chapter IX—THE CHRISTIAN LIFE

Chapter XII—ROMAN CATHOLICISM

Chapter XIII—FALSE RELIGION IN PROFESSING CHRISTENDOM

Chapter XVI—MISCELLANEOUS QUESTIONS

Index of Scripture

INDEX OF SCRIPTURE